SEXUAL ORIENTATION
AND SCHOOL POLICY

Curriculum, Cultures, and (Homo)Sexualities

Edited by James T. Sears

SEXUAL ORIENTATION AND SCHOOL POLICY

A Practical Guide for Teachers, Administrators, and Community Activists

Ian K. Macgillivray

ROWMAN & LITTLEFIELD PUBLISHERS, INC.

Lanham • Boulder • New York • Toronto • Oxford

ROWMAN & LITTLEFIELD PUBLISHERS, INC.

Published in the United States of America
by Rowman & Littlefield Publishers, Inc.
A wholly owned subsidiary of The Rowman & Littlefield Publishing Group, Inc.
4501 Forbes Boulevard, Suite 200, Lanham, MD 20706
www.rowmanlittlefield.com

P.O. Box 317, Oxford OX2 9RU, UK

British Library Cataloguing in Publication Information Available

Library of Congress Cataloging-in-Publication Data

Macgillivray, Ian K. 1967–
    Sexual orientation and school policy : a practical guide for teachers,
administrators, and community activists / Ian K. Macgillivray.
        p. cm. — (Curriculum, cultures, and (homo)sexualities)
    ISBN 0-7425-2507-4 (cloth : alk. paper) — ISBN 0-7425-2508-2 (pbk. :
alk. paper)
    1. Homosexuality and education. 2. Education—Social aspects. 3.
Gays—Identity. 4. Lesbians—Identity. I. Title. II. Series

    LC192.6.M33 2004
    371.826'64—dc21

                                                            2003011932

Printed in the United States of America

∞™ The paper used in this publication meets the minimum requirements of American
National Standard for Information Sciences—Permanence of Paper for Printed Library
Materials, ANSI/NISO Z39.48-1992.

Dedicated to the High Plains Safe Schools Coalition.
Keep up the great work!

Contents

Series Editor's Foreword

James T. Sears, Ph.D.

O UR NATION'S SECONDARY SCHOOLS HAVE experienced remarkable progress in addressing lesbian, gay, bisexual, and transgender (LGBT) concerns. From the formation of gay–straight alliances to the adoption of antiharassment policies, being a queer high school student is in some ways quite different from my experience a generation ago.

Progress, however, can only be judged from my *Ozzie and Harriet* vantage point—an era when every state criminalized homosexuality, when the psychiatric profession diagnosed it as an illness, when no religious denomination sanctified homosexual relationships, and when teachers were entrapped and summarily dismissed because of their sexual orientation. Even today, relatively few schools have recognized gay student groups (the drama club notwithstanding); little protection is provided to LGBT educators or pupils; the curricula that include the contributions of acknowledged lesbians and gay men are rare as are pedagogical practices that are inclusive; and queering elementary education is more likely found on a bookshelf than in the classroom.

Within this historical context a new generation of scholars and researchers are peering into the black box of schooling. They are asking difficult questions, often challenging our simple-minded equation that policy reform equals school change. One of these inquirers is Ian K. Macgillivray, an openly gay classroom teacher with an earned doctorate who came out to the music of Boy George and George Michael.

Macgillivray takes us to America's heartland through an exemplary ethnographic inquiry. In *Sexual Orientation and School Policy*, we enter High Plains

School District, which has already included sexual orientation in its nondiscrimination statement but over the ensuing years has done little more—to the point that its existence has been all but forgotten. When a new initiative is proposed, not surprisingly, the participants experience conflict. Here, voices and images of local gay activists and moral conservatives are lucid and lively as they (and we) are drawn behind the battle lines in the Rocky Mountain high country. The result is as compelling as it is disturbing.

In this case study, what is most provocative is not the finding that there are slippages or loose couplings between policy adoption and implementation. Those of us engaged in policy analysis or everyday school practice are well aware of this divide. What is thought provoking is how democratically committed, social justice–oriented persons apply the principle of equality in their pursuit of the "gay agenda." Macgillivray's position is clear: "I am asking the schools to teach democratic principles like equality and reciprocity; I am not suggesting that the school teach or require students to 'value' homosexuality." And, it is at this juncture—where the high terrain of political philosophy and the bog of educational practice meet—that sexual orientation can be squared with school policy. If we *can* marshal our resources here, then the next generation of queer youth—from the High Plains of the Rockies to the Low Country of the Carolinas—need not suffer through either Ricky Nelson or Boy George. (Re)visioning *Sexual Orientation and School Policy* is worth the effort.

Foreword

Kevin Jennings

A S BOTH A HISTORY TEACHER and a social justice activist, I sometimes think that the popularized history of the life of Martin Luther King Jr. has given rise to profound misconceptions about how justice and equality are won. In the "made for television" version of King's life that we celebrate each January, one could think that justice is won by giving one moving speech invoking a "dream"; after which, lawmakers enact the right legislation, and the citizenry falls in line. I am sure that, were King alive today, he'd watch this and say, "I wish."

Hollywood prefers a version of history focused on charismatic individuals who resolve all the hard issues in less than two hours. Real change is not so easy. While individual leadership and the enactment of legislation play important roles, social justice is won by citizens who commit themselves to the painstaking, slow, and trying work that winning it involves. The passage of a law is the beginning of the end, not the end of the beginning, of the process by which equity is made a reality in everyday life for those who have been denied it. The hard work of winning such laws, and then ensuring they are implemented in ways that make a difference in our lives, is a complex story rarely told on the silver screen.

There is no denying that equity in our schools is not forthcoming for lesbian, gay, bisexual, and transgender (LGBT) students. The 2001 Gay, Lesbian, Straight Education Network (GLSEN) National School Climate Survey found that over 80 percent of these students experience verbal, physical, or sexual harassment while at school. The 2001 Massachusetts Department of Education/Center for Disease Control and Prevention (CDC) Youth Risk Behavior Survey found that LGBT students were over three times as likely to skip school and over four times as likely to attempt suicide as their non-LGBT peers. The ideal upon which our public education system was founded—a free education that would enable every child to achieve their human potential and become a full citizen in society—is far from a reality for most LGBT students.

Over the past decade, awareness of this inequity has been growing, and efforts to address it have been increasing. Eight states (California, Connecticut, Massachusetts, Minnesota, New Jersey, Vermont, Washington, and Wisconsin) now protect students from harassment and/or discrimination based on sexual orientation. Three states (California, Minnesota, and New Jersey) now protect students from harassment and/or discrimination based on gender identity. Student leadership has played an important role in changing our schools: high school–based and student-led gay–straight alliances have spread from a lone one in Concord, Massachusetts, in 1989, to over two thousand in all fifty states as of 2003. As LGBT students and their supporters have become visible and have begun to insist on more equitable treatment in our schools, authorities at the local, state, and even federal level have begun to take note and, in many cases, take action.

But those seeking equity for LGBT people in our schools confront a basic problem: because this work is of such recent vintage, no road map exists to show how to best achieve this goal. In *Sexual Orientation and School Policy: A Practical Guide for Teachers, Administrators, and Community Activists*, Ian K. Macgillivray gives us a much-needed and long-overdue case study of how this process actually unfolded in one community. The story of the struggle to make the High Plains School District a more equitable place for LGBT students is an instructive, fascinating one. We learn how citizens organized the High Plains Safe Schools Coalition to push for change—the tactics they employed, the obstacles they encountered, and the victories and setbacks they experienced along the way. What emerges are lessons for those activists organizing for change and for those education leaders seeking guidance on how to change their schools to be more inclusive.

Macgillivray makes a singularly unique contribution to our understating of the process of change by his analysis of the "slogan systems" of those supporting and those opposing the changes advocated by the High Plains Safe Schools Coalition. Macgillivray helps us understand where each side is coming from and why conflict results. While Macgillivray shows that the two sides can demonstrate profound (and in some ways irreconcilable) differences in their worldviews, his analysis can nonetheless help more communities move productively through the process of change, whereby they minimize the "shouting matches" that too often occur.

Eleanor Roosevelt once said, "Where do universal human rights begin? In small places, close to home." In *Sexual Orientation and School Policy: A Prac-*

tical Guide for Teachers, Administrators, and Community Activists, Ian K. Macgillivray shows us how the process of winning one of the basics rights included in the Universal Declaration of Human Rights that Mrs. Roosevelt inspired—the right to an education—unfolded "close to home," in the real world of a typical American community. It is my hope that this insightful, incisive study of the process of winning social justice for LGBT students in the High Plains School District will help more school systems become places where this universal human right is afforded to all young people, regardless of sexual orientation or gender identity.

Kevin Jennings, Executive Director
Gay, Lesbian, Straight Education Network (GLSEN)

Acknowledgments

W RITING THIS BOOK HAS TRANSFORMED ME, and I wish to thank many people for their love and support in this endeavor. First and foremost I
would like to thank my parents and best friends, Tom and Barbara
Macgillivray, who have supported me in numerous ways and who always encouraged me to stand up for my convictions. I could not have done this without their love and support. I would like to thank the rest of my family, who
helped raise me and helped make me the person I am today. Many thanks to
my grandparents, Ian Callum and Marjorie Aitkens Macgillivray and Kenneth
Henry and Dorothy Grefe Ruf. Thanks also to my sister and brother-in-law,
Magi and Aaron Ramirez, my nephew, Riley, and my niece, Phoebe, for their
love and support.

I would also like to thank all of the participants of this research who took
time out of their busy schedules to be interviewed, to talk on the phone, to answer e-mails, and to make this book complete. Special thanks goes to Dorothy,
president of the High Plains Safe Schools Coalition, who is tireless in her advocacy for the rights of gay, lesbian, bisexual, transgendered, intersexed, and
queer/questioning (GLBTIQ) students and adults. Many thanks also to other
members of the High Plains Safe Schools Coalition, including Roger and
Marge, who pointed out numerous grammatical errors in my manuscript!
Tons of love and respect go out to Violet, director of the High Plains GLBTIQ
Youth Support Group for her passion and drive to help queer youth develop
into adults with healthy GLBTIQ identities. Finally, I offer a very special thank
you to Nancy of Concerned Citizens for her forthrightness and tenacity.

I wrote the bulk of this book as a doctoral student and have my dissertation committee to thank for helping me to turn out a product of which I am very proud. Many thanks to Emily Calhoun, María Fránquiz, Ken Howe, Karen Harbeck, and especially to my co-advisors, Margaret LeCompte and Steve Guberman. You have my love, admiration, and respect, not only as academics, but also as just-minded individuals. I would also like to thank Dean William Stanley and the professors and staff of the School of Education at the University of Colorado at Boulder, where I completed my Ph.D., made many wonderful friends, and made my entrée into the world of academia. Thanks also to the late John Rawls, philosopher and author. You inspired me.

Words cannot express what I feel for Steven D. Hopp, Delores B. Kellman, David Lynden Francis, Robert Davis, Manuel Alvarado R., Erick Brunner, Tom Dempsey, and Daryl J. Walker, who continue to teach me about life, love, and the human spirit. Thanks also to my high school theater friends, especially Karen Atkinson, who helped me be strong. And tons of hugs and kisses to Gerardo. You are so special.

Last, but certainly not least, I thank all of my teachers. I especially thank Bill Nielsen, my high school biology teacher, for making his classroom safe. One teacher can make the difference between life and death.

I

Implementing School Nondiscrimination Policy That Includes Sexual Orientation: A Case Study in School and Community Politics

Never doubt that a small group of thoughtful, committed people can change the world. Indeed it is the only thing that ever has.

—Margaret Meade

This book is a true story about a small group of thoughtful, committed people who changed their own corner of the world. I wrote this book to share with others the strategies that this group employed in making their world a better and more just place to live. It is my hope that the accomplishments of this group will inspire you, as they have me.

Part I introduces this group, details their advocacy on behalf of gay, lesbian, bisexual, transgendered, and queer/questioning students, and makes suggestions for other community groups and school districts in cultivating school cultures of safety and respect. I open part I with a little bit about myself to help the reader understand my personal commitment to and involvement in this issue.

1

In the Beginning

ALLOW ME TO STATE MY BIASES UP FRONT. I am a gay man. I am the survivor of a middle and high school experience filled with antigay abuse. Day in and day out, I was punched, kicked, spit upon, shoved into lockers, and called terrible names. Although I learned to walk very quickly from class to class in an attempt to avoid abuse in the hallways, I was not completely safe in the classrooms either. Teachers rarely stopped name-calling and often missed the punches and objects hurled at me when their backs were turned. Several times I came close to taking my own life to end the pain inflicted on me by other students, teachers, and even administrators. The message I received every day for six straight years was, "You are not worthy. You do not deserve to be here. You are despicable. Die, you faggot."

Looking back at my childhood, I was a boy who identified more with girls and women. I identified with the nurturing roles women and girls often took in relationships with others. I did not identify with boys my age who were constantly punching one another and frequently torturing neighborhood cats and other defenseless animals. However, when I first started to develop sexual feelings, they were directed toward men. I don't know if I was born gay, but I do know that my sexual orientation was set in place from the time of my earliest recollections. I was born to and raised by heterosexuals. I grew up in a culture that valued heterosexuality above all other sexual and affectional expressions. As a boy I was prodded to take on heterosexual and masculine roles by family members who bought me BB guns and toy trucks and inquired as to how many girlfriends I had. My peers admonished me when I "acted like a girl." I should have turned out straight, but I didn't.

I quickly realized that I was different from other people, and I learned to monitor my thoughts and actions so I would fit in with the heterosexual majority. I didn't know what it meant to be gay until I was in middle school. When I learned what it meant, I began to wonder if that was what I was. I didn't want to believe I was gay because I knew the negative context in which being gay was discussed by other people. By the time I entered my freshman year of high school, however, I had accepted the fact that I was gay. I told no one. I felt that I was the only gay person in the world and that no one could possibly understand how I felt—that is, until Culture Club hit the popular music charts and I caught my first glimpse of Boy George on an album cover. I remember it vividly. I was shopping with my family when the words *Culture Club* caught my eye. I was just becoming interested in music and knew the band's name from listening to the radio. What really caught my attention, though, was the figure on the cover. Was it a man? Was it a woman? I couldn't tell. I examined the back of the album cover and discovered that the androgynous figure who caught my eye was named Boy George. "He must be a man," I thought. "But why is he dressed like a girl?" I had to know more about this person. My parents bought me the album, and Boy George became not only my pop idol but, oddly enough, my savior.

At last, I knew that someone else out there was like me. I bought every one of Culture Club's albums. I bought every teen magazine, poster, and any other artifact that was emblazoned with Boy George's image or had anything to do with this magnificent being who broke all the rules of gender. The walls of my bedroom were plastered from floor to ceiling with images of Boy George. When I wasn't in school, I was locked in my bedroom listening to Culture Club's albums, staring at Boy George all over my walls, and dreaming of running away to London (where he lived), and being his friend. This was how I spent two years of my early high school life. This was how I dealt with the physical pain and emotional misery inflicted upon me by my classmates, teachers, administrators, and the larger society that devalued people like me. Deep inside I knew that Boy George was like me. Knowing that at least one other person out there in the world felt like I did made life almost bearable. The fact that I had no access to Boy George—the one person who I thought would accept me for who I was—made it all the more difficult to cope with my pain and isolation. I often contemplated suicide as a way of ending my misery and loneliness. I also dreamed of killing the students at school who physically and verbally tortured me, who humiliated me in front of others and denied me human dignity. I knew they had no right to treat me the way they did, and I was furious at the injustices they perpetrated against me; yet I was powerless. Years later, when two young gunmen massacred their teachers and classmates at Columbine High School in Colorado, I understood how years of teasing and bullying by other students may have helped push the two young gunmen to their act of rage (Pankratz 2002). Though I do not condone their actions—indeed, I am as horrified as everyone else—I was not surprised to hear that the two young men were often the victims of antigay bullying by the more popular students and by the students who were active in sports (Greene 1999). I have since made peace with my public school experience. I survived the situation and came out of it with a greater understanding of human suffering, the ability to empathize with others, and a great deal of compassion. Now the memories of those days drive me to make this world a better place for other young gay, lesbian, bisexual, transgendered, intersexed, and queer/questioning (GLBTIQ) people who find themselves in similar positions.

I do not blame my teachers and administrators who did little or nothing to stop the abuse and who, in fact, often perpetuated it. I do not blame the students who tormented me. We were all trying to make sense of a situation that was new to us. By the time I was a junior in high school, I had found some solace in the drama club. Many students in theater were also social outcasts, and they accepted me into their group. There were tensions between students who were in sports and those in theater and choir. At one point "the Klan," a self-named group of boys in sports, organized in opposition to "the theater fags," the term they used for students in theater and choir. The Klan appointed leadership and a "Klan artist" and began littering the hallways with hand-drawn flyers containing derisive messages aimed at students in theater. At this point the school's administration finally stepped in, determined who "the Klan" members were, put an end to their organization, and offered counseling to those of us in theater who were being harassed (notice that the victims were the ones treated as though they had a problem to get over). We were told to come to the office every time another student harassed us and report that student. I reported offenders for a while, and, if my recollection serves me correctly, a few students were temporarily suspended as a result. However, I realized that I was fighting a battle much larger than myself and that nothing really changed despite my reporting, so I finally gave up.

When I became a senior, I was given the opportunity to attend a university in a nearby town in the mornings and finish my high school courses in the afternoons. The first course I signed up for at the university was a multiculturalism course called *Nonoppressive Relationships*. This course taught me about sexism, racism, classism, homophobia, and other oppressions; and finally, my world started to make sense. I took on a view of society much larger than the one afforded by my microcosmic high school experience. I began to understand the discrimination directed at me by my peers. By no means did this greater understanding paint a rosy picture of my future life as a gay person. It did, however, offer an understanding of why oppression and discrimination exist. This discovery was a huge relief, and it at least gave me hope that I could change life for the better. I was mentored by a professor who was bisexual and in a lesbian relationship. She told me about the university's Gay and Lesbian Support Group, and I knew I had to attend. Although it was difficult for me as a high school student to walk into a room full of college students, I was immediately accepted by the group, and my intimidations subsided. The group was facilitated by a Catholic priest—who later came out of the closet and was forced to leave the church—and it included GLBTIQ college students as well as community members. I was young and naïve, and the potential existed for me to be manipulated by and preyed upon by older gay men in the group. Several older men in the group tried to get my interest, but by and large other group members took me under their wings and helped me grow into a confident and savvy young gay person who could navigate gay male culture and avoid being manipulated by others. At last, I was no longer alone in the world.

Thus, my initiation into gay culture occurred while I was still a senior in high school. I was not yet out to my parents, so to hide my sexual orientation, I pretended that I was going to my part-time job when I was actually going to the Gay and Lesbian Support Group meetings. I would walk out of the house in my blue polyester McDonald's uniform with a change of clothes in my bag, and I would change in the parking lot when I got to the support group meetings. Because my newfound friends were of college age, I was also initiated into the world of parties, club going, and drinking. On weekends I would join my friends on treks to Minneapolis, where they would help me sneak into gay bars. At last I was surrounded by people like myself, and I reveled in the experience of feeling free for the very first time. As a young person still in high school, I was certainly vulnerable to being corrupted by these experiences, but I was raised by parents who instilled strong values in me. I did not succumb to the temptations of drugs and alcohol, and I did not "take to the streets" as some young GLBTIQ people in my position often do. I finished my studies, graduated from high school, and went on to postsecondary education. Nor did the older GLBTIQ people with whom I was associating ever take advantage of me sexually. Aside from a couple of older gay men who told me they wanted to have sex with me (but did not pursue it when I told them no), none of the other group members ever tried to manipulate me for sex. On the contrary, they were protective and supportive of me, and they educated me about safe sex practices just as HIV/AIDS was making its entrance into our social world. I was very fortunate.

With the support of my new gay friends, I was encouraged to come out to my parents, even though some of my friends had been disowned by their families when they came out. Coming out to my parents was something I wanted to do because I felt that I was lying to them about who I was. I was also lying to my parents about where I was going, what I was doing, and with whom I was associating. I was tired of the lies, yet I was terrified of being rejected by my parents. Coming out to my parents was the most difficult thing I have ever done. When, as a high school senior, I finally worked up the courage to come out, I armed myself with a book, at the suggestion of my professor mentor, entitled *Now That You Know: What Every Parent Should Know about Homosexuality.* I decided to come out to my mom first, as I thought she'd take the news better than my dad. On the Saturday morning I decided to come out to my mom, she was lying in bed reading a book. I stood outside my parents' bedroom door, clutching the copy of *Now That You Know* tightly in my hands, and trying to work up the courage to enter the room. Just as I had lost the nerve and was turning around to leave, my mom saw my reflection in the glass of a picture hanging in the hallway. She asked, "What are you doing?" I took a deep breath, walked in and kneeled down on the floor next to her. I don't remember my exact words, but I prefaced what I had to say with something like, "Mom, I want you to know that I love you and don't want to hurt you and that I'm the same person I've always been but . . ." And then I said it—"I want you to know that I'm gay." She took it pretty well. She tried to act as though she wasn't upset, although she visibly was, and she said that I shouldn't tell my dad. I gave her the book and left the house to get away. When I returned that evening, she had told my dad. My dad took it better than I had expected. He told me he loved me and that I would always be his son. That was just what I needed to hear. Finally, the burden I had been carrying all of those years was lifted from my shoulders. I didn't know what lay ahead, and I knew there would be a period of getting reacquainted with my parents, now as their "gay son"; but I was relieved. The love and support of my friends from the Gay and Lesbian Support Group, along with the love and support of my parents, started me on the way to becoming a well-adjusted and happy young gay man. Though my parents requested that I not come out to others, including relatives, I started to come out to more and more people at school.

I became the first openly gay student in my school district in my small town in central Minnesota in the early 1980s. I had the opportunity to go back recently and talk to the teachers and administrators about my school experience. Many of them were new to the district, but the older ones remembered me. They expressed remorse for not knowing what to do back then to stop the abuse.

Students are still the victims of antigay abuse in my old school and schools across the country. Teachers and administrators are still unsure of how to address the situation. Few schools have made real commitments to end antigay abuse, although some schools are trying and that gives me great hope. Antigay bias must be eradicated from America's schools. GLBTIQ students, as well as students who are perceived to deviate from heterosexual norms, deserve equality of educational opportunity. Bullying—both physical and verbal harassment—needs to end, and the curriculum and practices of the school must include GLBTIQ people and perspectives to the extent that heterosexual people and perspectives are already included.

I believe the principles of democracy, upon which this country was founded, and the U.S. Constitution demand that all students, including GLBTIQ students, deserve equality of educational opportunity in America's public schools. These are my biases. One goal of this book is to illustrate by example one school district's attempt to stop antigay abuse in its schools. My hope is that other school districts will use this information to stop antigay abuse in their own schools and use the philosophical foundations I present here to help bring about equality for GLBTIQ students.

How This Book Came About

"I wish someone would publish a guide for this sort of thing. We need strategies that work." This sentiment has been repeatedly told to me by school administrators, teachers, and community activists who are working to increase safety and equity for their GLBTIQ students. All over the country, school programs and groups of local activists are creatively employing strategies and taking advantage of various opportunities to make their local schools safe and welcoming places for GLBTIQ students. In speaking with these individuals, however, I learned that they are so busy with their advocacy that they do not have the time to record their accomplishments and how they achieved them.

The idea for this book grew out of these conversations with directors of programs such as:

- "Project 10" in the Los Angeles Unified School District,
- "Support Services for Sexual Minority Youth" in the San Francisco Unified School District,
- "Out for Equity" in the St. Paul School District, and
- "Out 4 Good" in the Minneapolis School District.

All of these programs provide support services to GLBTIQ students; professional development to teachers and administrators; advice on legal requirements; and assistance in forming policies and in developing inclusive curricula. All of these programs have faced opposition in one form or another, whether from resistant school boards and administrators or from religious fundamentalist parents in the community who felt the schools were advancing a "pro-gay" agenda.

Several years ago I became acquainted with a community group who were concerned that GLBTIQ students were frequently the victims of antigay abuse in their local schools. This group of people formed a coalition; garnered support from churches, a synagogue, a state senator, and a commissioner on the city's Human Relations Commission; and approached the school board with their concerns. When word got out to the community that a "Safe Schools Coalition" was working with the school board to get "sexual orientation" added to the school district's Diversity Goal policy, a group of morally conservative parents organized in opposition. Thus began a long debate, often highly contentious, about the rights of GLBTIQ students and families versus the rights of morally conservative parents and their children.

Thinking back to my conversations with the directors of programs in other school districts, I got the idea to record the strategies employed by the Safe Schools Coalition. I observed the Safe Schools Coalition working strategically and creatively to enhance school safety for GLBTIQ students. They came up with many creative ways to outwit or educate the opposition, and I wanted to share those strategies with others. This book is a history of the Safe Schools Coalition's efforts to work with their school district to bring about school safety for GLBTIQ students, the strategies they employed, the local conditions they took advantage of, and how they managed resistance to their efforts from morally conservative parents in the community. It is my hope that this book will serve as a useful guide in helping teachers, administrators, and community activists increase safety and equity in their own schools for their GLBTIQ students.

Similar studies relevant to my research—like Perrotti and Westheimer's *When the Drama Club Is Not Enough: Lessons from the Safe Schools Program for Gay and Lesbian Students* (2001)—focus on the problem of abuse directed at GLBTIQ students and suggest remedies to curtail the abuse. Others, like Harbeck's *Gay and Lesbian Educators: Personal Freedoms, Public Constraints* (1997), document societal struggles for gay rights. None, however, describe and analyze the case of a school district's attempt to implement and enforce policy to curtail harassment, or explicate the effects of local factors involved in the success or failure of the implementation and enforcement of the policy.

Studies such as Button, Rienzo, and Wald's *Private Lives, Public Conflicts: Battles over Gay Rights in American Communities* (1997) focus on gay rights public policy and provide methodological guidance and a framework for assessing the community groups and school districts who are working together to enhance school safety for GLBTIQ students. Those variables that operate in the community and that affect the success or failure of gay rights public policy likewise operate in the culture of the school. These variables are useful in helping to describe the process of implementing and enforcing school policies that include sexual orientation. Considering the related literature, this research seems like a good way to proceed in adding to our understanding of how school policy designed to enhance school safety and equity for GLBTIQ students is implemented, enforced, and resisted.

Sexual Orientation

I use the acronym *GLBTIQ* to refer to gay, lesbian, bisexual, transgendered, intersexed, and queer/questioning students. I believe it is important to be as inclusive as possible and to raise awareness about what each of these letters stands for. Not everybody uses all the letters, and some people order them differently—for instance, LGBT or QQITBLG. Sometimes the order of the letters reflects a political position. I use GLBTIQ simply because it is the order with which I am most accustomed to using.

The *G, L, B,* and *Q* in GLBTIQ have to do with sexual orientation. Sexual orientation involves whom one is attracted to sexually, emotionally, and spiritually (Savin-Williams 1990; Remafedi 1990; Thompson 1994). *Gay* most often refers to gay men; *lesbian,* to women who are attracted to other women; and *bisexual,* to people who are attracted to men and women (rarely is the attraction equal, but varies depending on specific circumstances). *Questioning* allows an individual not to claim a sexual orientation identity, which is important in letting individuals come to their own understandings of who they are.

Queer is a somewhat politically charged term (Warner 1993) and is used positively by many GLBTIQ people. Some also consider *queer* to be an umbrella term, like "GLBTIQ," which includes all nonheterosexual people; however, if it is to be all-inclusive, the term needs to be redefined beyond just sexual orientation to include transgender and intersex. In general, *queer* is no longer the dirty word it used to be. Many GLBTIQ people, especially the younger ones, proudly identify as *queer* because it is a way of reclaiming the word and removing the stigma attached to it. Some members of the GLBTIQ communities, however, believe the word *queer* carries too much of a negative connotation and should not be used. Finally, it is important to remember that *heterosexual* is a sexual orientation too. Thus, laws and policies that protect people from discrimination based on sexual orientation protect heterosexuals as well.

Gender Identity

Transgendered (the *T* in GLBTIQ) has more to do with gender identity (Macoby and Jacklin 1974; Money and Ehrhart 1972) than with sexual orientation. Gender identity refers to one's self-identity as a man, woman, or somewhere in between, and it also involves how an individual presents her or himself to the rest of the world. In other words, *transgendered* is the term used for individuals whose physical or genetic sex (male or female) does not correspond with their gender identity as a man, woman, or somewhere in between. *Transgendered* is included with G, L, B, and Q because many of the issues facing transgendered individuals are similar to those faced by GLBQ people. It is important to remember, though, that sexual orientation and gender identity are two separate issues.

Intersex

Whereas *transgender* refers to variant gender identity, *intersex* (the *I* in GLB-TIQ) refers to variant sexual anatomy. According to Cheryl Chase, executive director of the Intersex Society of North America (ISNA), *intersex* refers to individuals who were born with an anatomy not traditionally regarded as standard male or female. A good source of information on intersexuality is ISNA's website (www.isna.org). An important distinction to make is between being transsexual and being intersexed. The former involves transitioning from one sex to the other with hormone therapy and/or sex reassignment surgery; the latter is defined by the physical anatomy the person was born with. Although some transsexual individuals may have been born intersexed, most transsexual individuals were born with normally developed male or female anatomy. Furthermore, explains ISNA's website:

> While some intersex people also identify as transgender, intersex people as a group have a unique set of needs and priorities besides those shared with trans[gendered] people. Too often, intersex people's unique needs are made invisible or secondary when "intersex" becomes just another subcategory of "transgender." It is for this reason that we prefer to have "intersex" spelled out explicitly rather than have it "included" in "transgender."

There always have been, and always will be, individuals who do not fit traditionally and arbitrarily defined categories of male or female—genetically, anatomically, or in how they identify. Understanding this fact helps us understand the full range of human sexes, sexual orientations, and gender identities; and it helps us understand that these differences are normal, natural, and nothing to be afraid of. One way of demonstrating the social importance of heterosexuality and identification with the gender that matches one's genitals is the separation of men's and women's bathrooms, locker rooms, barracks, and so forth. The first assumption is that everyone is either a man or a woman and will be accepted by others in the bathroom or barracks. The second assumption is that all women in the women's barracks are attracted to men and vice versa. The fact that a woman in the women's barracks might be attracted to other women or that a person in the women's barracks might be intersexed confounds our separation of the sexes. Our system for talking about, thinking about, and dealing with the presumed gender differences between men and women falls apart when intersexed, transgendered, and queer people enter the equation. I propose that if GLBTIQ people had been invited from the beginning to help construct society's conceptions of what it means to be a man or a woman, the way we separate the sexes today would be radically different, much more inclusive, and far less oppressive.

How Schools Are Affected by Heterosexism

At a fundamental level this debate is about a challenge to the worldview that all people are or should be heterosexual. Friend (1993, 1998) terms this worldview as *heterosexism*. Friend explains that heterosexuality is held to be "normal," such that society's norms and institutions are based on the logic that men are sexually and affectionately attracted only to women, and women likewise only to men. Two results of heterosexism are that GLBTIQ people are disadvantaged and that, conversely, heterosexual people are privileged simply for being heterosexual. For instance, one way GLBTIQ people are disadvantaged is that same-sex marriages are neither socially sanctioned nor legally recognized, resulting in a host of social, emotional, and economic costs to GLBTIQ people. Moreover, heterosexuals are privileged because their identities as straight people, as well as their opposite-sex relationships, are affirmed and celebrated in every facet of the culture, from the popular media to the law. GLBTIQ identities are rarely celebrated in the popular media and even less often affirmed in the law.

Another effect of heterosexism is the use of homophobia to reinforce rigid gender role stereotypes (sexism), thus keeping men and women in their respective places. Homophobia is not so much a fear of GLBTIQ people; rather, it is a fear of how GLBTIQ people are perceived by some to threaten the heterosexual order of traditional male and female gender roles. An effect of homophobia is to squeeze men and women into rigid gender role stereotypes. For instance, I wrote in 2000:

> The fear of being perceived as gay restricts boys to making choices that will affirm what it means to be "a man" in our society, and restricts girls to making choices that will affirm what it means to be "a woman." Consider the number of men whose lives could have been enriched by exploring their interests in ballet

or other arts, but chose instead competitive sports because of chastisement from their friends, and maybe even their parents. And consider the women who could have had successful careers in math and science but picked up on the societal message that "That's not what girls should be interested in."

The heterosexism of the larger society affects schools in that GLBTIQ people and perspectives are most often excluded from the curriculum and practices of the schools, which results in physically, emotionally, and developmentally hostile environments for many GLBTIQ students.[1] Nondiscrimination policies that prohibit discrimination on the basis of sexual orientation and gender identity are sound ways to help make the schools safe for GLBTIQ students. Anecdotal evidence suggests that the awareness raised by these policies and the class discussions they motivate help reduce levels of antigay abuse in schools (Buckel 2000; Sears and Williams 1997). Including gender identity in nondiscrimination policies to protect transgendered students is so foreign a concept to most people that it appears nowhere in the literature.

Though local climates for gay rights advocates vary and some school boards have a relatively easy time of supporting GLBTIQ students, often times antigay hostility makes it extremely difficult for schools to consider including sexual orientation in board policies. Moreover, hostile climates make it all the more risky for teachers and administrators to be proactive when it comes to taking a firm stance against antigay abuse in their classrooms and schools (LeCompte 2000). In many cases teachers and administrators have become pawns in social and legal battles between advocates and opponents of GLBTIQ student rights.

Why Should Educators Care about This Topic?

Recent court decisions have increasingly interpreted the law in favor of the rights of GLBTIQ students. Public schools and school officials may no longer ignore the abuse and exclusion of GLBTIQ students, or they risk being sued. One of the first and most well-known cases that helped pave the way for greater rights for GLBTIQ students was that of Jamie Nabozny. Nabozny was an openly identifying gay student who sued his Ashland, Wisconsin, school district, two principals, and one assistant principal for $900,000 in federal court for failing to protect him from peer abuse (*Nabozny v. Podlesny* 1996). When Nabozny complained to his middle and high school principals that he was being targeted for antigay abuse, he was told that openly gay students should expect such treatment. School officials did not attempt to stop the abuse, which included a beating that resulted in Nabozny's being hospitalized. The trial proceeded to court

Chapter 1

on the grounds that school officials treated Nabozny differently because he is gay and because he is male (similar abuse directed at female students by male students was halted). Buckel (2000) explains:

> The different treatment because he is male gave rise to a sex discrimination claim [under Title IX]. We often find that male students are treated differently on their complaints of harassment because school administrators believe that boys should fight back physically rather than request help from administrators. The different treatment because Jamie is gay gave rise to a sexual orientation claim [under the equal protection clause of the U.S. Constitution].

One of the most important points that school officials should realize about the *Nabozny v. Podlesny* case is that failing to protect GLBTIQ students from sexual harassment based on their sex, such as telling a gay male student to "act like a man and fight back," while stopping similar abuse directed at female students, may constitute discrimination based on sex, a violation of Title IX—and schools risk losing their federal Title IX funding if found guilty in court. Buckel (2000) also points out that antigay abuse of students may also violate state and local civil rights protections, state tort law, and criminal law. Furthermore, individual administrators and teachers may be sued, as well as the school district.

A more recent case, *Colín v. Orange Unified School District* (2003), proved victorious for Anthony Colín—a sixteen-year-old high school student from Orange County, California—and several of his peers, who formed a gay–straight alliance (GSA) in their high school. The school board voted unanimously to prohibit the GSA from meeting on school property in response to complaints from parents in the community. According to attorneys from the Lambda Legal Defense and Education Fund (2000), "the school board, in preventing the GSA from meeting on school property, violated the federal Equal Access Act ... [and] the students' right to free speech, association, and equal protection under the U.S. Constitution." The case, now settled, gives the GSA the rights to "meet on school grounds, to use the school's public address system to announce club meetings, and to be featured in the school yearbook"—just like all other student clubs (Lambda Legal Defense and Education Fund 2001).

Finally, in *Henkle v. Gregory* (2003), Lambda Legal Defense and Education Fund attorneys assisted twenty-one-year-old Derek Henkle in a suit filed against Washoe County School District in Reno, Nevada. "The complaint also asserts that school officials violated Henkle's First Amendment rights by trying to silence his self-identifying speech and retaliating against him for being openly gay." Henkle suffered verbal and physical abuse almost daily from classmates. His principal told him, "Stop acting like a fag." Two school guards stood by and watched as Henkle was beaten until bloody by other students. School officials had him take classes at a local community college to obtain a GED, rather than create a safe educational environment in their own school. In an August 2002 settlement, the school district agreed to pay Henkle $450,000 and make eighteen policy changes. Moreover, a federal judge affirmed in the ruling that students have a constitutional right to speak openly about their sexual orientation in school without retaliation. In many other cases, courts are increasingly ruling in favor of GLBTIQ students who complain that their schools did little or nothing to stop antigay abuse directed at them.[2]

High Plains Safe Schools Coalition

This book illustrates how the High Plains Safe Schools Coalition (HPSSC) worked creatively to increase safety for GLBTIQ students in its local schools. The HPSSC is currently a coalition of forty individuals: twenty-one members and nineteen associate members. Dorothy, president of HPSSC, explains, "The associate members are allies. I think of it as two rings of bull's-eyes. Allies are an outer ring, further from the center of action, but still interested in being informed and helpful as opportunity allows." The members include thirteen people from the community (among these are three retired school teachers and two mothers of school-age children), three teachers, three other school district employees, an elementary principal and a high school student, who represent and have garnered the support of various community churches, government offices, and other organizations. Current HPSSC members represent the local chapter of Parents, Families, and Friends of Lesbians and Gays (PFLAG); a local synagogue; a Committee for School Improvement of an elementary school; Citizens United against Racism (discussed later); a local Unitarian Universalist Church; the High Plains County Health Department; and the city's Human Relations Commission. (At the time this research was originally conducted, HPSSC's membership was seventeen individuals.)

Four years after the High Plains School District (HPSD) school board added sexual orientation to the nondiscrimination policy, GLBTIQ students were still being harassed in the district's school. Learning of this, members of the local chapter of Parents, Families, and Friends of Lesbians and Gays (PFLAG) invited members of the local Unitarian Universalist Church; representatives from a local chapter of Gay, Lesbian, Straight Education Network (GLSEN); a school board member; GLBTIQ youth; the director of the county health department's GLBTIQ youth support group; and five other churches and one synagogue to join them in creating a "put-down free environment" for all students—with a particular emphasis on students who are harassed for real or perceived differences in gender identity or sexual orientation. As a result, on June 16, 1998, the

High Plains Safe Schools Coalition was born and held its first meeting. At this meeting the GLBTIQ youth in attendance were asked, "What would it take for you to feel safe and to have a sense of belonging in school?" Based on the youth's responses, the group came up with a mission statement and a list of goals for the HPSSC to accomplish. Dorothy, president of the HPSSC, explains that the meeting was youth-driven and that the resulting mission and goals were devised according to the youth's needs.

The group's mission statement reads, "A coalition of organizations and individuals, concerned especially with issues around sexual orientation and gender identity, working to make High Plains Schools a safe place, where every family can belong, every educator can teach, and where every child can learn." HPSSC also partnered with the state's Safe Schools Coalition, which disbanded two years later.

Members of HPSSC are involved for various reasons, including being GLBTIQ themselves, having a gay child, or simply sharing an understanding of the need to stop antigay harassment of students. The HPSSC has worked in numerous ways in the community and the school district to advocate implementation and enforcement of the district's nondiscrimination policy in regards to sexual orientation. The HPSSC was also partly responsible for the addition of sexual orientation to the district's Diversity Goal. Subsequently, the HPSSC has come to be recognized as an entity in High Plains by showing up at school board meetings, attending work sessions of the school board, and by talking with others in the community to raise awareness and support for safe schools. The HPSSC now serves as an official advisory committee to the superintendent and the school board on GLBTIQ issues.

Concerned Citizens

Besides GLBTIQ individuals and their allies, this book is concerned with the views of people who oppose the inclusion of GLBTIQ people and perspectives in the schools. Concerned Citizens is a group of parents who oppose schools' teaching about homosexuality and who organized in opposition to the inclusion of sexual orientation in the district's Diversity Goal policy in 1998. I use the name Concerned Citizens because that is how members of this group referred to themselves in a document they distributed to the school board, in which they outlined their objections to the district's policy. Also, though I refer to Concerned Citizens as a group, it should be noted that these individuals insist they are simply citizens working independently, but who share common concerns and are not part of any formal group. Furthermore, I include with Concerned Citizens other morally conservative individuals who were involved in the school board debate over the nondiscrimination policy in 1994 because they express the same beliefs. While opposition to GLBTIQ equality comes from people of many different religious faiths, all of the opponents I interviewed who disclosed their religion to me were Christian, and two were further identified as Mormon.

An interesting turn in this research is that while most Concerned Citizens base their objections to homosexuality on religious grounds in general, their objections to the school district's handling of sexual orientation issues in the classroom and district policy are not categorized as being religious in nature. Their arguments against the policies are based more on libertarian principles, such as government nonintervention and parental autonomy. For this group, *moral conservatism* is a philosophical and political stance that binds them together.

Moral Conservatism

Kenneth R. Howe (1997) in his book, *Understanding Equal Educational Opportunity*, describes "moral conservative" beliefs about school choice. He explains that moral conservatives believe in a "morally best way of life" and want to "foster correct beliefs and dispositions in their children and to insulate them from the corrupting influences of modern society." Of paramount concern to morally conservative parents is any threat to their autonomy as parents to instill in their children their beliefs. In my research, morally conservative parents expressed to me their concern that public schools, with a liberal and secular agenda, would usurp their parental authority to instill in their children their antigay beliefs. Thus, I believe the term *moral conservative* appropriately defines this group, and at least one moral conservative parent I interviewed agreed with this assessment (see Nancy's comments in the epilogue). The opposition to GLBTIQ equality from the moral conservatives I interviewed stems from their deeply held fundamentalist religious beliefs. John Vaughn, a self-proclaimed Christian fundamentalist, provides some insight into religious fundamentalist beliefs in Sears (1998). He explains:

> For the Christian fundamentalist, God communicates to us through Scripture— our most objective source of information about God. . . . Principles evidenced in the Bible are objective truths as revealed by God. . . . The Bible is His voice. . . . God made no mistakes when he transmitted the Bible to us. . . . everything He wanted is in it, and . . . everything that is in it is perfect. . . . We believe that the Bible is the final authority for faith and practice.

Vaughn goes on to explain, "We are militantly unyielding about what God has revealed, but Christian grace requires us to be patient, humane, and gracious at the level of policy." Furthermore, he says, "one of the conclusions that a true bib-lical fundamentalist must come to is that he has no right—ever—to impose by force his beliefs onto another person even if it might seem the expedient thing to do." Vaughn's statements would seem to imply that Christian fundamental-ists are not interested in affecting laws and policies or the legal processes that de-cide such issues as abortion and gay rights. In the case of this book, however, and with many other national issues, Christian fundamentalists have tried to wield their influence upon laws and policies to shape them according to their own religious beliefs and values.

William Martin, in his book *With God on Our Side: The Rise of the Religious Right in America* (1996), describes a "culture war" (Hunter 1991), where reli-gious right organizations like the Moral Majority, Christian Coalition, and Focus on the Family are rallying members to political causes such as school prayer, abstinence-only sex education programs, the banning of books from school and public libraries, and the calling for creationism to be taught along-side evolution in science classes. Martin also illustrates the tactics of such groups in promoting the election of Christian fundamentalist candidates to school boards, city councils, hospital boards, state legislatures, and the U.S. House and Senate while at the same time blocking the passage of federal, state, and local ordinances that would grant GLBTIQ people equal rights.

James W. Fraser, author of *Between Church and State: Religion and Public Education in a Multicultural America* (1999), explains that religious right lead-ers have a "negative view of the public schools" and that they support vouch-ers and other tax credits that would make it easier for morally conservative parents to send their children to religious schools "that would be free of the taint of the [National Education Association] and the public school cartel ide-ology." Fraser gives numerous examples of how moral conservatives increas-ingly perceive public institutions, including the schools, to be hostile toward people of faith. More than anything else, moral conservatives fear their chil-dren will learn secular values and beliefs with which they disagree. Fraser quotes Ralph Reed of the Christian Coalition as saying, "[The school's] pri-mary job is to reinforce the basic values taught at home, not experiment with alternative value systems." Thus, a major tension between moral conservatives and the public schools is that morally conservative parents resent their chil-dren being exposed to ideas, beliefs, and values in school that clash with the values they are taught at home and in church (Provenzo 1990).

Marty (2000) points out that "much of the debate is not about education itself but instead is about the culture that education produces." In his book, *Education, Religion, and the Common Good*, he asks, "If citizens expect educa-tion to be devoted to transmitting culture, to whom should they entrust it?" Herein lies the root tension between moral conservatives and advocates of

GLBTIQ equality. Moral conservatives believe that homosexuality is wrong and do not want their children to be taught in school that "it's okay to be gay." They believe that when schools officially include sexual orientation in nondiscrimination policies—along with gender, age, race, religion, and so on—it gives GLBTIQ students and staff "special rights" and will lead to the legitimization and promotion of homosexuality as normal and natural. Moreover, asserts Hills (1997):

> Some conservatives sound alarms that antidiscrimination laws are barely concealed weapons aimed at their beliefs. According to this view, antidiscrimination laws stigmatize traditional moral beliefs by outlawing action based on such beliefs. . . . Conservative critics charge that the message sent by such laws—their "social meaning"—is that the religious believer who disapproves of homosexuality is just as bigoted as a racist (whose actions are also prohibited by similar legislation).

Frank, a Concerned Citizen, opposed the district's statement regarding "valuing diversity" and instead favored the language "respect diversity" because the school district shouldn't "tell people they have to value certain lifestyles." Members of this group believe the topic of sexual orientation is a social issue, and social issues should be the exclusive domain of the family and perhaps the church. Concerned Citizens often reported feeling slighted by the school district; they believed their rights as parents were being trampled upon by an administration that was bowing to the demands of gay rights advocates. Richard, another Concerned Citizen, asserts that "Most of the parents, once they said their piece and lost [when the school board adopted the policy despite opponents' objections], have basically given up. I hear more of that group threatening to pull their kids [out of the public schools]. They're fed up." Frank, expressing his frustration that his rights as a parent are not being acknowledged, states, "It seems okay to discriminate against Christians."

Fraser (1999) reiterates a common sentiment expressed by moral conservatives nationwide. He states that members of this group "tend to feel discriminated against. . . . They feel modernity is against them—in matters dealing with sex, crime, pornography, education. . . . many felt themselves to be victims of 'anti-Christian bigotry.'" Carol, a Concerned Citizen who is devoutly Mormon, agrees. In her discussions with school officials she explains, "I've felt a feeling of condescension that because I'm trying to live a moral life in accordance with my conscience and the outlines that God has given in the scriptures that I'm some kind of a narrow minded bigot." Thus, this group can be characterized as opposing any district or state intervention that would challenge or override their attempts to instill in their children their belief that homosexuality is wrong. Finally, while their belief that homosexuality is wrong is rooted in religion, their arguments against the school district's handling of sexual orientation issues are rooted in libertarian themes of government non-intervention and parental autonomy.

Moral conservatives often complain that policies like these are forcing them to agree with something with which they personally disagree and are making them look like bigots in the eyes of the more liberal and tolerant public. On the other hand, advocates of equality for GLBTIQ people want the schools to declare "It's okay to be gay" and are asking for the same legal protections and rights that heterosexuals already have. Thus, a way of resolving this seemingly irreconcilable difference must be addressed, and this book does just that.

First Amendment Rights for All Students

The fact that students are often targeted for abuse and discrimination by other students, and sometimes teachers, when they speak out on the topic of gay rights begs the question of protecting free speech rights for students. Advocates of GLBTIQ student inclusion contend that GLBTIQ students are denied First Amendment rights because the fear of reprisal forces them into silence. Moral conservatives, in turn, counter that including sexual orientation in school policy violates their First Amendment rights. Thus, a deeper exploration of the First Amendment is necessary to wade through both sides' competing claims. The First Amendment to the United States Constitution states:

> Congress shall make no law respecting an establishment of religion, or prohibiting the free exercise thereof; or abridging the freedom of speech, or of the press; or the right of the people peaceably to assemble, and to petition the Government for a redress of grievances.

Forrest Gathercoal, author of *A Judicious Philosophy for School Support Personnel* (1996), affirms that students in public schools have constitutional rights. According to Imber and van Geel, authors of *A Teacher's Guide to Education Law* (2001), the First Amendment right to "freedom of expression is a cornerstone of personal freedom and democracy [and applies] to the actions of state government by virtue of the Due Process Clause of the Fourteenth Amendment." Imber and van Geel give four major themes, drawn from court decisions and political theorists, for upholding individuals' right to freedom of expression. They write:

> Freedom of expression is essential to effective operation of a system of self-government. People are unlikely to reach reasoned decisions unless they are free to debate the issues confronting them. Without freedom of expression, uncovering and challenging false ideas would be impossible, thereby drastically reducing the

possibility of advancing knowledge and impeding personal and political improvement. Freedom of expression fosters self-realization and achievement. Freedom of expression operates as a social and political safety valve permitting people to let off steam without resorting to violence.

Imber and van Geel explain freedom of association "is not explicitly guaranteed by the First Amendment [but] the Supreme Court has recognized it as a corollary of free speech. [However,] there has been little litigation exploring the right of association of [public] school students."

The First Amendment has direct bearing on public schools in our democratic society, and it bears on GLBTIQ students' abilities to take part in the systems of schooling and self-government that affect their lives. The U.S. Supreme Court, in its 1969 *Tinker v. Des Moines Independent School District* decision, declared, "It can hardly be argued that either students or teachers shed their constitutional rights to freedom of speech and expression at the schoolhouse gate" (Imber and van Geel 2001). Simultaneously, however, the "Court recognized that 'the special characteristics of the school environment' may create one of those circumstances that require modification of the way freedom of speech is understood and applied" (Imber and van Geel 2001). The implications for schools of this decision are:

> Schools must endure some risk of disturbance in order to protect the expression of ideas. . . . Schools are justified in regulating student speech only if and to the extent that regulation is necessary to prevent "material and substantial" disruption of the educational process or to protect the rights of others within the school community. [For instance, schools] may enforce reasonable regulations limiting the time, place, and manner of student expression as long as the regulations are necessary for the school to perform its educational function. . . . The Constitution require[s] the school[s] to operate as a marketplace of ideas in which students retain the right to disagree, to formulate their own positions, and to express their dissent to others. . . . School officials may not punish or prohibit speech merely because they disagree with the ideas expressed. Nor may they act to suppress or punish speech because of a generalized fear of disruption. (Imber and van Geel 2001)

The U.S. Supreme Court's 1988 decision in *Hazelwood School District v. Kuhlmeier*, gave school officials greater power in that it "ensures that schools have ample authority to pursue their legitimate educational goals by regulating student speech in curricular contexts" (Imber and van Geel 2001). Again, however, this decision does not give school officials license to act on personal subjective preferences in deciding when, where, and how to regulate student speech. In the area of students' free speech rights, there are no hard and fast rules, and courts have taken both narrow and broad interpretations of the

Tinker and *Hazelwood* cases in deciding subsequent related cases. In recent years, however, the U.S. Supreme Court has permitted the government to put more restrictions on what First Amendment rights can be exercised in a public school setting. Nonetheless, courts still generally invoke a broad principle of First Amendment rights in deciding cases of student free speech.

Religious Expression in Public Schools

The debate over the expression of GLBTIQ issues in schools often comes down to a contest between GLBTIQ rights advocates and those who oppose them on the basis of religion. In addition, opponents often claim they do not have the same right to express religious beliefs in the public schools. Therefore, it may be helpful to outline the ground rules for religious expression in the public schools issued in 1998 by Secretary of Education Richard W. Riley, at the direction of President Clinton.[3] A synopsis of the federal guidelines for religious expression in public schools is as follows:

1. Students have the same right to engage in individual or group prayer and religious discussion during the school day as they do to engage in other comparable activity.
2. Local school authorities have "substantial discretion" to impose rules of order but may not structure the rules to discriminate against religious activity or speech.
3. Students may attempt to persuade peers about religious topics as they would any other topics, but schools should stop such speech that constitutes harassment.
4. Students may participate in before- or after-school events with religious content, such as "see-you-at-the-flagpole" gatherings, on the same terms they can participate in other noncurricular activities on school premises.
5. Teachers and administrators are prohibited from either encouraging or discouraging religious activity and from participating in such activity with students.
6. Public schools may not provide religious instruction but may teach *about* religion.
7. Students may express their beliefs about religion in homework, artwork, and other written and oral assignments. The work should be judged by ordinary academic standards and against other "legitimate pedagogical concerns."
8. Students may distribute religious literature on the same terms other literature unrelated to curriculum can be distributed.

9. Schools have "substantial discretion" to excuse students from lessons objectionable on religious or other conscientious grounds. But students generally don't have a federal *right* to be excused from lessons inconsistent with religious beliefs or practices.
10. Schools may actively teach civic values and morals, even if some of those values also happen to be held by religions.
11. Students may display religious messages on clothing to the same extent they may display other comparable messages.

In essence, the law gives the same protections to students who express religious beliefs as it does to students who express other types of beliefs and opinions. Thus, morally conservative students and parents who claim that they are discriminated against because the schools limit their abilities to express their religious beliefs have no valid claim because the same rules apply to everyone equally. However, application of the rules is unequal for school personnel. Gathercoal (1996) explains:

> [Teachers] have no constitutional rights in the student/school personnel relationship. Public school authorities have the legal responsibility of respecting and ensuring student rights, but they do not enjoy the same rights in the school setting as their students. The constitutional rights public school personnel do have are those which flow between them and the school board. In other words, their rights come down to them from the employer/employee relationship, not up to them from the student/employee relationship.

Thus, teachers' and other public school employees' rights to freedom of expression are restricted to preserve a nonthreatening classroom atmosphere. For instance, racist teachers do not have the right to discuss their racist beliefs with students. Similarly, heterosexist teachers should not share their personal antigay opinions with students. This policy, however, should not stifle classroom discussion. Just as Catholicism and Judaism can be discussed by the teacher without explicitly stating or implying that one is better than the other, so too can different sexual orientations. Teachers should take a firm stance in instilling in students democratic principles such as equal rights for all people, and they should teach that discrimination based on religion or sexual orientation or other protected classes is wrong.

In This Book

This research was conducted in the city referred to as High Plains between May 2000 and April 2001. I changed the names of the city, the school district, the community groups, and individuals involved to protect their privacy (see appendixes A, B, and C for details on how this study was conducted). This book is about the High Plains Safe Schools Coalition (HPSSC) and how they advocated inclusion of sexual orientation in two of their school district's policies. The book also details the resistance they encountered from Concerned Citizens, a group of morally conservative parents in the community who opposed the inclusion of sexual orientation in the district's policies. Part I focuses on the implementation of the policies. I illustrate the strategies employed by the HPSSC in advocating the policies, and I end with suggestions for other school districts and groups who advocate equality for GLBTIQ students and families. I recommend that teachers, administrators, or those who may not have time to finish this entire book focus on part I. Part II supplements part I and highlights my data analysis. Everyone, however, should read chapter 9, as it sums up the entire debate between moral conservative opponents and GLBTQ rights advocates.

Part II provides a deeper understanding into moral conservative opposition to school policies that include sexual orientation, and it concludes with a guiding framework based on democratic principles to provide a way around the apparent stalemate of each sides' conflicting claims. I describe how the different sides in this debate understand the policies and what they believe the effects of such policies to be. HPSSC maintains that the policies are intended to prevent antigay abuse of GLBTIQ students, while Concerned Citizens contend the policies will lead to the promotion and legitimation of homosexuality. The main contention is that while schools may rightly work to change students' behaviors (i.e., prevent harassment on the part of students), it is not as clear a matter for schools to work to change students' beliefs (i.e., promote equity for GLBTIQ people in the minds of students). Finally, in the epilogue, I reflect upon the process of conducting this research, and I provide critiques of my finished study from several members of HPSSC as well as Concerned Citizens.

Notes

1. Other works that address how schools are physically unsafe for students perceived to be GLBTIQ include Arriola (1998); Kielwasser and Wolf (1994); Owens (1998); Reis and Saewyc (1999); Rofes (1994); Telljohann and Price (1993). Other works that address how schools are emotionally and developmentally unsafe places for GLBTIQ students include Anderson (1994); Besner and Spungin (1995); Committee on Adolescence, American Academy of Pediatrics (1993); D'Augelli (1998); Friend (1998); Garofalo et al. (1998); Remafedi (1990); Rotheram-Borus and Fernandez (1995).

2. In 1998, a former high school student in the Kent, Washington, school district received a settlement of $40,000. Two teachers stood by as he was assaulted, and an-

other remarked, "I already have twenty girls in my class. I don't need another" (Lipkin 1999). Also in 1998, a twelve-year-old from Pacifica, California, received $125,000 in an out-of-court settlement, and his school "agreed to teacher training and better enforcement" of nonharassment policies (Lipkin 1999).

In 2000, a Kansas student who was sexually harassed by peers who *thought* he was gay was awarded $72,500, and his school district "agreed with the U.S. Justice Department to establish a two-year program to 'prevent, identify and remediate harassment and discrimination' on the basis of sex or sexual orientation" (Morris 2000). In October 2000, a superior court in Brockton, Massachusetts, ruled that a middle school may not prohibit a transgender student from expressing her gender identity even if that expression does not conform with the sex ascribed to her at birth. The court ruled that disciplining the fifteen-year-old biological male student for wearing girls' clothing would violate her First Amendment right of free expression and constitute sex discrimination (name withheld, personal communication, October 13, 2000).

In September 2000, the Salt Lake City school board voted to overturn its 1996 ban on noncurricular clubs, which they originally instituted just to prevent a gay–straight alliance from meeting on school property. In October 2000, as part of the settlement for this case *(East High Gay/Straight Alliance v. Salt Lake City Board of Education)* and the related *East High PRISM Club v. Seidel*, the Salt Lake City School District agreed to recognize, as student clubs, both the East High Gay/Straight Alliance and the PRISM Club (a group that supplements the curriculum with GLBTIQ topics). The lawsuit claimed violation of the First Amendment and the Federal Equal Access Act of 1984. Both clubs can now meet on school property; use school bulletin boards, the public address system, and the school newspaper; and have their pictures in the school yearbook, as do other student clubs (Lambda Legal Defense and Education Fund 2001).

3. According to a spokesperson for the Bush administration's Center for Faith-Based and Community Initiative, these guidelines, like all guidelines passed under former administrations, are "under review" and may be either supported, revised, or replaced by the current administration. Until a decision is made, however, the spokesperson confirmed that these guidelines can still "provide guidance" (personal communication, July 11, 2002).

2

A History of the Two Policies

T HE HISTORY OF THIS DEBATE ILLUSTRATES HOW a mix of fortuitous and unpredictable events led to many unexpected turns, which finally resulted in
the inclusion of sexual orientation in two of High Plains School District's
policies. A history of the community and the personal histories of the key
players in these events are important in helping us understand the outcomes
of this debate. The district's nondiscrimination policy was adopted in 1994
under unusual circumstances. The second policy, the Diversity Goal, is part of
the district's Strategic Plan, a three-year plan that outlines priorities for the
school district. The history of the policies as described in this chapter is a syn-
thesis of information from interviews and school board meetings.

Adoption of the Nondiscrimination Policy

Historically, High Plains has had a well-organized GLBTIQ community and
has supported local gay rights public policy. High Plains is relatively affluent,
and, according to Button, Rienzo, and Wald (1997), affluent communities
tend to support gay rights legislation more than poorer communities. In the
early 1990s the district and the school board were relatively supportive of
GLBTIQ student issues, although the support was largely unspoken. One of
the reasons for the "behind the scenes" support was that the superintendent,
Bruce, was a closeted gay man. Bruce covertly supported several closeted lesbian staff members and program directors in the central administration who
were conducting teacher in-services that included GLBTIQ issues. In June

1992 the board adopted policy JFH-R: Student Complaints and Grievances, which details the steps for students to follow in resolving conflicts, including those based on sexual orientation. This policy, the district's first to mention sexual orientation, was passed in one vote with almost no discussion and without resistance. However, it was seemingly forgotten and never mentioned in the following debates over the inclusion of sexual orientation in the nondiscrimination policy and the Diversity Goal.

During this time in the early 1990s, Trisha, who is lesbian, was a program director in the district's central office. She offered a class on how to work with GLBTIQ adolescents for teachers, administrators, and other people in the district. The class focused on school safety issues and motivated participants to become more politically active in advocating for GLBTIQ student's rights. Trisha recounts, "There was a lot of interest in it. We offered it several times. There were probably twenty people [in each] class." Then, in 1992, the passage of a statewide ballot initiative that sought to limit legal recourse for gay, lesbian, and bisexual people had a galvanizing effect on Trisha and others who took her class. She explains:

I personally got really pissed off and decided I'm not going to take it anymore. And so I decided to come out more at work. I came out in the class and that touched a lot of people in the class. [It] got several [of them] motivated to do some more active things in their schools.

The passage of the state ballot initiative posed a direct threat to GLBTIQ individuals and their supporters. It spurred them to address the topic of discrimination based on sexual orientation within the district and in their own schools. In January 1993, Trisha, along with other district employees and community members, formed a group called the Coalition in order to, in Trisha's words, "offer support to gay, lesbian, bisexual and transgendered youth." Trisha continues:

And that coalition then became, for me, a front that I could hide behind, really, that I could be politically active and not worry about having my name out there or having repercussions in the district. So I did a lot of behind the scenes political work through that group.

After several meetings, the Coalition came up with various goals to pursue with the district in supporting GLBTIQ students. According to Trisha:

One of the things we really wanted to do was to get it into the curriculum. We wanted gay issues taught; we wanted it infused into the curriculum so when you taught about literature you'd talk about gay artists and gay authors and that kind of thing. But we decided that was the last priority because that's the hardest.

Instead of pursuing curricular inclusion at the outset, Trisha stated that the Coalition "worked quietly behind closed doors" and "started offering trainings and collaborating [with the local GLBTIQ youth support group] and putting together Safe Teacher Trainings" through the district's central administration. The Coalition also kept in touch with district staff who had been a part of earlier classes on working with GLBTIQ students by keeping them apprised of other classes and meetings on the topic. Trisha explained, "Doing things quietly is more effective to prevent opposition"; it is a good first step so that the group can then make "promotional efforts."

The Coalition's next objective was to get sexual orientation included in the Diversity Goal of the district's Annual Goals (later called the Strategic Plan), a set of five or six districtwide goals that served as a guide for each school's own set of goals. Trisha admitted, "We thought that was going to be pretty hard." The Coalition began working behind the scenes with several top-level administrators, including the superintendent who, according to Trisha, "would publicly deny any knowledge of the Coalition" so as not to bring scrutiny upon himself. At this time the school board began rewriting the district's Annual Goals. One of the goals was a Diversity Goal, in which the Coalition wanted the district to include sexual orientation as a protected class along with race, ethnicity, gender, age, disability, and religion.

Trisha explained that in order to make it appear that the community, as a whole, supported the inclusion of sexual orientation in the Annual Goals' Diversity Goal, the Coalition got someone under the superintendent to

set up several community meetings without a whole lot of notice. [The district was] trying to get community input [on the Annual Goals] so they set up these [meetings] in schools around the district and what we did was we networked with all of our contacts from the classes and we got representatives to go to each of those meetings and to bring up the issue [of adding sexual orientation to the Diversity Goal]. And so there were six meetings held and we had representatives at all of them. Some parents would come but they weren't super well attended so we got a voice there just through this behind the scenes networking. When you had two or three people speaking up like that in a group of ten it got noticed. [District officials] couldn't overlook that in all the meetings this was a common theme, people saying, "Sexual orientation should be included."

As a result, including sexual orientation in the Diversity Goal "was on the table and the school board had to start looking at it." The Coalition knew, however, that adding sexual orientation to a district policy would be a big leap for the new school board, especially since the new board president and other members had reputations as being politically conservative. Thus, the Coalition decided to approach the inclusion of sexual orientation as "an area for future study."

The Coalition's strategy with the school board was to request the formation of a committee that would meet for one year simply to "study and recommend to the board ways to encourage tolerance and respect for all people," which was in line with the Diversity Goal's intent. The committee's objective, to study and recommend to the board ways of "encouraging tolerance and respect for all people," would include GLBTIQ students. Trisha added that a related objective would be to explore ways that the district might be able to work sexual orientation into the curriculum.

The first two times the Coalition met with the school board, they took with them various "local experts," such as adults who work with GLBTIQ youth and who testified about "how hard developmentally it was for gay kids in school and how much they're discriminated against." The Coalition also took GLBTIQ youth themselves, who testified to the levels of antigay abuse they suffered in the schools and how it affected them. Trisha recalls the first two sessions of discussion went well. At the third session, on May 12, 1994, the school board would vote on whether or not to form the committee to study for one year how to ensure that schools are safe and secure for GLBTIQ students and if it would be possible to incorporate sexual orientation issues into the curriculum.

However, explains Trisha, by that third meeting the "Right Wing had got wind of what was going on and they had flyered and they had e-mailed and they were going to have their people there en masse." Trisha recalled that many of the protestors were from outside the district and even from out of state. Bruce recalled that some of the protesters were representatives of the Boy Scouts of America. Members of the Coalition knew that the local chapter of Parents, Families, and Friends of Lesbians and Gays (PFLAG) was meeting that same night and telephoned them for support. Immediately, all the PFLAG members rushed down to the school board meeting to help counter the message of the protesters. An emotional and somewhat violent debate ensued.

Trisha related that at some point during the meeting, a gay man in attendance with his male partner leaned over and kissed his partner. Trisha recounts:

And one of the Right Wing people freaked out and started screaming, "Oh my God! There are faggots here! There are faggots here! Oh my God! They're kissing!" and ran from the lobby into the boardroom screaming this. Well this [gay] high school student that we had taken to talk got really upset. This woman came running in the room screaming and the [gay] student came running in the room and I thought she was after him. And he started saying, "Yes, I'm a faggot! So what?" and flaunting himself down the aisle. And I just thought, "Oh my God." So I went over and I grabbed this woman by the arm and just intervened. I just got in her face and said, "You need to back off right now. You need to get control of yourself. You need to cool it." So she stopped and somebody else got the high school student and calmed him down, sat him down. So that was this wild thing. So I stood in the back of the room next to her just kind of watching her for a long time and then at one point she started going off again. She started getting hysterical so I turned to her and I said, "You need to leave now" because it was about to turn into a riot and my heart was just pounding. And so she turned around and left with her boyfriend. People were kind of converging on her so they just ran out. They jumped in their Jeep and took off and a few minutes later security came and it was really intense. And a really cool thing that happened for me personally was that the next day, another administrator called me up and she said, "I saw what happened in the meeting and I saw what you did. I really think that took a lot of guts. I don't know how you did it with so much tension and so much hatred being spewed out in that room." You know, that felt really good that she acknowledged that and was supportive.

Seventy people signed up to speak at the school board meeting that night. The allotted time for community input was quickly exhausted, however, and not all who signed up were able to speak. During the community input portion of the meeting, one protester exclaimed:

Sexuality of any kind should not be taught in the public schools. It is a very divisive issue and the schools are already facing many difficulties without adding this to them. We should focus on excellence in academics and leave social programs to individual families. I do agree, though, that violence against anyone is wrong. We all can agree on that.

Another added:

I believe the foundation of life is God the Creator. And I believe the moral absolutes that his word presents. [He quotes a passage from the Bible here and continues.] God created Adam and Eve and not Adam and Steve. God ordains and supports heterosexual union in marriage, only. He condemns homosexual behavior. I believe allowing my children to be taught anything that contradicts God's word and commands is irresponsible to the wonderful privilege of being a father. I implore you to teach my children academics but leave their moral and character training and discipline to me and their creator, God. Do not add any curriculum as it regards homosexuals, gay, lesbian, bisexual, pedophilia, homophobia or otherwise to my children's training and I added those others even though they have not been discussed because I feel that they will creep into the curriculum.

The two most common themes evident in the messages of those protesting were that schools should focus on academics, not social issues, and that God does not approve of homosexuality. Another protester mentioned that the majority's tax dollars should not be spent on an issue that affects only a minority (i.e., homosexuals). Other themes surfaced: the school district encouraging children to experiment with homosexuality, homosexuals leading shorter and less healthy lives, and gays not being given special rights. Other protesters mentioned that teachers shouldn't be burdened with this type of issue and threatened to homeschool their children if the district did not provide an alternative education for families who did not want their children exposed to a curriculum that included sexual orientation.

Trisha recalls:

> The Right Wing people had been coached. I mean I saw a flyer that they were given on what to say. Some of them didn't even really know what was going on or what [the meetings were] about. They just showed up enraged, fired up, and they were gonna say whatever they were told to say. So all of them got up there and said, "We don't want anybody hurt. We don't want anybody to be discriminated against. We just don't want this in the curriculum."

After community input, it was time for the board to vote on whether a committee would be formed to "study and recommend to the board ways to encourage tolerance and respect for all people." Colleen, the conservative school board president, explained that she saw both sides of the issue. Getting very emotional and choking up, Colleen disclosed that she has two brothers, one of whom is gay. Between short sobs, she explained she was very fond of both of her brothers but also agreed that schools should focus on academics.[1] Colleen and other board members opposed the inclusion of sexual orientation issues in the curriculum, seeing it as "values instruction" and thus opposed the formation of a committee to consider it as an area for future study. Drawing on both sides' expressed agreement that no student should be subject to peer harassment in school, Colleen proposed a compromise to "prevent this [controversy] from going any further." She proposed a districtwide nondiscrimination policy that would state, "The HPSD will not tolerate discrimination, harassment, or violence against anyone including students or teachers regardless of race, ethnicity, gender, sexual orientation, or religion and will encourage respect for all people."

Another board member then made the point, "The policy itself won't be enough. If we're serious about nondiscrimination, then we need some guidelines about how we're going to handle it when it happens." (These guidelines already existed in policy JFH-R: Student Complaints and Grievances, which lays out a procedure for students to follow in resolving cases of discrimination, including discrimination based on sexual orientation. The school board president and other board members, however, were unaware of this policy, which was adopted two years prior under another board.) Insisting that guidelines were necessary, a motion was made to amend the original statement to read, "Study and recommend to the board ways to encourage tolerance and respect for all people, clarify the board's policy intent to prohibit harassment and discrimination, resolve conflicts that arise, and develop accountability procedures for those instances where conflicts are not resolved." However, Colleen and a majority of board members were opposed to the "extremely broad language of that statement," and the motion failed.

Colleen then moved to have her previous statement added, and the motion passed. What started out as an attempt to get sexual orientation in the Diversity Goal took some twists and turns and ultimately resulted in a nondiscrimination policy. Thus, HPSD's nondiscrimination policy that includes sexual orientation was adopted (see appendix D). Trisha recounts:

> So it was really a coup, I think, for our group that Colleen did the thing of, "I have a gay brother" and "But I can't see putting this in the curriculum either. But what I hear you people saying is you don't want gay people hurt. So can't we make a policy to that effect?" And they went and they created the policy right there in the meeting, voted on it, and we were sitting there. I mean it was very difficult emotionally to be in that room, it was so tense. But we were sitting there going, "Oh my God. They're writing a policy! We're getting a policy out of it, not a committee!" [laughing] And, "Okay, who cares about the curriculum stuff. That's gonna come later anyway." And the Right Wing people felt like they had won, like they had charged in there by God and they had "stopped them from doing this thing" and they were totally fine with the policy [Colleen] came up with. And we just sat back sort of smirking going, "Okay, once it's in the policy, that's so much more than what we were asking for. We can really build on that. We can really take it and run." So, it was cool.

Dorothy, president of the High Plains Safe Schools Coalition, agrees that the resulting policy was "kind of quirky" and that it was "a fluke" that the school board voted to add sexual orientation to a nondiscrimination policy as a compromise. I asked Colleen if everybody went home happy from the school board meeting that night. She responded:

> I think there were some people who were unhappy. There were some parents who had come and spoken about their children who were gay and had difficulties coming out with the gay issue when they were in high school and they were not happy [because more was not done to advocate GLBTIQ students' rights]. The crowd, in general, went away reasonably pleased. Pretty much everybody, except for some real fringe people said they, "Didn't support discrimination against anyone, couldn't we just leave it at that and move on?" There were some fringe folks who said things that were extremely painful, as someone who has a brother who is gay. Afterwards I felt terrible because I thought I had created a good compromise but it was with people who I otherwise had absolutely nothing in common, particularly the more radical ones. So it was a traumatic evening for me. It's the only time I ever cried after a board meeting.

I also asked Colleen, "Looking back, do you have any regrets about making that policy?" Colleen replied, "No." She went on to explain:

> My entire family is supportive of my brother and his partner. They're a part of our family. It hurt my feelings for people to think that I was homophobic. . . . I talked to my [gay] brother ahead of [the meeting] and he is in education also. He's the vice president of a college in California. His partner is a member of ACT UP [an activist gay rights organization] so they are very aggressively gay issue oriented. He felt that what we needed to do was to have more academic emphasis and less values. So much money was going into values education and not enough into core curriculum and he agreed with me and I wouldn't have done something that would have offended him. I have no regrets.

I asked Trisha, "If Colleen had not had a gay brother, what do you think would have been the outcome of that meeting?" Trisha responded:

> That's hard to speculate. [Colleen] still wanted to look reasonable. She may still have gone that route of, "Okay. We don't want [GLBTIQ students harassed]." But I don't know. Maybe it took her having a gay brother because she was just so, flaming, you know radical [right].

When I asked Colleen if she thought having a gay brother influenced her decision at the meeting, she replied that having a gay brother "made me sensitive to it." Finally, the other board member's statement—that "The policy itself won't be enough. If we're serious about nondiscrimination then we need some guidelines about how we're going to handle it when it happens"—was forgotten and never acted upon. Although the nondiscrimination policy was implemented, it was inconsistently done. For instance, several program directors in the district's central administration took the policy as encouragement to start offering more in-services to district staff on how to stop antigay peer harassment. The nondiscrimination policy also appeared in a 1995 edition of the district's *Students' and Parents' Rights and Responsibilities* handbook, distributed to all students at the beginning of the school year. Even with these measures to implement the policy underway, many teachers and administrators remained unaware of the policy until 1998, when *(a)* the HPSSC demanded that the district do more to implement and enforce the nondiscrimination policy, and *(b)* when a subsequent school board added sexual orientation to the Diversity Goal of the district's Strategic Plan (previously known as the "Annual Goals").

Antigay Abuse in HPSD after the
Adoption of the Nondiscrimination Policy

After the adoption of the nondiscrimination policy in 1994, Trisha and others continued to offer classes and workshops for teachers and administrators in the district. One such workshop focused on how to handle antigay name-calling, as well as other types of name-calling. Trisha recalls:

> There are always some teachers, even in the best schools, who aren't comfortable with [stopping antigay name-calling] for whatever reason, religious or their own sexual issues. . . . Some do actively resist, and with others it's gonna be, "I'm just not comfortable with that and do we really have to go there? Why do we have to do this? I'm not gonna do it." They feel like it's more a personal choice, whereas with most district policies, it doesn't matter what your personal beliefs are, you enforce it because it's policy. But it seems like people feel like they can make their own choice on this one [whether to enforce the policy or not]. And religion does play a part.

Even with the addition of sexual orientation to the nondiscrimination policy and even with occasional workshops on the topic, many GLBTIQ students in High Plains continued to suffer emotional and physical antigay abuse from peers and even teachers. The director of the local health department's sexual orientation and gender identity support group for GLBTIQ youth under twenty-one told me about the following examples from the High Plains School District:

> Verbal harassment saturates every GLBTIQ youth's experience—I hear that every day. . . . Another gay youth got surrounded by other kids and was dowsed with water. He reported it in the office and was told to fill out a form, and nobody in the office offered to help him. . . . One lesbian girl was verbally harassed on a daily basis by the same group of boys. She filed numerous reports and nothing was done. Finally she was transferred to another school and I just think that's so ludicrous. Instead of addressing the problem, the school got rid of it by blaming the victim and transferring her out. . . . A female sophomore was the victim of continuous antigay verbal harassment and she was pushed and shoved into lockers. The counselors offered to help but she was too afraid and didn't trust the counselors—she didn't want to be re-victimized—and so she dropped out. She was afraid the situation would just get worse. . . . A transsexual youth, who self-identified as female to male, found no recognition of the transsexual experience anywhere in the school except in psychology class where transsexualism was listed under "disorders" and the teacher made incredibly "transphobic" and discriminating comments about transsexuals. So the only information this kid received was how trans folks are confused and mentally ill people. This kid was socially isolated—he had only one friend in a different school. He had

no support and was afraid to talk to anyone. When he discovered the GLBTIQ youth support group, it changed his life because he found social support and acceptance for the first time. He found the GLBTIQ youth support group in his senior year and now he's in college and doing well. (Personal communication, December 3, 1999)

Sexual Orientation in the Diversity Goal: "Valuing" versus "Respecting" Diversity

In 1998, four years after the High Plains school board added sexual orientation to the nondiscrimination policy, Dorothy, the president of the HPSSC, says she was "appalled that nothing had changed." GLBTIQ students were still being harassed in school. For example, some schools had posted the first paragraph of the nondiscrimination policy, which, for some reason unknown to everyone I interviewed, does not reflect the addition of sexual orientation. Many administrators and most teachers were unaware that the policy existed. GLBTIQ students who were being harassed had few, if any, resources for support, although a few GLBTIQ-friendly teachers, counselors, and intervention specialists were scattered around the district and offered informal support to GLBTIQ students in their schools.

A new school board was elected in 1997, and Colleen, as well as other conservative board members, were replaced by new members characterized as being more liberal. HPSSC reports the new and current board is much more supportive of issues affecting GLBTIQ students in general. Concerned Citizens concede that they had more support from the previous board. Serendipitously for the HPSSC, two school board members wrote a letter to the editor of the local paper in the summer of 1998 inviting the public to give input on the district's Strategic Plan, which was being reconsidered by the current school board. HPSSC used this opportunity as a foothold to give its input into getting the school district to enforce the nondiscrimination policy and to put sexual orientation in the Strategic Plan's Diversity Goal (see appendix E), as the Coalition had attempted to do four years previously and which resulted in the current nondiscrimination policy. The HPSSC's rationale was that the Diversity Goal—which listed the protected classes of race, ethnicity, gender, age, disability, and religion—should be brought in line with the district's nondiscrimination policy and should therefore include sexual orientation.

In response, Concerned Citizens, who were suspicious that the district would be promoting a gay-positive social agenda, mobilized in opposition to the HPSSC's efforts to get sexual orientation included in the district's Diversity Goal. Besides morally conservative parents, opposition to the inclusion of sexual orientation in the Diversity Goal came from Citizens United against Racism (CUAR), an official advisory committee to the school board composed of people of color. CUAR sensed a sea change from a focus on race and ethnicity to sexual orientation insofar as the district's efforts at promoting diversity. An alliance was eventually formed between the HPSSC and the CUAR advisory committee, with both sides recognizing commonalities in their efforts. (This relationship is detailed in the next chapter.) However, what took a great deal of effort, a wealth of resources, and a wide variety of strategies was to not only persuade the school board to include sexual orientation in the Diversity Goal but to also counteract the efforts of the opposition.

Videotaped school board meetings reveal that for seven months, beginning August 1998 and carrying through to February 1999, school board meetings were often consumed by the debate around adding sexual orientation to the Diversity Goal. The main contention of Concerned Citizens to the inclusion of sexual orientation in the Diversity Goal was the word "value" in the Diversity Goal, which read "Value Diversity and Promote Understanding." Opponents expressed the belief that if sexual orientation was listed as a type of diversity, along with race, ethnicity, gender, age, disability, and religion, the Diversity Goal would be sending the message that everyone must "value homosexuality." Furthermore, it raised fears that homosexuality would creep into the curriculum. In an October 28, 1998, letter to the school board president, a parent in the district wrote, "I received an e-mail from a member of my church [that] states 'Valuing sexual orientation will become a part of what is talked about in all district programs,' i.e., we will now be promoting the homosexual lifestyle in our curriculum."

In preparation for what lay ahead, HPSSC secured the support of churches and a synagogue, as well as community organizations and government officials, including a commissioner from the local Human Rights Commission and a state senator. Then, in August 1998, Dorothy took a group of gay, lesbian, bisexual, and transgendered youth to a school board meeting to testify about the harassment they faced in the district's schools. She did this to "warm up [board members] to our goals." A gay former student who had recently graduated from a High Plains school stated:

> I overheard two teachers talking and one referred to a student she was describing as "the faggot." In class, while watching a video, a table behind me was gay-bashing a student the entire time. I looked over and the teacher was sitting right beside us reading a book ignoring the entire conversation. I also couldn't find any information in the hallways posted anywhere. When school's not safe you can't explore and you're closeted and there's no way of coming out.

Another former student, who is bisexual, said:

I am a [class of 1997] High Plains graduate. I had a math teacher once who referred to a student as a faggot and all the other students laughed. There were constant remarks in the hallways and often times it was in front of teachers and hallway monitors who did nothing. I had an English teacher once who was trying to
describe a Shakespeare character who was weak and effeminate and she laughed
and agreed when other students yelled out faggot and fairy. These daily occurrences made me feel unsafe in my school. It was a hostile environment. It was not
conducive to learning experiences at all. I had one teacher who didn't allow
name-calling and set a safe space for learning for all students.

A former student who is female and transgendered testified:

I'm an out lesbian and a high school dropout of this district and my reason for
dropping out is nothing short of the discrimination and harassment I felt as a
student based on my sexual orientation. In my world literature class as a sopho-
more, we were given a poem in which a man describes what he looks for in a
woman romantically. Our assignment after reading the poem was to write an
essay about what we looked for in people of the opposite sex romantically. This
is not something I could participate in because I do not look for anything other
than friendship in men. I felt very upset and confused by this and even more
upset when the teacher separated the class, women on one side and men on the
other side and we had to tell the people on the opposite side what we're looking
for romantically from them. This sort of stuff should not be going on in the
school district.

Finally, a current student spoke for other GLBTIQ students who were afraid
to speak for themselves. The student relayed:

I'm here on behalf of many students who couldn't be here for fear of being outed
and discriminated in the High Plains schools they'll attend this year. . . . I'm also
here to state my fear. I will not feel safe in school this year. I hope you'll consider
requiring training for teachers so teachers can help make High Plains schools a
safe place for GLBTIQ youth.

As a result of the youth's testimonies, Dorothy recalled, "The school board
members were touched and agreed that the abuse and harassment should not
happen." That board meeting was also in preparation for a school board work
session the following month, during which, the HPSSC would make a presentation to the board on the needs of GLBTIQ students and why the board
should include sexual orientation in the Diversity Goal.

Prior to the work session, Dorothy gave all the board members a packet of
information that included testimony from GLBTIQ youth as well as legal con-

cerns, like Title IX, in the hopes that board members would read it and be better prepared for HPSSC's presentation. At the work session, Dorothy recalled that two board members appeared not to have read it, were noncommunicative, and seemed not to care about what HPSSC was presenting. Dorothy went through the district's nondiscrimination policy line by line and talked about what it entailed and how to enforce it. Again, she had GLBTIQ students present their own stories of harassment and recalled, "This was the most compelling part of the presentation." A principal added, "When speakers from the [GLBTIQ youth group] come in and talk, it helps legitimize it. There's an air of legitimacy to it that helps." Dorothy described the two reticent board members as a "brick wall" but said the five other board members favored HPSSC's proposal to include sexual orientation in the Diversity Goal. The five board members' support would soon be challenged, however.

During the work session, a woman whom Dorothy did not know, asked Dorothy for a copy of HPSSC's presentation. Dorothy explained that the woman then used it to "rile up conservative parents." Dorothy contends the unknown woman misquoted the presentation, which led "a minister of a local Fundamentalist Christian church" and other parents to believe "there was going to be a secret vote [on the part of the school board] to include discussions of sexual orientation in the curriculum." In response, Dorothy set up a meeting with the minister, which, coincidentally, happened to take place just after Matt Shepard's murder and the ensuing media blitz. During the meeting Dorothy explained to the minister that HPSSC was concerned only with safety and had no intentions of "teaching homosexuality" in the classroom. Dorothy thinks that, in part, the minister was swayed by the beating death of Matt Shepard, as well as her arguments, and he ended up agreeing with HPSSC's premise that the schools should be safe for all students.

Shortly thereafter, parents opposing the inclusion of sexual orientation in the Diversity Goal organized and took their opinions to the next and subsequent school board meetings At first, their arguments focused on the contention that harassment of students for any reason was already prohibited by the nondiscrimination policy, and it was not the place of the school board to tell students what types of diversity they should value. For instance, an opposing parent asked, "What's being done to enforce the current [nondiscrimination] policy? I've read it over myself and it seems to be a very strong policy on its own. I think it just needs to be enforced. What's being done in that regard?" Another parent said the language of the Diversity Goal

> seems to imply that schools will be teaching morals and ethics in order to value diversity and promote understanding. I'm really alarmed at any program that addresses one's personal attitudes even if the program is well intentioned. If the

program happens to clash with one's personal beliefs, how are you going to guarantee that this program won't be used to, say, intimidate the teacher? A much better plan would be to greatly enforce and strengthen the present nondiscrimination policy and then use the state law as a model for teaching diversity which states we are to teach the history and culture of ethnic minorities.

Another argument posed by morally conservative parents, as well as the two school board members who supported them, was that spelling out protected classes would lead to further divisions between people. One of the opposing school board members contended, "By enumerating privileged categories we are forcing children to identify themselves into various groups, therefore, balkanizing our student body. We are forcing people into polarization." The other opposing school board member agreed saying, "As we promote cultural plurality we tend to disunite as Americans."

In an attempt to get beyond the controversy spurred by the phrase "value diversity," another board member suggested the phrase "respect diversity" in its place. Opponents agreed that the word "respect" would be an acceptable compromise and would largely take care of their concerns about the implication of the word "value"—that is, it circumvented the implication that students would be forced to "value homosexuality." However, the HPSSC and other advocates strongly resisted replacing "value" with "respect." Dorothy, the president of the HPSSC, later explained to me that she would have been okay with "respect diversity" were it not for another member of HPSSC and a school board member who both wanted to keep the language "value diversity." According to Dorothy, "They wanted to alter attitudes and they thought 'respect' would let people off too easy. They convinced me that 'valuing' over 'respect' was indeed what we wanted to help change attitudes about accepting differences, not about accepting homosexuality." A school board member who supported "value diversity" explained:

> "Value" encompasses more than just "respect." We cannot expect students to succeed if we do not value them. [Concerned Citizens] propose the change because they believe the word "value" meant that the district would be forcing their children to accept gays. This point sends the message that gays do not have value. This is the last thing that students who are struggling with their sexual identity need to hear. We must be supportive without judgment of all students and validate their experience. . . . "Respect" may be a safe neutral word but we cannot be neutral. We must be active in promoting a safe learning environment for everyone.

On the surface, the debate turned into a "war over words." At a deeper level, however, the meanings each group ascribed to their words of choice reflected differing opinions over the purpose of schooling; that is, schools should or should not legitimate a gay lifestyle.

Subsequently, school board members and administrators from the district's central office met with members of Concerned Citizens. The objective was to hear their concerns in an attempt to work out a compromise draft of the Diversity Goal and its accompanying beliefs by incorporating language acceptable to both the HPSSC and Concerned Citizens. One meeting between members of Concerned Citizens and a high-level district administrator resulted in a document containing recommendations for changes in language that were subsequently presented to the school board by Concerned Citizens. Their recommended changes replaced the word "value" with the word "respect," in line with their contention that while they cannot "value all differences," they can "respect that all people have differences."

At the school board meeting of January 28, 1999, the deputy superintendent, having met with Concerned Citizens, recommended changes to the Diversity Goal and its accompanying beliefs, resulting from that meeting. Concerned Citizens believed that spelling out protected classes of people was not as inclusive as saying "all people" and that acts of discrimination based on characteristics like height, for example, might go unpunished because "height" is not spelled out as a protected class. For instance, a concerned parent explained:

> There was a case recently where a short child shot a tall child. There was discrimination going on there by size. So we just sense that if you just leave "all students" then we have a very good solid base to say, "That means everybody."

Another proposed change was a compromise between spelling out the protected classes, which Concerned Citizens believed to be limiting, and trying to account for other characteristics upon which individuals might be discriminated against, like height. The compromise was to use the following language: "All students regardless of diversity . . ." Along with this wording, "diversity" would be defined as "Group and individual differences that are characteristic of all human beings which include, and are not limited to, race, ethnicity, gender, sexual orientation, age, disability, or religion." The deputy superintendent, speaking for Concerned Citizens, explained that by using the language "which include but are not limited to" would help to account for other characteristics (like height) for which individuals might be discriminated against. Interestingly, a member of the audience who advocated spelling out the protected classes understood this point of contention and offered the following suggestion in an attempt to allay the opponents' concern:

> I would like to offer an alternative slightly more inclusive statement which is as follows: "All students regardless of race, ethnicity, gender, sexual orientation, age, disability, religion, *or physical or emotional differences* deserve a quality education in an environment free of discrimination, harassment and violence."

This suggestion, it seems, would have covered all other characteristics, like height and weight. However, it was either forgotten or ignored by the school board.

By this time, the school board members had grown tired of the word-smithery being proposed as compromises to try to make both sides happy. Finally, one board member exclaimed, "Let's just leave the goals alone. They're clear. Tinkering with more changes will just confuse the community and that's not a good idea." This began a heated discussion amongst board members in which each board member made her or his position clear. A board member who supported HPSSC's position all along explained his position on the issue:

> If we adopt a document that creates the impression that difference in hair color or height or the type of clothes you wear are of as much significance to the district as differences in race or ethnicity or religion or sexual orientation, we make a serious mistake. If we create a climate in our schools in which teasing a kid because he has a red shirt and not a blue shirt is considered as serious as teasing a kid because he's Jewish or gay or African American, we make a real serious mistake. . . . We have to make it clear that this type of harassment is particularly serious. We have to be very clear about that. . . . Families, of course, rightfully develop moral beliefs, and so do churches and synagogues and friends and our government, to some extent, and so do schools. And I don't want to create the impression that somehow it's part of this document that we believe that families have a unique right to teach morality. Many families are completely dysfunctional and teach no morality at all and it's up to the rest of us in society through the schools and other institutions to step in and to help kids develop morality. (Videotaped school board meeting, January 28, 1999)

In response, one of the two opposing board members charged, "This brings us back to where we were two months ago! Once again [you've] included sexual orientation that I believe you heard many members of the community do not hold as a value for their children and students." The other opposing board member asked, "What about the fat kid who is harassed and severely beaten? Will we tolerate it because he does not belong to any privileged group?" (videotaped school board meeting, January 28, 1999).

A supporting board member then attempted to explain how he understood "value diversity" and made an impassioned plea to end the "war over words":

> This [debate] has been disheartening because I've heard people say "Well, I just want to win," like having this language in here means that somebody's won and somebody's lost. This is about providing a safe environment for our kids. It's not about us as adults winning or losing something. . . . It's been quite a conversation just to see the extremes and the behaviors and the way that we've come about

this. At this point I just think we should be succinct and put [value diversity] in there and list the categories, or not, and vote on it that way. (Videotaped school board meeting, January 28, 1999)

This concluded discussion on the Strategic Plan's Diversity Goal at this meeting, where it was moved to action so it could be voted on at the next school board meeting.

At the next school board meeting on February 2, 1999, Concerned Citizens made their final effort to convince the board to change the language of the Diversity Goal to "respect diversity." A new approach was taken by a morally conservative parent in an attempt to change the opinions of board members. The parent first referred to another belief statement from a different part of the Strategic Plan, which read, "Diverse student characteristics are accommodated through a variety of learning options and classroom environments." The parent contended that "diverse student characteristics" could be interpreted to include sexual orientation. He explained, "Sexual orientation implies a behavior and a lifestyle and I don't believe that should be accommodated in school through a variety of learning options and classroom environments." The parent went on to criticize belief number two, which states, "All students, regardless of race, ethnicity, gender, sexual orientation, age, disability or religion, deserve a quality education." He contended:

> By attaching certain groups with quality education it implies that, by virtue of belonging to that group, a student may not be receiving a quality education in the High Plains School District now. Speaking to the issue of quality education and not harassment, I ask, "What is lacking in the quality [of] education to students now of the groups identified under harassment? Are they not being prepared to enter the university or workforce like the rest of the students?" Successfully writing a business letter or solving physics problems has nothing to do with diversity. It has everything to do with quality education. For this reason belief two should be revised to say, "A quality education is the goal for all children."

Other Concerned Citizens repeated their arguments from previous school board meetings, and one of the opposing school board members proclaimed, "Enumerating special protected classes will lead to quotas and I have a serious problem with that." For a brief period, the arguments of the Concerned Citizens appeared to be having an effect on some of the school board members. The board president agreed with another board member that, "The protected classes should be pulled out of the definition of diversity because the definition of diversity is something much broader than just the protected classes." To this, another school board member, whose opinion had not wavered, responded:

We're dealing with trying to establish a certain attitude and culture, if you will, in the schools. . . . We have to deal with the categories because these are the categories that I firmly believe have traditionally and identifiably suffered harassment and intimidation and all kinds of discrimination and it's important to me that the school district state these categories here. (Videotaped school board meeting, February 11, 1999)

The two originally dissenting school board members continued to oppose the language "value diversity" and the inclusion of sexual orientation as well as the other protected classes. The other board members, some of whose opinions had slightly wavered, were brought back to their original position of retaining the language "value diversity" and the inclusion of sexual orientation along with the other protected classes. The Diversity Goal, along with its accompanying beliefs, was adopted by a five–two vote, with school board members ultimately keeping their original positions on the issue.

How the Policies Have Made a Difference

Most staff I interviewed agreed that, since the policies' adoptions, "the climate is better" for GLBTIQ students, although it is still far from ideal. Interestingly, however, many staff were reluctant to point to the district's policies as the source for this change. Rather, they attributed the change in climate to a change in consciousness or awareness. It is doubtful this change would have occurred without the policies, however. One staff member explained:

It's directly related to the beliefs of our teachers and staff and their tolerance for behaviors that are different than their own. Our Dean of Students found a couple of young men kissing and he was shocked because he hadn't seen that [before] and I'm proud that he handled it like any public display of affection. We frown on kids making out in the halls. So he dealt with that as if it were a male/female [couple], as if they were heterosexual and there were no repercussions from [being a same-sex couple]. I think what's contributed perhaps is we've been consistent in dealing with that kind of an issue and not making a big deal out of it.

Along with a better climate has come more support and inclusion for GLBTIQ people and perspectives. Examples given by interviewees included:

- alternative assemblies on same-sex marriage, instead of a mock heterosexual wedding, at one high school;
- students' showing interest in starting gay–straight alliances;
- teachers and school libraries' having on their shelves books with GLBTIQ characters and families;

- teachers' posting SAFE ZONE posters, or other posters advocating respect and tolerance for all students;
- teachers and student groups' inviting GLBTIQ speakers to address students;
- teachers' beginning to use inclusive language and other curricular examples that don't assume heterosexuality or traditional gender roles;
- GLBTIQ staff's coming out of the closet, and
- heterosexual staff's bringing up the topic of being inclusive of GLBTIQ people at staff and other meetings.

Another factor has provided evidence that adoption and implementation of the policies have helped make a difference: district staff and students are now taking responsibility for monitoring their own language and actions, as well as those of others, to help create an inclusive and safe atmosphere for GLBTIQ students and staff. More and more often teachers are stopping the name-calling, bullying, and other forms of harassment. One teacher told me she has witnessed this transformation in the teacher's lounge on the part of teachers:

> Other teachers [make] comments about, "That's not appropriate" and make the staff lounge a positive environment by asking that people make positive comments about other staff, people, and students and that's in reaction to some [intolerant] comments that are just not appreciated.

Teachers report that one effect of their stopping harassment and addressing it when it happens has been that their students do the same. A teacher explained, "One thing I've noticed is how much the kids monitor each other. I've really seen kids jump on each other when they say, 'That's so gay' and I say to them, 'Thank you.' I see this everywhere in the school." Another teacher said, "Kids will come to me and say, 'I know you would want to know this. This is written on the bathroom wall down in the seventh grade pod.'" Thus, teachers report a new consciousness and raised awareness about GLBTIQ people and perspectives in the district. They believe it is helping to create a culture of respect and inclusion where individuals are taking responsibility for helping to implement the district's nondiscrimination policy.

The director of the county health department's GLBTIQ youth support group shares somewhat contradictory evidence, however. I asked her, "Based on what you're hearing from your youth groups, do you think antigay harassment has lessened any in the last couple years in HPSD?" She responded, "I don't really see a recognizable decrease. Kids are still wary of reporting for the same reasons [fear of being revictimized by an unsympathetic staff and other students]. It's hard to say, though, because we don't keep stats on it." Thus, whether or not the district's policies truly have created a safer environment for

GLBTIQ students has not yet been definitively resolved and was not within the scope of this study to determine.

Conclusion

The events leading up to the passage of the policies took many unexpected turns. A fortuitous mix of the right opportunities and personal histories of key players also helped set the stage for successful creation and adoption of the policies. First, the superintendent was gay, although closeted. Second, several lesbians, like Trisha, held high-ranking positions in the district's administration and worked covertly with the superintendent to advocate for GLBTIQ students. This group (the Coalition) helped lay the groundwork for the inclusion of sexual orientation in the nondiscrimination policy and, later, for HPSSC to promote the inclusion of sexual orientation in the Diversity Goal.

Furthermore, the fact that Colleen, the school board president, has a gay brother (with whom she spoke before the meeting to get his advice) may have been a factor in her decision to add sexual orientation to a nondiscrimination policy as a compromise of sorts between the two opposing sides. Other unpredictable factors in the political and social climates of the community also helped have a galvanizing effect on the Coalition and later the HPSSC. For instance, an antigay statewide ballot initiative in 1992 helped motivate sympathetic GLBTIQ rights supporters into more outspoken activists. What also helped sway popular opinion in support of taking measures to make schools safer for GLBTIQ students were the beating death of Matt Shepard and the school shootings at Columbine High School in Littleton, Colorado, where it was reported the gunmen were the victims of peer harassment that included antigay taunts (Cullen 1999; Greene 1999). An administrator points out how certain events push this issue to the forefront: "A lot of times what happens is, it's things occurred that bring us to revisit these things. They're usually grim reminders."

Finally, the community of High Plains has a long history of supporting equal rights for GLBTIQ individuals. School districts that adopt policies that include sexual orientation tend to be a part of communities that previously adopted gay rights legislation at the local level. Button Rienzo, and Wald (1997) explain, "It was not the legal statute itself that seemed to encourage efforts to address sexual orientation issues in schools, but the factors that produced a gay movement strong enough to get an ordinance passed" in the first place. All of these things combined helped to make this case unique and provided the right mix of opportunities for the successful inclusion of sexual orientation in the policies. Other communities, with differing histories and opportunities, can still learn from the case of High Plains and attempt to recreate many of the same conditions. The next chapter highlights the strategies employed by the HPSSC in garnering support for the inclusion of sexual orientation in the Diversity Goal. Also discussed are the social and political factors in this case that either facilitated or impeded the adoption and implementation of the district's policies.

Note

1. There appeared to be no reaction from the morally conservative crowd to Colleen's disclosure of having a gay brother. This school board meeting was audiotaped, and no discussion or any remarks were made in regards to Colleen's disclosure.

3

Strategies Employed by the High Plains Safe Schools Coalition to Build Community and District Support

A FORTUITOUS AND UNPREDICTABLE MIX of opportunities no doubt played a part in the successful passage of the policies. I would argue, however, that the meticulous planning, organizing, and strategizing on HPSSC's part, as well as the Coalition's before it, was at least as much the reason for the two groups' success as was the fortuitous and right mix of opportunities. The commitment and passion of the group's members also played a part. The HPSSC's strategies helped them be better prepared to take advantage of the opportunities that presented themselves. They also made mistakes, however. Other community groups and coalitions can thus learn from the example of the High Plains Safe Schools Coalition. The following illustrates the strategies the group used, the mistakes they made, and the commitment its members demonstrated.

Establishing a Relationship with Citizens United against Racism

When the HPSSC petitioned the school board to include sexual orientation in the Strategic Plan's Diversity Goal, members of Citizens United against Racism (CUAR), an official advisory committee to the school board, were afraid their focus on equity for students of color would be overshadowed by a new focus on sexual orientation. Members of CUAR believed that the HPSSC, and the GLBTIQ community in general, had more resources and received more attention than people of color in the community. A member of CUAR pointed out, "If you have a racial/ethnic parade in a community, you don't get the newsprint that you would if you had a [gay] pride parade. 'Who's got more resources?'" Similarly, an administrator who is also a person of color contends, "I found the central office, that when they were talking about discrimination, they weren't talking about ethnic minorities. They were talking about gays." A member of HPSSC recalls:

> I definitely felt like we, the Safe Schools Coalition, were the outsiders, the intruders, and that CUAR was suspicious of what we might do that would co-opt them into losing ground on their issues. CUAR was the one with the history of working hard to make changes for students and families of color in the district. One member, who did not attend [the initial] meeting, told me in a private discussion that the goals of HPSSC and CUAR were "apples and oranges." She saw nothing that could be gained for CUAR if the two groups worked together.

Despite this apparent rift, there were members in both CUAR and HPSSC who realized that potential advances could be made in the area of nondiscrimination for all students if CUAR and HPSSC would join forces. In late summer 1998, a meeting was scheduled for the two groups to come to an understanding of each other's goals and issues. According to a CUAR member, the two groups agreed on a neutral meeting place and neutral facilitators. However, a CUAR member explained that the HPSSC made last-minute changes to the agreed-upon protocol as a "small example to stack the deck in their favor." First, the meeting got scheduled where HPSSC held their regular meetings, not a neutral place, as was previously agreed. Second, though both groups agreed on a lesbian of color as a neutral facilitator, somebody in HPSSC invited a second facilitator with whom HPSSC had an established relationship. The CUAR member lightly recounted, "I just noticed that somebody slipped something in there and it was minor, but little things like that just make a difference, especially if you don't talk about them."

Interestingly, members of HPSSC remember the circumstances differently. According to the HPSSC, the two groups never agreed to meet anywhere other than HPSSC's regular meeting place. Also, the City of High Plains' Office of Mediation Services provided the facilitators, and it was they who sent two facilitators. A member of HPSSC recalls, "I believe that I was told that they would send two people because they work in teams." A representative of the Office of Mediation Services said neither of the facilitators sent by their office had any membership connections with either group and should not have had any personal connections with members in either group. He admitted, however, it could have been possible that one of the facilitators was acquainted with one or more members of HPSSC just as a simple fact of living in the same community.

Regardless of any possible lapses in diplomacy, the two groups met and told their stories about what it was like to be a person of color and what it was like to be an Anglo GLBTIQ person. A member of HPSSC explains:

> This first meeting of wariness was all about building trust—learning to meet and talk with one another, share personal stories, understand our motivations and concerns—are the things I remember from that first meeting. It was "walking on egg shells," but it was a first step and it was done in goodwill on both sides.

A CUAR member recalls:

> It was real important that we went through that process. You reach a level of understanding that you didn't have before as it relates to the issues—things about gay people that I didn't understand, and the gay white community didn't understand in terms of my issues as a person of color, and the discrimination that we experience all the time. I think going through that circle that we had that evening was pretty powerful in coming to a clear understanding of what we could do together.

When asked about any lingering animosities that HPSSC might be riding on the coattails of CUAR, a CUAR member responded, "No, I haven't heard that. If some people make some progress then other people should be there making progress too. It's not a competition, social justice." CUAR and the HPSSC continue to work together and support each other's causes. They even cosponsored a school board candidate forum regarding candidates' positions on educational equity for students of color and GLBTIQ students. The two groups also coauthored a statement for the superintendent: "Enhancing Institutional Equity Programs in High Plains School District." It detailed problems and statistics of discrimination against students of color and GLBTIQ students in the district, and it offered suggestions for enhancing equity in these areas.

Building Bridges: Cultivating Understanding between the HPSSC and Concerned Citizens

Strong ideologic stances and hurt feelings often prevent opposing sides in any public debate from engaging in dialogue with each other (Sears and Carper 1998). In this case, however, the HPSSC reached out to, and were more or less warmly received by, Concerned Citizens. Members of HPSSC met individually and as a group with Concerned Citizens. The group meeting took place in a church that donated its space. Individuals on both sides report it was good to sit down face-to-face with each other and have a civil dialogue. The meeting led to a greater understanding on both sides of where the other was coming from. An HPSSC member recounts:

I think what really helped [the conservative parents] to understand was . . . we can have kids being picked on here, being called queer or faggot or whatever, because they may be in the band or are really smart. So I think that actually helped [the conservative parents] to realize, "So it's really not that it's just kids that are [gay] but it could be any kid to get that form of harassment."

The meeting resulted in a letter to the school board, signed by a member of both HPSSC and Concerned Citizens, explaining that the two groups had met, shared their concerns with each other, and reached agreement on four points:

1. Staff, teachers, and students should respect everyone—all means all.
2. We want a put-down free environment in all of our schools.
3. Even if our values are different, we can still respect each other's right to be different.
4. The HPSD Nondiscrimination Policy should be known so well at all levels that anyone who harasses or experiences harassment should expect swift, direct, effective action.

Dorothy said the letter was presented to the school board so that they would know the two opposing sides "were working together" to resolve their differences. Dorothy further explains the letter "was done to give some satisfaction to the opposition. They needed to be heard and to be taken seriously. We let them vent and we listened without arguing." Likewise, members of Concerned Citizens told me they were grateful for the opportunity to sit down with members of HPSSC and to be heard. One of the parents in Concerned Citizens recalled:

What I liked was that we sat down together as individuals and we actually spoke to one another instead of being in a large room speaking at a podium [after months of the two groups presenting their issues at school board meetings]. We had a discussion and I came out of it with a great deal more respect and understanding where they were coming from. It didn't change my religious conviction, didn't change my point of view. I just had greater understanding, which is what we really want with this deliberative process, where we can sit down and talk to people and understand where they were coming from without changing who we thought we are. And by doing that, by having that better understanding, we can make changes in the community that are positive, that are for everybody.

Dorothy recalls that the meeting and resulting letter had a profound impact on members of Concerned Citizens. "They thought they'd had some type of victory," explained Dorothy, "I thought the letter was innocuous [because the points of agreement were vaguely worded and did not mention sexual orientation] but it was terribly meaningful to them." Dorothy concluded that by allowing Concerned Citizens to share their concerns and by putting the points of agreement in Concerned Citizens' language—that is, by saying *all* people, instead of spelling out protected classes—the two groups built a great deal of trust and significantly reduced the animosity. Although the letter did not stop HPSSC from advocating the inclusion of sexual orientation in the Diversity Goal and although it did not stop the board from finally approving the inclusion of sexual orientation, the meeting and the letter helped Concerned Citizens to feel that they were being taken seriously and, according to Dorothy, "that may be why they backed off a bit."

Building a Strong Coalition:
Alliances with Other Organizations and Individuals

Besides forming a relationship with CUAR and Concerned Citizens, HPSSC sought the support of other community organizations. Dorothy, president of HPSSC, explains the group's strategy:

> One group alone shouldn't go into the district or they're perceived as a single interest group. When we named ourselves a coalition and included other groups, especially churches for broad based community support, that was key. You have to find your allies in the community and get them to write letters [of support]. Get religious organizations to sign on so the school board knows [you] have [support in] the community. You have to form a coalition; you can't do it as loners and lone rangers. Networking and working as allies, rather than adversaries, is important.

A commissioner on High Plains' Human Relations Commission served as liaison to HPSSC and helped the HPSSC secure funding from the city to print five thousand brochures. The brochures, distributed to every school district staff member in fall 1999, contained a photo of the superintendent and quoted him as saying, "I expect you to join me to create a positive, fear-free, prejudice-free environment in every school, every hallway and every classroom." The brochure also included phone numbers of organizations that provide support and resources to GLBTIQ youth and to teachers wanting more information. When the new superintendent took office in 2000, he gave HPSSC permission to use his photo and a quote for a new batch of updated brochures.

The HPSSC has also forged a working relationship with the school district's director of institutional equity and multicultural education, as well as an administrator and program coordinator in the district's central administration.

These district employees have relied on the HPSSC to help develop and facilitate in-services and other trainings for district staff on sexual orientation and gender identity issues. A member of HPSSC reports the group is happy and grateful to have established these relationships. "The [previous director of institutional equity] was not forceful in enforcing the policy. It has to be from the top down. If your boss is not going to be forceful in enforcing the policy, why should you?"

The group has also cultivated a solid working relationship with the school board. A member of HPSSC recalled her conversation with a board member who gave her "the inside scoop on school board politics and how to deal with the [other] board members and make the changes we wanted to make. [I was given] phone numbers and ideas for how to talk to other board members." Subsequently, the HPSSC came to be recognized as an entity in High Plains by showing up at school board meetings, attending a work session of the school board, and by talking with others in the community to raise awareness and support for implementing and enforcing the nondiscrimination policy. As of 2003, HPSSC now holds its meetings at the district's central office and is working under the superintendent as an official advisory committee to the school board.

Demonstrating the Need for Inclusion: More Strategies for Building Support and Raising Awareness

The testimony of GLBTIQ youth has been one of the most effective strategies for building support and demonstrating the need for including sexual orientation in district policy. The director of the local GLBTIQ youth support group, which is run through the county health department, explains that personal accounts from GLBTIQ youth are "very powerful in terms of putting faces on real life issues." When skeptics hear stories, such as from a local high school student testifying at a school board meeting, it becomes hard for them to deny that antigay harassment is a problem. The student in question had a brick thrown through his car window in the school's parking lot. Attached to the brick was a note that read, "The only good fag is a dead fag." GLBTIQ youth have also spoken at in-services for staff and have done peer education in various schools to raise awareness about the problems of antigay harassment in the schools and heterosexism in the larger society.

Another strategy for raising awareness was a School Climate Survey that the HPSSC took to all of the high schools in the district, where they met with each school's governance team (composed of students, staff, and parents). The self-surveys asked the governance teams to rate their schools on points, such as the number of antigay remarks heard in the hallways, the number of GLBTIQ-related books in the library, whether or not the nondiscrimination policy was posted somewhere in the school, and if forms were readily available for reporting harassment. During one of these meetings, a principal was inspired to print the "Harassment Report Form" in the student handbook, on a perforated page, to ensure that each student would have easy access to the form. Since then, the new district regulations for implementing the nondiscrimination policy require that the report form be printed in the student handbook.

Two related strategies that members of HPSSC have followed are to move slowly and to win people over on a personal level. One group member explains, "I feel like with school policies it's better to sort of build slowly and not pick a necessarily revolutionary path so as to not alienate folks who would write us off as 'whackos.'" HPSSC members constantly mention that the best way to win support is one person at a time, by opening dialogue with people—"and then they'll listen to what your ideas are." Insofar as how to bring up the issue, she explains, "I always try to liken it to a civil rights issue and the similarities between that and sexual orientation." Another contends, "You're always on safe ground when you're talking about respect and dignifying each human and safety. People are always ready to rally around safety." Thus, the HPSSC often relied on the slogan "student safety." Not only did it garner support among district staff, but it also got their foot in the door with administrators and the school board because everyone agrees that students should be safe. At one point, though, I wondered if members of HPSSC were being somewhat dishonest by saying they were concerned only with safety. I was also hearing some members say they would like sexual orientation issues included in the curriculum. I asked Dorothy about this and she explained:

> We see it as an evolutionary process. We have to start where we can. We began with the nondiscrimination policy already in place and "safety" was the best way to begin so we would not be accused of this big gay agenda. It becomes clearer, as a process, if we start with safety and policy. Then we can talk about Restorative Justice and education. So it's not a secretive thing—it's an understanding that you can't do everything all at once.

One strategy the HPSSC did not make great use of was utilizing the media, and several members expressed regret about this apparent oversight. Dorothy, however, disagreed and said the HPSSC used the media sufficiently and "strategically." For instance, "We wanted the reporters there when we had GLBTIQ youth speaking about their experiences so that the youth's own words would get printed." Dorothy contends that at other times, "Working behind the scenes is a more important strategy. It's important not to go overboard with the media." When the HPSSC was working with the superintendent to get recognized as an official advisory committee to the school board, Dorothy was concerned that media coverage would "pull out the conservatives." She relates, "We wanted to be a quiet presence that didn't cause anxiety with the district's administration or risk fanning the flames of fear [with moral conservatives in the community]." When a reporter from the local newspaper learned of HPSSC's pending official advisory committee status and asked Dorothy for an interview, Dorothy responded, "There's no story here." However, recalls Dorothy, "They did the story anyway." Dorothy expressed relief that no community opposition arose as a result of the media coverage.

The group had attempted to cultivate a relationship with the media by cosponsoring a luncheon with PFLAG for members of the media at a local restaurant in February 2000; but according to Dorothy, "No reporter has ever written a story on the history or work of the HPSSC." Members of the HPSSC have written several guest opinions and letters to the editor, and the local GLBTIQ youth support group takes out monthly advertisements in every school newspaper in which they can get one printed. Some high schools, especially smaller ones, do not accept outside advertising. For those that do, the support group director reports, "It takes persistence. Since we're a program of the health department, that has helped tremendously. [Schools] who didn't want us to advertise didn't return my calls or answer letters. I just kept calling until I got a hold of them." When she reaches the person who makes the decision, she explains she uses a "I have the ad—I have the money—I'm sending it in" kind of approach (personal communication, November 30, 2000).

Maintaining Group Cohesion: Keeping the Coalition Strong

Several important features internal to the HPSSC helped motivate members and allow them to achieve their goals. One highly motivated individual often inspired the group. In the case of HPSSC, this individual was Dorothy. Dorothy is described by other members as "tireless," "passionate," "an activist who's come into her own right," and "a role model." Dorothy, a retired schoolteacher from HPSD, also has a good reputation with many insider connections in high places in the district. She has also developed a keen sense for just how much pressure to exert on individuals to garner their support, sometimes by going to their superiors.

As far as group cohesion is concerned, members report similar reasons for staying involved, including "shared values," "working to make the schools better for kids is fulfilling," and "my involvement brings me personal satisfaction." Other members acknowledge the risks for involvement by including, "There's a little risk for me as a business person in the community," "I always feel like I'm kind of walking on egg shells with certain bosses in my job," and, "There's little chance that I could ever be hired in this district as a teacher."

At times, the group experienced intragroup conflicts. One example was over HPSSC's conflicting commitments to parents and the district. The tension arose out of their wanting to be a "watchdog" group to advocate the rights of parents and students while at the same time being careful not to damage the trust the group had built with the district. One HPSSC member, who was a strong advocate for a student who suffered harassment, explains:

> I was attacked [by the rest of the group] for taking initiative without asking permission from the other members. So there's a conflict there that I have never felt comfortable with because parents have seen us as an ombudsman; that we're an organization they can go to, to seek some support. But we've tied our hands [because we don't want to damage our relationship with the district] and we can't give support [to those parents who come to us] and I find this very frustrating.

Marge, another group member who understands this potential dilemma, feels the group can serve in both capacities. She explains that even though HPSSC is an advisory group for the district, HPSSC can still be an advocate for parents and students who file grievances with the district. The difference, she maintains, is how it is done. Marge explains that the HPSSC "must empower the person with the grievance to work within the system as long as some resolution within the existing grievance policy remains a possibility." For instance, Marge told me that HPSSC once worked closely with a family whose child was the target of antigay harassment. They provided the family with the appropriate district forms and (with the assistance of an HPSSC member who is also a district employee) helped them work within the system to file a formal grievance with the district. Marge concludes:

> The HPSSC can advocate behind the scenes and support those, who are finding themselves having to navigate the system, with information, suggestions, and assistance in understanding and using the avenues that are available while still honoring the position of Advisory [Committee] to the district.

She further explains, "I try to make sure HPSSC doesn't alienate itself from the district by burning bridges. I try to inform them of existing procedure and make sure they are given the information and tools to work within existing [district bureaucracy]."

Another example of intragroup conflict results when the district employees who lend their support to HPSSC are reprimanded by their colleagues or bosses for appearing to be too closely allied with the HPSSC. Several examples arose where HPSSC members inadvertently dropped names of district employees in discussions with people outside the district who later questioned why the district employees appeared to be giving so much support to the HPSSC. Thus, the district employees who are also members of HPSSC walk a somewhat tenuous line between their loyalty and duties to their employer versus the HPSSC, with whom they also feel aligned.

Other members of the group report feeling dissatisfied at times because of a sense of "floundering or not seeing change" and "feeling unclear about the goals of the group." They disagree about use of language, including the hesitancy of some group members to include "Transgendered" and "Queer" with "Gay, Lesbian, and Bisexual" ("Intersexed" was never discussed by the group).

Despite tensions that occasionally arise, a shared sense of commitment and strong leadership keep the group together. Old members have dropped out and been replaced by new ones, and the group, as a whole, sees this transition as a healthy and natural process.

Conclusion

The HPSSC and CUAR realized that if they could join forces, work together, and share resources, then together they would have a larger voice in the school district. Though it took time and effort to build a relationship of trust and common goals, HPSSC and CUAR's union proved beneficial for both groups. The two groups support each other's causes and show a strong and united front, which helps to establish credibility for both groups. By setting aside some ideological differences and by engaging Concerned Citizens in a civil dialogue, they helped quell some of the fears that Concerned Citizens had, and they probably made them relax their efforts to oppose inclusion of sexual orientation in the Diversity Goal.

Coalition building and grassroots organizing—by winning the support of other community and state organizations and of the higher-ups in state and local governing bodies—also helped HPSSC to gain credibility. Strategic use of the media helped HPSSC get their message out without revealing too much "behind the scenes" information that could potentially "fan the flames of hysteria" and lead the opposition to organize. Conducting School Climate Surveys, taking GLBTIQ youth to school board meetings to testify as to abuse they suffered, and helping the community understand that schools are not safe places for many students all helped HPSSC demonstrate the need for including sexual orientation in the policies.

Finally, the passion and commitment of the group's members, as well as Dorothy's leadership, helped the group remain strong and achieve their goals. Though they made their mistakes, the group maintained a clear sense of direction. They frequently met to discuss which goals had been achieved and where more effort needed to be concentrated. The support of district employees who are also members of HPSSC helped the group navigate and work within district bureaucracy.

4

Lessons from the Case of High Plains

O NE OF MY GOALS FOR CONDUCTING THIS RESEARCH was to help other school districts and communities adopt and implement nondiscrimination policies that include sexual orientation and gender identity in their own districts. In this chapter, I summarize the factors that facilitated compliance with the High Plains School District's (HPSD) nondiscrimination policy so that other school districts can avoid some of the pitfalls identified in this book. I also suggest some practical strategies for dealing with the factors that act as barriers to implementation and enforcement.[1]

Strategies That Facilitate Compliance
with HPSD's Nondiscrimination Policy

According to HPSD staff, the following strategies facilitate compliance with the district's nondiscrimination policy. Administrators, teachers, and other staff members said they have personally benefited from the following in helping them understand the policy and implement and enforce it.

Professional Development

Almost every HPSD staff member interviewed said that educating staff was extremely important. Many agreed that the district does not offer adequate professional development on what sexual orientation in the nondiscrimination policy means for all staff in their various positions. Nor does the district offer sufficient practical strategies and guidelines for identifying harassment, stopping it, reporting it, and ending it in the classroom. The fact that staff gave different answers to my interview question regarding what constitutes harassment points to the need for staff development on how to identify harassment; how to distinguish the difference between exercising freedom of speech and harassing behavior; how to address First Amendment rights in the classroom; and how to recognize students' rights.

Moreover, the training should stress that the policy involves changing certain behaviors (i.e., name-calling and bullying) and not beliefs regarding the social acceptability of homosexuality. That is, while schools rightly instill in students democratic beliefs, (i.e., "all types of people deserve equal rights") schools should not force teachers or students to personally agree that "it's okay to be gay." Also, teachers certainly should not require that students agree with their personal beliefs. It is the teacher's duty to ensure that all sides of a debate are represented in the classroom and that all students will be guaranteed the safety to express their opinions. When it comes to promoting democracy, however, teachers should steer students toward certain beliefs. Teachers have the duty to uphold the law, and they should tell students that it is wrong to discriminate against people based on race, religion, sexual orientation, and so forth. When it comes to students' beliefs that are more personal in nature, such as whether or not they approve of homosexuality, teachers must allow students to form their own conclusions and should encourage students to seek the guidance of their parents in so doing.

These sorts of discussions require that teachers be able to address sexual orientation both neutrally and comfortably with students. However, teachers in the HPSD were unsure that the district would back them up in this respect. To feel comfortable in addressing sexual orientation with students, teachers themselves said they needed more training to better understand differences in sexual orientation. The teachers needed to know what can be said and what cannot be said to students in regards to human sexuality. The teachers in the district also wanted assurance that the district would not reprimand them for allowing class discussions on sexual orientation differences—such as when they arise as a matter of student inquiry, when they are appropriate to the curricular material being discussed, or when a panel of GLBTIQ speakers is invited to lead a discussion.

Staff also said that discussing the nondiscrimination policy and its associated regulations in staff meetings was helpful; that mandatory in-services might be a good idea to better reach staff who would otherwise skip them; and that it would have been helpful if their preservice teacher coursework had addressed issues of sexual orientation, gender identity, and GLBTIQ students. Teachers reported that they need more opportunities for engaging in discussions with their colleagues on this topic. Sociologist Herbert Blumer (1969) explains that reality is constructed through the interaction of individuals, who react to situations through a process of interpretation. Thus, allowing teachers to discuss, in a structured way, what GLBTIQ inclusion means for them can help cultivate a sense of shared responsibility among teachers for creating a school environment that affirms the rights of GLBTIQ students. Michael Fullan (1991), an expert on educational change, contends that "all real change involves loss, anxiety, and struggle." The way in which the policy is implemented has direct bearing on how the new policy is received and perceived by the teachers. Including teachers as a group in the implementation process, by giving them opportunities to talk to one another and make decisions about how to effectively implement the policy, helps them take ownership over the rules and responsibilities they are expected to uphold. Blumer explains, "It is the social process in group life that creates and upholds the rules, not the rules that create and uphold group life."

One administrator suggested study groups, as opposed to one-day in-services, as a way of stimulating discussion and change. She believes in-services are the least effective form of professional development and that the district can in no way make them mandatory. She explained that teachers can always take a personal day to avoid an in-service. When the districts suggest restricting teachers' use of their personal days, the teachers' unions threaten to strike.

School districts and state departments of education should encourage universities with colleges of education to include sexual orientation, gender identity, and GLBTIQ student issues in their teacher education programs. The district can also require that teacher candidates demonstrate an understanding of how to ensure an equitable classroom for GLBTIQ students as well as students from diverse racial and ethnic backgrounds. All new district employees should go through this type of mandatory training as part of their employee orientation.

One practical strategy to assist teachers is to have district lawyers review school law with principals and explain the legal definitions of *harassment, discrimination,* and First Amendment rights of students. The principals could then review the information with their teachers. For peer support, principals of schools who are just beginning to address this issue can "partner up" with a principal from another school who has more experience in equity issues for GLBTIQ students. To bring in speakers to do trainings for students and staff, schools can draw on local resources, such as GLBTIQ youth support groups, county health services, local chapters of GLSEN and PFLAG, Safe Schools Coalitions, and gay teachers in the district. Hearing personal stories helps faculty and students who oppose homosexuality understand that stopping anti-gay harassment is not about forcing anyone to agree that "it's okay to be gay."

Furthermore, since GLBTIQ issues are a new and sometimes uncomfortable topic for teachers, in-services should frame classroom practices for teachers in specific and concrete examples, like "do this" and "do not do this." One teacher explained, "At first people really need things 'languaged' for them. It's kind of like, you get 'a script' because at first some issues are tough and if you haven't dealt with them before you don't want to bungle them." Teachers also need to know how to present sexual orientations neutrally so as not to promote one over another, thus leaving it up to the individual student to form their own opinion with the guidance of their family.

Implementing the Nondiscrimination Policy

First, the nondiscrimination policy and its associated regulations must be written in clear and consistent language. HPSD's policy contains two paragraphs, both of which spell out the protected classes, but one of which excludes sexual orientation. This was a source of confusion and suspicion when some schools chose to post the first paragraph of the policy, which does not include sexual orientation. The associated regulations to the nondiscrimination policy that HPSD adopted in 2000 (see appendix F) holds principals, as site-based managers of their schools, accountable for seeing that claims of discrimination and harassment are investigated and followed through. Staff consistently reported they needed this type of top-down support, with clear mandates from the administration making certain individuals accountable for resolving complaints of discrimination—otherwise, nobody takes responsibility.

Staff also mentioned that having a full-time director of institutional equity and multicultural education in the district was helpful in that this office provides training and support on the nondiscrimination policy, its enforcement, and related issues. The person in this position, however, should *not* have responsibility for ensuring that the policy is being enforced. HPSD's director of institutional equity contends, "I don't think my position is to do investigations or enforcement because once I start doing that then I lose my ability to support schools in the transition for safe environments because I become more of the finger pointer and the 'mandater' than somebody who's there to help them transition." This director recently began a series of equity leadership trainings, where selected staff members from each school go through extensive training on diversity issues, including sexual orientation, and then are expected to return to their schools to educate other staff. It is too soon to evaluate this training, but it holds great promise.

Posting the nondiscrimination policy with its associated regulations in every school and in student/parent handbooks was cited as a good way of raising awareness about the policy. Finally, designating a Safe Person (one who has been trained to deal with GLBTIQ student issues) in every school was said to be a good way to help staff and students know that a trusted person was available, should they feel the need to lodge a complaint of discrimination. Posters advertising who the school's Safe Person is should be hung on every classroom door.

A practical strategy for implementing the nondiscrimination policy is that the superintendent can mention the need to stop harassment of GLBTIQ students in addresses to staff, parents, and students. Also, staff should not be deluged with information at the beginning of the year. The district should spread it out and make it continuous and consistent in both quality and quantity. Through the use of anonymous School Climate Surveys, students should be allowed to evaluate teachers', administrators', and their schools' handling of GLBTIQ and harassment issues. Students can give a different perspective and an honest critique of how well their schools are addressing these topics. Finally, posters should be hung up around the school, with toll-free numbers where students can call anonymously to report incidents of abuse. This ensures a safe way to report incidents that students have heard about or that happened to them, especially if the student is concerned about backlash.

Enforcing the Nondiscrimination Policy

Again, top-down support—from school board to superintendent to central administration to principals to teachers—was cited as very important to send the message to staff and students that the nondiscrimination policy should be taken seriously. Parents and teachers also said that they and students need to see results after reporting incidents of harassment; otherwise, they feel that nothing is being done, and they subsequently stop reporting. One mother of a student who is frequently picked on described this policy of follow-up as "continuity of care"—that is, district officials let victims know what corrective actions were taken to improve their safety. This policy also helps with accountability.

Some schools in the district have a "Zero Tolerance" policy for name-calling and bullying, and they cite it as a factor in helping them enforce the nondiscrimination policy. Most important, however, staff consistently called for education, not just discipline. That is, when students violate the nondiscrimination policy, they should be educated as to why their actions were wrong, as opposed to simply being punished, so as to foster understanding and reduce rates of recidivism. Staff called for involving parents in the discipline process and for the education of parents as to the requirements of the nondiscrimination policy.

A practical strategy to assist with enforcement is to devote class time to discussing the nondiscrimination policy with students. Teams of teachers, principals, counselors, and peer educators can discuss, with small groups of students, the requirements and responsibilities of the policies for students; what students can do when they witness or are the victims of harassment; and associated issues like, "What does it mean to be GLBTIQ?" "What is harassment?" and "What are my rights as a student?" In addition, monitoring the hallways and bathrooms between classes to stop peer harassment is important. Some teachers make a sincere effort to do so and feel resentment for those teachers who sit in their classrooms between classes. As a teacher myself, I know how difficult it is to give up passing periods when we could be preparing for our next class. For the safety of our students, we should make a sincere effort to maintain a presence in the hallways and bathrooms in between classes, and gym teachers, as well, should monitor students in the showers. Had my teachers done so when I was in school, I could have avoided much of the abuse I suffered while walking from class to class, using the restroom, or showering after physical education. Showering with other boys is enough of a humiliating experience for a young gay man without being beaten while naked and vulnerable. The restrooms, also, were such terrifying places for me that usually I held my bladder or used the private restroom in the nurses' office.

Students also reported that school busses, where the only adult is the person driving, are one of the places they experience harassment and feel the least safe. A teacher explained:

> When a student is disrespectful to another student, I require an apology on paper, and if they do a very sarcastic job of it, I make them rewrite it. I tear it up and make them rewrite it until it's right. I have a private conversation with them about their bullying behavior. What they're doing is both social and emotional bullying and we don't accept that. On the job they'd get fired for it. So it's not an option. Furthermore, it could cause litigation.

Finally, to encourage participants to go through extensive diversity training, like the Equity Leadership Trainings, the district should continue to pay for substitute teachers for staff who attend the trainings; they should offer a stipend to those who attend; and they should give professional development or university credit to their staff in attendance.

GLBTIQ Parent Involvement

Representation from GLBTIQ parents should be at all levels of decision making, such as at parent–teacher organizations (PTOs) and at each school's governance team or school improvement team. Virginia Casper and Steven B.

Schultz, authors of *Gay Parents/Straight Schools: Building Communication and Trust* (1999), offer an excellent resource for school districts working with GLBTIQ parents. GLBTIQ parents need to be actively recruited and personally asked to serve on these committees, so they understand they are sincerely wanted (Kozik-Rosabal 2000). The excuse "We don't know any GLBTIQ parents" does not hold water. Boards that actively recruit underrepresented populations have diversity. Boards that do not do so have no diversity. In addition to recruiting traditionally underrepresented groups, a member of Citizens United against Racism (CUAR) explains:

> Often times groups that attempt to be more equitable by including underrepresented communities do it without a deep understanding of why they are doing it. Groups should truly understand and believe in the benefits of having diverse membership. Groups should also be aware that they may need to modify their organizational structure if it is not equitable, i.e. decisions by majority vote. If these conditions do not exist, new members from traditionally underrepresented communities may feel unwelcome, misunderstood, or not appreciated, even though the current group members have gone out of their way to recruit them. Ironically, current group members may also develop the very same feelings over time. It's true that group dynamics change whenever you add new members to any group. Therefore, leaders [of such groups] should provide structured opportunities for the group to prepare for and work through changes.

He goes on to explain that one way groups can work through such changes is to plan some type of extended meeting or a retreat, facilitated by an outside facilitator. Such opportunities allow members of the group to create a safe space to come to deeper understandings of how oppression affects them and to realize that nondiscrimination practice is an ongoing process that requires regular maintenance. He concludes, "I can almost guarantee that after members of underrepresented communities hear that your group is going through this process, it will be easier for you to recruit them as members!"

A member of CUAR gave the following practical strategies for a group retreat to enhance understanding and diversity. First, do an opening activity that helps members develop a "heart" understanding of the issue—that is, it's not enough to simply understand with only your head. Then, define some commonly used terms, like "equity" and "diversity." Afterward, have the group list reasons why it wants to be more representative of diverse communities. You could also have the group list and prioritize communities that need to be represented on parent–teacher organizations and school governance teams. Have the group list barriers to success, and use this list for planning. Develop a "Membership Action Plan," using information from the brainstorming activity and discussion. Subsequent training should occur so that the group can continue equity work. Be ready to facilitate the process with "structures," that is, dyads, small groups, and panels. Be ready to help the group define "heterosexism," "racism," and "sexism." Be ready to discuss how institutions can perpetuate various forms of oppression and how the role of the individual can facilitate institutional change. Finally, he says, "If you do activities that help people understand with their heart, then you should provide tissue for tears."

Peer Education

Staff consistently reported that they have seen tremendous and effective results stemming from students' talking to and educating other students about issues of diversity, nondiscrimination, and respect. Most teachers I interviewed overwhelmingly favored having the schools address social issues and help students through their personal problems. Parents who say schools should not address social issues really mean that they want schools to continue to teach social issues with which they agree, such as morally conservative values. Likewise, they do not want schools to teach so-called social issues that they feel go against their religious beliefs, such as the idea that GLBTIQ people deserve equal rights. A teacher who works with students on issues of diversity explains why it is important for schools to address "social issues":

I really think the schools need to adopt this notion of social-emotional learning. If a kid comes to school and they have emotions that they're sitting on it can get in the way of their learning. Teachers need to build into their time with their kids an opportunity for them to really share with each other what's going on, share their stories with each other, and do that in a structured way. You have those concentric circles or dyads or the talking stick or you could use small group discussions with focus questions and focus on how kids are feeling. And over time, if that's done consistently, then you have a classroom environment where people really have a much better understanding of themselves and each other and the environment is safer. So if somebody says "fag" and they say, "That really hurts, I want to talk about this," then they can move into this because the teacher's already set it up so that kind of a thing can happen. What happens now is nothing because, it's off the subject, you know, "Let's move on." Well what about this kid who's just been called a "fag," if they're sitting there in this emotional state or the person who was the perpetrator feeling like, "Oh, I got away with that!" There has to be more relationship building between students and between students and the teacher.

In contrast to the above model, one morally conservative teacher in this study said that he thinks students who are dealing with such problems should just "suck it up" and "deal with it." Morally conservative parents believe that such problems are for families and churches to deal with. Having families and churches, not schools, deal with all the "social problems" that students face may be a model that works for morally conservative families. However, not all students have families and churches that are willing and able to help them deal with their problems. According to educational historian Carl F. Kaestle (1983), one of the reasons public schooling was formed in this country was to address social issues and take care of students' social and emotional needs.

One high school in the district employs an adult from the community for eight hours per week to work with the school's Multicultural Action Committee. The committee consists of peer educators, most of them students of color, who receive specialized training on issues of diversity, including sexual orientation diversity. They educate their peers by visiting classes and by facilitating discussions, school assemblies, and other initiatives. This type of peer education, as well as teacher in-services, can be done in collaboration with community groups like the Safe School Coalition. Similarly, other schools in the district have support groups for GLBTIQ students. Often facilitated by the school's intervention specialist or guidance counselor, programs like LINKS (a training program that prepares juniors and seniors to mentor freshmen) can incorporate issues like sexual orientation differences. HPSD also has a Student Advisory Accountability Committee, composed of high school and middle school students and facilitated by a faculty member. The committee members' objectives include educating their peers on a variety of issues—such as nondiscrimination based on sexual orientation—and advocating for all students by acting as a liaison between the student body and the school board.

A model called "Restorative Justice" was cited as the most effective model for educating students as a part of their discipline. Restorative Justice empowers students to take responsibility for themselves and others, and it teaches firsthand lessons about democratic social relations. Several schools in the district utilize Restorative Justice models of student discipline, which involves a face-to-face meeting with the victim, the perpetrator, and the other members of the student community, who are usually represented by an elected advisory board of students. Often times the three parties decide on the appropriate punishment and/or restitution, with the goal of healing the relationship between victim, perpetrator, and student body to prevent further harms. One way this scenario can play out was described to me by a teacher who had the idea of holding the perpetrator accountable for any acts of retribution against the victim. Therefore, it is up to the perpetrator to ensure that his or her friends do not seek retribution against the victim for "ratting on their friend." Not only does this help prevent revictimization, it also helps educate the perpetrator's friends. Restorative Justice can also be used in the workplace with teachers, administrators, and other staff who violate district policy. Districts can also look to research on building community among students as a way to prevent peer harassment (Berv 2002).

Finally, a current debate in the HPSD regarding peer education is the district's policy of prohibiting noncurricular student clubs, which effectively prohibits gay–straight alliances (GSAs). GLBTIQ and straight students alike are currently organizing to present their case to school officials. They claim that the district's policy unfairly prohibits student clubs because such clubs cannot, to some administrators' satisfaction, tie in with the school's curriculum. The students' case is that the clubs' members can offer support to students and engage in peer education. According to district officials, only one high school in the district, an alternative school with a progressive staff and student body, offers a course on GLBTIQ literature; thus, only this high school can justify allowing a GSA student club. Students organizing at several other high schools, with some assistance from the High Plains Safe Schools Coalition, are joining forces to ask the school board to allow for the formation of GSAs. A member of HPSSC cautions, however, that there is a temptation on the part of HPSSC to "do the work for the students." She advocates instead "that we work with the kids to understand the policy, help them write their proposal, find the curricular support it needs, and assist them in doing their own advocacy work." She goes on to explain, "If the students' GSA proposal is turned down after exhausting the system, then I think HPSSC can advocate more on their behalf" (personal communication, March 12, 2001).[2]

Some schools in the district hold "Diversity Days" and the like; however, teachers' opinions were torn on this issue. Many of the teachers I interviewed dislike the practice because they think it sends the message to students that they need be nice to one another only on Diversity Day. Rather, teachers called for changing the culture of the school so that "every day is Diversity Day."

Finally, schools with significant ethnic minority student populations were reported to have an easier time of discussing all diversity issues, including sexual orientation diversity. A member of HPSSC reports that the attempt to "tackle minority issues lacks momentum when there aren't many minority students at the school." Similarly, a principal who is a person of color contended that his being a minority certainly helps him to understand the subject of discrimination.

Barriers to Enforcing HPSD's Nondiscrimination Policy

High Plains School District staff and members of the High Plains Safe Schools Coalition identified the following areas as barriers to enforcing the district's policies in regards to sexual orientation.

Not Enough Top-Down Support

Schools are bureaucracies, and as with any hierarchically organized social institution, the potential exists for a breakdown in communication between the various levels. According to a school board member, "Our main role is to create the policy and then send a clear message to the superintendent about how important it is and then it's his job to make sure that it has been enforced all the way down the line with teachers, staff, and parents and everyone who's involved." This process is easier explained than carried out, however. Almost nothing was done in regards to nondiscrimination based on sexual orientation from the policy's adoption in 1994 to the time the HPSSC started advocating for the rights of GLBTIQ students in 1998. Furthermore, policy JFH-R, adopted in 1992, which makes provisions for students to file grievances when discriminated against because of sexual orientation, was forgotten and still has not been utilized. At the school level, some teachers complained that their principals and assistant principals did not take seriously the issue of disciplining students, in general, and of disciplining students for making antigay remarks, in particular.

Staff Do Not Understand, or Are Unaware of, the Policy

Until the High Plains Safe Schools Coalition began its advocacy in the district, many principals, teachers, and students were unaware that their schools were terrifying, and often physically and emotionally abusive, places for GLBTIQ students and students perceived to be GLBTIQ. Many staff, mostly elementary and middle school teachers, continue to deny that antigay harassment is a problem in their schools, but now most district staff are at least aware that antigay abuse is a problem.

As mentioned previously, the district's nondiscrimination policy contains two paragraphs, one of which does not include sexual orientation. Some schools chose to post the first paragraph, which excludes sexual orientation, thereby leaving advocates to wonder if this was a deliberate maneuver on the parts of some administrators. Although the policy still contains the two paragraphs, all schools are now required to post the second paragraph, which includes sexual orientation. Still, some teachers, mainly those who oppose homosexuality, claim to be unaware of what the nondiscrimination policy says. Given that the district has conducted in-services on the policy and that the policy has been in the spotlight, this alleged ignorance is probably a smoke screen for teachers who don't care or don't want to know what the policy says. Before the district adopted the associated regulations for the nondiscrimination policy in 2000, nobody was held accountable for following up on claims of discrimination, and no clear protocol existed for staff to follow. Now that the district has adopted, and is implementing, these guidelines, the HPSSC is hopeful that schools will seriously address antigay abuse and curtail it. Assessment, however, will have to come at a later time, when more data is available.

Lack of Resources for Effectively Implementing the Policy

Time and money were cited as the most common resources that the district lacks to implement the nondiscrimination policy most effectively. Granted, school districts are notoriously underfunded and are often forced to make budget cuts. What it seems to come down to, however, is establishing priorities, and many staff claim that the district has not given enough priority to issues of diversity and nondiscrimination. Lack of time and money leads to inadequate trainings for implementing the nondiscrimination policy. Many teachers reported they don't know how to stop antigay harassment and that in-services were inadequate in quantity and sometimes in quality. Moreover, supportive teachers reported disdain for their colleagues who skip in-services on GLBTIQ issues or take a sick day to avoid having to deal with the issue. Supportive teachers suggested making these in-services mandatory.

Another barrier that helps people remain "in the dark" about antigay abuse is the lack of statistics regarding reported incidences of abuse. Before the associated regulations for the district's nondiscrimination policy were adopted in 2000, no statistics were recorded on incidents of harassment unless discipline was involved. The new guidelines call for all reports of discrimination to be recorded in a central office, which will help illustrate any patterns of discrimination on which the district can then focus.

The fact that GLBTIQ people and perspectives are not formally included in content areas of the curriculum (besides health education) makes it difficult for teachers and students to facilitate discussions on GLBTIQ issues and raise awareness and support for the nondiscrimination policy. Formal inclusion of GLBTIQ people and perspectives in all content areas of the curriculum sends the message that sexual orientation diversity is a legitimate topic for teachers and students to discuss. As a result of curricular exclusion and inadequate training, elementary schools especially are less prepared to deal with antigay bias and abuse. A program director told me, "I know one elementary school that's been confronted with it and has had to deal with 'What do we do with an eight-year-old boy who wears a dress to school?' It's something elementary schools usually aren't faced with so they're not always as aware as high schools are on how to deal with these issues." Finally, along with class sizes that are too big, teachers report that they can't be everywhere all the time and can't catch every single antigay epithet. Teachers often mentioned their workload and complained, "We don't have time for this." Like designating funding to priority areas of the budget, teachers choose what they make a priority. As a teacher, however, I do not mean to dismiss teachers' complaints that we are often overburdened with too many students and too many bureaucratic requirements.

Fear

Fear, plain and simple, is a major barrier when adopting, implementing, and enforcing school policies that include sexual orientation. Acknowledging staff and students who are GLBTIQ is new terrain for school districts in a society that has only recently begun to acknowledge and grant rights to its GLBTIQ citizens. GLBTIQ students fear self-disclosure of their GLBTIQ identity, and they fear being revictimized by an unsympathetic administrator, should they report abuse. This issue points to the need for a "Safe Person" in every building and the need for report forms to be easily accessible, in a place where students can take one without having to ask for one. Many teachers and administrators fear backlash from morally conservative parents if they support or advocate safety and equity for GLBTIQ students. The district needs to make a strong statement that it will stand behind its employees in this regard. One high school in the district offered a facilitated discussion on the current debate over same-sex marriage as an alternative for students who did not want to attend a general assembly depicting a mock heterosexual wedding. Word got out to morally conservative parents, who barraged the principal with phone calls. They even complained to a state legislator, who then accused the superintendent of supporting a mock gay wedding. The backlash from morally conservative parents almost resulted in the cancellation of the forum on same-sex marriage. The district in this case, however, held its ground and attempted to explain to parents the reason for the alternative assembly and to allay their fears.

For good reason, then, GLBTIQ staff are most often afraid to come out of the closet. However, at least one school in the district has an out-of-the-closet GLBTIQ administrator and several openly identifying GLBTIQ teachers. This school has cultivated an ethos of safety and inclusion for its GLBTIQ students and staff, much to the credit and hard work of its heterosexual teachers. Most GLBTIQ staff in the district, and even most heterosexual staff, reported that they doubt the district's real commitment to support GLBTIQ teachers who come out of the closet and who may then come under attack from morally conservative parents and teachers. Staff who do not commit to enforcing the policy were cited as a major barrier by their colleagues, who see them as fearful of appearing to condone homosexuality. Many teachers told me that they felt helpless and had little hope for their colleagues whose anti-gay views prevented them from creating a safe and inclusive learning environment for GLBTIQ students and GLBTIQ staff.

Finally, the district's prohibition of all noncurricular student clubs is partly based on the fear that should such clubs be allowed to meet, then students will want to form Ku Klux Klan and neo-Nazi skinhead clubs. The Equal Access Act of 1984 would seem to support allowing such clubs to meet on school property if other noncurricular clubs are also allowed to meet on school property. While the district cannot do anything that would violate either the First Amendment principle (that government cannot impose content-based restrictions on private speech) or a private club's First Amendment rights of association (see *Boy Scouts of America v. Dale* 2000), it could prohibit "clear and present danger" speech or speech that is otherwise illegal under laws that survive First Amendment strict scrutiny. Thus, as was the case with *East High Gay/Straight Alliance v. Board of Education* (2000) in Salt Lake City, Utah, school districts often take the route of banning all noncurricular clubs, rather than having to deal with the political fallout from the formation of a student club that espouses unpopular ideas. I maintain, however, that the discussions such groups would spark in the schools and community would teach students and adults important lessons about tolerance, democracy, and First Amendment rights.

The district's policy prohibiting noncurricular student clubs (including GSAs) may itself be in violation of the First Amendment and the Equal Access Act of 1984 (this would need to be determined by a court of law). GSAs allow GLBTIQ students and their straight allies to educate their peers and offer support to other students on sexual orientation issues. Thus, the prohibition of noncurricular student clubs is a barrier in that it prevents students from organizing and engaging in peer education (i.e., free association).

Notes

1. In my dissertation (Macgillivray 2001), I used Button, Rienzo, and Wald's (1997) model of policy adoption to create an analytic framework. Their model of policy adoption includes four parts—urbanism/social diversity, political opportunity, resource mobilization, and communal protest—which I applied to this case to explicate the factors that affect whether or not a policy gets adopted, implemented, and enforced. This chapter is an analysis of those factors using Button, Rienzo, and Wald's work as an analytic framework.

2. Students finally won the right to form gay–straight alliances in HPSD. As of October 2002, GSAs were meeting in six schools. Dorothy explained: "Once one high

school paved the way, all the others were a piece of cake. We were working with a gay-friendly administration who wanted to help it happen, not prevent it from happening, so the legal advice was consistent with the position. We coached the students to argue with posing the state standards compliance to health education, social studies and the HPSD stategic goal of Diversity—Valuing ALL. It worked." (Personal communication, October 15, 2002)

5

Suggestions for Other School Districts and Safe Schools Coalitions

S CHOOLS MUST CREATE CULTURES OF INCLUSION to become welcoming places for GLBTIQ students and their families. GLBTIQ students and parents are currently excluded from the schools in that GLBTIQ people and families are not represented in the curriculum or acknowledged in the practices of the school. Schools must send the message that GLBTIQ parents, students, and their families are welcome to participate in the functions of the school. A good first step in "reculturing" the school is to lay the legal groundwork for inclusion of GLBTIQ people.

School districts should, if they have not already, adopt a nondiscrimination policy that includes both "sexual orientation" and "gender identity." Refer to "Developing a District's Anti-harassment Policy" (U.S. Department of Education 2000a, 2000b) and your local ACLU chapter[1] for guidance in wording the policy. If the policy is worded too broadly, it risks violating First Amendment rights to freedom of speech. In this case it can easily be struck down if challenged in a court of law, just as one Pennsylvania school district's antiharassment policy was deemed by the court to violate First Amendment guarantees to freedom of speech (*Saxe v. State College Area School District* 2001).

School districts should also adopt associated regulations to go along with their nondiscrimination policies. The purpose of the associated regulations is to clearly spell out a protocol for reporting, investigating, and resolving complaints of discrimination. It also makes certain individuals accountable for seeing that the intent of the policy is carried out. In addition, districts should hire a full-time director of institutional equity and multicultural education—devoted in part or entirely to GLBTIQ issues—and devote adequate resources and personnel to this office. As well, each district should offer adequate training on what the policy entails for each employee and how to understand GLBTIQ students, differences in sexual orientations, practical strategies for identifying and stopping all forms of harassment, and First Amendment rights of students and district employees. Finally, school districts should draw on national and local chapters of GLSEN, PFLAG, Lambda Legal Defense and Education Fund, and Safe Schools Coalitions to assist in bringing about equity for GLBTIQ students and staff. Likewise, they need to learn to rely on local resources, such as GLBTIQ youth support groups, religious organizations that affirm GLBTIQ identities, and community-based coalitions of GLBTIQ advocates.

Creating a culture of inclusion includes ensuring the following: that GLBTIQ students, employees, and families are covered by nondiscrimination policies; that teachers are given adequate training and resources to be able to implement the nondiscrimination policy; that teachers feel comfortable enough to neutrally discuss sexual orientation and gender identity issues with their students; and that students are given the opportunity to form gay–straight alliances. School districts that have adopted and implemented nondiscrimination policies that include sexual orientation and have offered training to teachers, students, and parents on GLBTIQ issues have shown success in creating safer places for GLBTIQ students and staff. Minneapolis School District, St. Paul School District, and San Francisco Unified School District, to name a few, are districts that have overcome many hurdles in implementing policies and educational programs to increase safety and equity for GLBTIQ students, staff, and families.

Suggestions for Other Safe Schools Coalitions

Although Button, Rienzo, and Wald (1997) are correct that successful adoption and implementation of policy is usually the result of a fortuitous and unpredictable mix of opportunities, this case proves that groups like High Plains Safe Schools Coalition can be better prepared to take advantage of opportunities when they arise through planning and by being well organized. Though HPSSC, and the Coalition before them, often worked quietly behind the scenes so as not to catch the attention of moral conservatives, others have discovered that putting controversial issues in the public spotlight can also have beneficial consequences. At times it may actually be better to involve the public and build grassroots support, even if it means running the risk of defeat. At least, then, the stage has been set to bring the issue up again later. Quiet passage of school policies that include sexual orientation and gender identity could have negative and unforeseen consequences. For instance, Wisconsin was the first state to pass a statewide nondiscrimination law that included sexual orientation. For years, nobody used the law or opposed it. Now that students and educators want to use the law, "Republican-controlled political bodies are enraged to find the law on the books. Little support is there for [students] because we have no educated policy group in support who helped pass the law in the first place" (K. Harbeck, personal communication, May 1, 2000). Amy Gutmann and Dennis Thompson, authors of *Democracy and Disagreement* (1996), concur:

> Moral debate in politics can reveal new possibilities and suggest new directions, making realization of the principles more feasible than was previously thought. Because deliberation has the potential for improving collective understandings of liberty and opportunity, the conditions of deliberation are an indispensable part of any perspective committed to securing liberty and opportunity for all.

In this case study, High Plains School District adopted its first policy (JFH-R) that includes sexual orientation in June 1992. The policy was adopted quietly by a liberal school board under the direction of a closeted gay superintendent. Subsequently, the policy was forgotten and never utilized by students or staff because no one knew of its existence, including the High Plains Safe Schools Coalition. Only one teacher and one administrator I spoke with were aware of the policy. Policies often do no good when adopted secretly because there is no support for their implementation.

General Strategies for Organizing

Safe Schools Coalitions and other community groups can employ the following organization strategies. First, forge working relationships and collaborate with other community groups that advocate similar positions, such as groups who advocate equity for students of color. Second, build a strong coalition and grassroots support by soliciting the support of other community agencies, organizations, local and state politicians, and churches. Don't go it alone. Third, attempt to cultivate understanding with opponents, especially those in positions of power. This can be done through either one-on-one or group meetings, facilitated by neutral facilitators if necessary. Next, demonstrate to the school board and district administrators the need for a nondiscrimination policy that includes sexual orientation and gender identity, by having GLBTIQ students testify to the abuse they suffer in the schools at school board meetings and teacher in-services. Finally, meet with each school's governance team to assess the climate for GLBTIQ staff and students, and what their school is doing, if anything, to enhance safety.

Community groups can also assist GLBTIQ students and their straight allies to advocate for themselves. Resist the temptation to do all the work for them. District officials are more impressed when students organize and request equal representation on their own behalf, rather than when a community group is doing it for them. This demonstration of autonomy also makes it more difficult for morally conservative parents to sell the idea that "youth are being manipulated by a national gay agenda." Move slowly, be persistent and patient, and win people over on a personal level—especially school board members, superintendents, and administrators, who can help your group establish credibility. Make friends with the media by keeping them informed of what you are doing—give them leads, send them information, and thank them for covering your work. However, remember to use the media strategically; that is, be aware that media coverage could cause moral conservatives to organize in opposition and make it more difficult to achieve your goals. Finally, when possible, work with the opposition to attempt to iron out differences and hear one another out.

Strategies for Keeping Your Group Healthy

Lessons learned from the HPSSC point to the following strategies for keeping your group healthy. First, appoint or elect a leader who has inside connections with the school district and who is energetic, diplomatic, and available for the position. Decide what the group's role will be. Will the group advocate for GLBTIQ students and staff and assist in the resolution of grievances? If so, then how can the group work within the system to prevent damaging their relationship of trust with the district? Take time to meet as a group, to set goals, and to reflect on accomplishments—what worked well and what did not. Otherwise, members may feel that the group is "floundering" and not accomplishing anything. This lack of communication could have negative effects on group morale.

It is important to respect that certain members of the group risk physical and economic harm if their participation in the group is disclosed to others, especially group members who are also employees of the school district. However, do not feel guilty about asking those group members to limit their participation in the group if their fear of being in a compromising position is limiting what the group can accomplish. Call on national organizations like GLSEN, PFLAG, and Lambda Legal Defense and Education Fund for guidance and support in keeping your group focused on clear objectives. Finally, allow members of the group to come and go without making them feel guilty about their ability to participate.

Note

1. Another great source: *Adding Sexual Orientation and Gender Identity to Discrimination and Harassment Policies in School.* A publication of ACLU Lesbian and Gay Rights Project, 125 Broad Street, 18th Floor, New York, NY 10004-2400, (212) 549-2627.

II

Understanding Moral Conservative Opposition to School Policies That Include Sexual Orientation

To change long-established habits in the individual is a slow, difficult and complicated process. To change long-established institutions—which are social habits organized in the structure of the common life—is a much slower, more difficult and far more complicated process.

—John Dewey

THE MORALLY CONSERVATIVE PARENTS AND TEACHERS I interviewed for this book all agreed that antigay harassment of students should be stopped. Why, then, do they oppose the passage of nondiscrimination policies that include sexual orientation? To better understand this paradox, we must look at the larger body of worldviews and beliefs that moral conservatives bring to this issue. This part of the book explores the worldviews of individuals on both sides of the debate and how their worldviews affect their understanding the district's policies. I then explore what those differences mean for policy implementation, and I discuss how both sides in this debate feel that their rights are being violated. This section closes with a way to evaluate the competing claims of each side, and it offers a way to get around the political stalemate regarding the conflict of violation of rights.

6

Opposition to Educational Change

T O UNDERSTAND THE PROCESS OF EDUCATIONAL CHANGE (like the implementation and enforcement of school policy) and the social interactions
among the various groups and individuals involved, we must understand the
nature of reality and meaning that those groups and individuals bring to their
understandings of the situation. The philosophical foundations[1] I lay out in
this chapter will help us understand the nature of the competing beliefs and
meanings that those in this study bring to the public debate about the inclusion of sexual orientation in the district's policies.

The Social Construction of Reality

Public schools are microcosms of the larger societal macrocosm. Michael W.
Apple (1992), Professor of Education, explains, "Education does not exist iso-
lated from the larger society. Its means and ends, the daily events of curriculum, teaching, and evaluation in schools, all of this is connected to patterns of
differential economic, political, and cultural power" (412). As social institutions arise out of interactions between individuals, a good place to start is with
the construction of reality through social discourse at the personal level.

Peter L. Berger and Thomas Luckmann (1966), sociologists of knowledge,
write of the "reality of everyday life" (23) as being intersubjective as it is shared
with others. It comes to be taken for granted as reality because it seems com-
monsensical and self-evident in one's social interactions with like-minded individuals. That is, what we know results from interactions with our parents,

our peers, the system of schooling, and so forth. Also, the way we come to understand the world usually goes unquestioned until someone with a different point of view challenges our knowledge. In this case, advocates of GLBTIQ inclusion are challenging the established norms of the heterosexual majority.

An example of how peoples' beliefs around sexual orientation are validated by the social institutions and other individuals in their lives is that heterosexuality comes to be accepted as normal or superior to other sexual orientations. As I described earlier, the institutionalization of heterosexuality as the norm privileges heterosexuals. For instance, heterosexuals can be married, and they expect both legal and social recognition for their marriages (from the government, and from their family and friends, respectively). Same-sex marriages, on the other hand, are neither legally recognized nor socially sanctioned. Therefore, heterosexual identity and the institution of heterosexuality are upheld. The law legitimates—as do others (government, religion, and family)—that heterosexual identity is a valid one, and it confirms to the heterosexual individual that it is the only proper one. Thus, it helps maintain that specific reality through the affirming social interactions of like-minded individuals.

Slogan Systems

Slogan systems help maintain the established order by preventing any redefinition by individuals. Though Apple (1992) is writing of standards in the teaching of mathematics, his discussion of slogan systems has relevance here in analyzing the employment of "official knowledge" in school reform movements. Slogan systems must grab us and provide something around which different groups can rally, thereby resulting in more widespread support. Thus, slogan systems draw on the norms and values of legitimate knowledge in such an ambiguous way as to garner broad support from different groups. The effect is that any potential threat to egalitarian ideas that the slogan system may entail is hidden by sentiments that, at face value, appear to be non-threatening, nonpolitical, and easily supportable. For example, all people can rally around the idea of "safe schools" until it becomes explicitly known that "safe schools" may entail the inclusion of sexual orientation in the policies or curriculum.

Subjective Realities

The norms of an established order are learned as truth and come to be internalized by individuals. At times, however, opposing ideas cause conflict and thus compete with one another to be legitimated. For example, a morally conservative teacher may have to negotiate her competing beliefs. Although she may hold that homosexuality is an abomination against God, she may also believe that it is her duty to provide a nurturing classroom environment for all of her students, including the GLBTIQ students.

School personnel who are told by their district to respect their GLBTIQ students' identities may be faced with a personal moral dilemma if they were socialized in a religious doctrine that teaches that homosexuality is a sin. They must negotiate between the doctrine of homosexuality as sin and the doctrine of respecting all of their students' identities. This paradox may pose a direct threat or challenge to the teacher's firmly held beliefs, her subjective reality. Berger and Luckmann (1966) explain, "The appearance of an alternative symbolic universe poses a threat because its very existence demonstrates empirically that one's own universe is less than inevitable" (108).

Thus, for educational change to take place—such as the legitimation of GLBTIQ identity (which was previously delegitimated)—the new message must be consistently maintained through discussion, the use of symbols (e.g., a "safe schools" slogan), and clearly defined steps for implementation. Thus, consistent implementation and education can repudiate the previous message of *homosexuality as deviance* and instill the new message of *GLBTIQ students as deserving of social justice*.

Official Knowledge and Legitimation

How are symbols manipulated to legitimate knowledge and help establish one group's knowledge as the "official knowledge"? Apple (1993) is largely concerned with the "official legitimacy of particular groups' knowledge" (11) and the fact that "those in dominance almost always have more power to define what counts as a need or a problem and what an appropriate response to it should be" (10). For example, to connect mathematics curricula to the lived realities of students, all sides could help students apply mathematics to their daily lives by focusing on social problems with which students are familiar. However, the construction of the social problems can be done in a variety of ways. One could choose and incorporate social problems into mathematical texts "in such a way that there would be education for leadership and education for 'followership' [organized] . . . on an ideological vision that [is] less than democratic" (Apple 1992, 424). That is, the way in which information is presented can evoke certain responses and thought patterns. For example, I queried math teachers about their level of comfort in framing a math word problem without assuming heterosexuality—for instance, "Bruce bought David one dozen roses . . ." Those in dominance, the heterosexual majority, have the power to frame what kinds of knowledge are presented to students and how they are presented, even in the simple case of assuming heterosexuality in a math word problem. For instance, most heterosexual math teachers would not even think about framing a word problem that asks students to "figure out the interest on Alice and Debbie's mortgage." How knowledge gets presented has very real implications for educational change in the area of policy. GLBTIQ students in particular, and GLBTIQ people in general, are a relatively voiceless and politically disempowered group. This disadvantage means that advocates of GLBTIQ inclusion in school policies must work hard to overcome the negative ways in which the general public is accustomed to thinking of GLBTIQ people. In addition, they must overcome the ways in which GLBTIQ people and perspectives are excluded from the schools.

Perceived Threats to Tradition

Contests between competing conceptions of reality—say, between moral conservatives and GLBTIQ rights advocates—often bring up issues of mistrust, fear, and a feeling that one's reality and way of life are threatened. Reform-minded movements, such as gay rights, challenge preconceived notions of the "naturalness" of social institutions, like that of the traditional family. The civil rights movement of the 1960s challenged whites' notions of what it meant to be white, and the feminist movement continues to challenge our notions of what it means to be a woman or a man. An unfortunate phenomenon for both sides is that gains for one minority group are often perceived to come at the expense of gains for other minority groups that are also vying for power. During Colorado's Amendment 2 campaign in 1992, a television commercial aimed at swaying popular opinion against gay rights was created by a group from the religious right. It depicted an African American woman professing the idea that there are only so many rights to go around, and if gays start getting them, then people of color will lose out. In this way, moral conservatives played on the fears of people of color to build support and protect what they perceived as a threat to their traditional way of life and their own hopes for change. The rhetoric and slogans that groups employ in preserving their dominance, or in challenging the dominant social order, often play on important symbols of the established social order. Any change in the established order, then, is perceived to entail a loss of control and a loss of economic and personal security.

Challenging Established Norms

For the dominant group whose knowledge is officially legitimated, the established order seems natural and neutral because it affirms their identity and way of life. For minority groups, however, the established order is not always natural or neutral; rather, it can be oppressive and terrorizing. The established social order of heterosexuality, along with its institutions and ideologies, affirms the lives and values of heterosexual people while delegitimating, or posing a threat to, the lives and values of GLBTIQ people. For example, "'minority' groups and 'minority' cultures have consistently been neglected in the media except for activities that are considered violent or confrontational" (Apple 1992, 107). Social reproduction theorists explain that this process enfranchises one group's cultural capital while disenfranchising the other's (Bourdieu 1977; Giroux 1983; Heath 1983). It is not surprising then that when minority groups have petitioned the government for inclusion and legitimation of their lives and values, explosive controversies have often erupted (Apple 1992, 48; Button, Rienzo, and Wald 1997; Harbeck 1997). Apple (1992) contends, "controversies over 'official knowledge'... really signify more profound political, economic, and cultural relations and histories" (48). This point is important here because moral conservatives challenge any attempt to affirm GLBTIQ identities in the public schools, seeing such attempts as threats to their traditional way of life and to their worldview that being GLBTIQ is wrong.

Intersubjective Meanings and Educational Change

Understanding how reality and meanings get constructed is important to understanding the social dynamics of the actors involved in the process of educational change. Fullan (1991) is concerned with what educational change looks like from the perspectives of teachers, students, parents, and administrators. Fullan sees educational reform as being about changing the cultures, or established orders, of the classrooms, schools, and districts; and as being about restructuring the roles of individuals within these settings (see also Sarason 1971, 1990, 1996).

Many of the factors that operate at a societal level to establish official knowledge and legitimate certain values and ways of life also operate within schools to create the culture of the school. Within schools, claims Fullan (1991), one readily finds direct and frequent communication about cultural norms, values, and beliefs, as well as the use of symbols to express the cultural values of the school (i.e., established order). For instance, teachers admonish students to "wait in line" and "raise your hand." All of these directives from teachers establish a modus operandi for movement and social interaction in the classroom. Examples of symbols that reinforce the culture of the school include the American flag, the recitation of the Pledge of Allegiance, posters of school rules, and other student codes of conduct. Thus, students, teachers, administrators, and others who are a part of the everyday life of the school come to embody the school's culture, or established order. This culture is often referred to as the school's "hidden curriculum." As far as sexual orientation, students come to embody the established order of the dominant heterosexual society, which is also taught (either explicitly or implicitly) through the hidden curriculum of the schools. For instance, students are socialized into a heterosexist worldview, where heterosexuality is presented as the only option (as previously discussed).

Contested Meanings of Educational Change

The way in which school policy is implemented has direct bearing on how the new policy is received and perceived by the social actors involved. Fullan (1991) writes, "An understanding of what reality is from the point of view of people within the role is an essential starting point for constructing a practical theory of meaning and results of change attempts" (144). Many policy reform efforts fail because the policy makers assume that all students, teachers, and other actors will accept the newly instituted policy because the intent of the policy is to make education better—and they presume that everyone wants to make education better. Blumer (1969) would caution administrators here not to reduce individual actors to the predefined patterns that guide their actions—in this case, they should not reduce teachers to mindless automatons of the school, who will blindly go along with the newly instituted policy.

In the case of teachers' willingness to accept new policy, Blumer reminds us that it is important to realize that human societies (and schools as microcosms) are "composed of individuals who have selves" and are not "merely organisms with some kind of organization, responding to forces which play upon them" (83). This distinction matters when one considers that reality is constructed through the interaction of individuals (in this case teachers, administrators, students, and parents) who react to situations through a process of interpretation (84). When it comes to school change and the implementation of policy, Fullan (1991) writes:

> Some proposals fail to acknowledge the personal costs, the meaning of change to teachers, and the conditions and time it will take to develop the new practices. Stated another way, teachers' reasons for rejecting many innovations are every bit as rational as those of the advocates promoting them. (130)

Especially when school change involves the alteration of beliefs we must

> adequately recognize how individuals come to confront or avoid behavioral and conceptual implications of change. Changes in beliefs challenge the core values held by individuals regarding the purposes of education; moreover, beliefs are often not explicit, discussed, or understood, but rather are buried at the level of unstated assumptions. (Fullan, 42)

Sears (1992) empirically affirmed that teachers' and counselors' personal feelings are related to their professional beliefs and that they affect educators' ability to support and intervene on the behalf of GLBTIQ students.

In addition, parents may have their own reasons for rejecting school policy that is intended by its initiators to make education better. For instance, one may argue that by including a gay-themed lesson in a literature course, education would be better for GLBTIQ students, who should see their lives represented in the school's curriculum, and for heterosexual students, who should learn about the GLBTIQ people in their lives. However, morally conservative parents can claim that the gay-themed lesson runs counter to their beliefs and that they do not want their children exposed to that material. Fullan (1991) reminds us that "innovations are 'rationally' advocated from the point of view of what is rational to the promoter, not the teachers [and others involved]" (130). The often overlooked part of the equation, however, is that "teachers have to have some understanding of the operational meaning of the change before they can make a judgment about it" (128)—and likewise for parents, students, and community members, as well as for other social actors in the schools, such as principals (167). That is, the actors involved cannot be expected to embrace the change without having at least some understanding of what the change entails for them. This point is especially important in considering the role of teacher in-services in helping staff understand and implement new policies. It would also be helpful for teachers to hear from teachers in other schools about how such change, when implemented, affected them.

Effectively Implementing Change

Reformers often fail to consider the impact of the proposed reform on teachers and others. So how does one get a school, including its students and staff, to accept and enforce a new policy? The new policy (educational change) must be made a part of the school's culture—that is, it must become the established order. The social interactions of all those involved are crucial to this establishment. "To state the aim another way, implementation is an ongoing construction of a shared reality among group members through their interaction with one another within the program" (Fullan 1991, 132).

Successful educational change that requires a change in belief or understanding on the parts of the actors takes time and perseverance. Fullan (1991) explains that it is easier to change peoples' behaviors than it is their beliefs; but ultimately, the beliefs must change, too, or the educational change will not have a lasting effect. He writes:

> When people try something new they often suffer what I call 'the implementation dip.' Things get worse before they get better and clearer as people grapple

with the meaning and skills of change. We see then that the relationship between behavioral and belief change is reciprocal and ongoing, with change in doing or behavior a necessary experience on the way to breakthroughs in meaning and understanding. (91)

Thus, asserts Fullan, "educational change is a process of coming to grips with the multiple realities of people, who are the main participants in implementing change" (95). Often times, though, advocates of new policy are blinded by their own reality and drive to implement the policy—no matter how good their intentions—and, thus, fail to consider the multiple realities of the people who will be affected. Fullan contends that this scenario is often the case where educational changes have failed—that policy innovators did not consider the meaning that others may have for the proposed policy. Thus, innovators of policy need to remain mindful that others will perceive the proposed policy differently, based on their worldview. Further, democratic deliberations between supporters and opponents may lead to a better thought-out policy and a smoother implementation for all involved.

In sum, innovators of educational policy must take into account the constructed realities and social meanings (worldviews) that all involved parties bring with them to the public forum. To discount a group's beliefs because they run counter to the proposed reform runs the risk of violating democratic principles that we as a nation claim to hold dear. Further, it can be destructive, insofar as it damages parent–school relationships; it can also be costly if the implemented reform fails because of resistance to it. However, resistance to a proposed reform alone is not a good reason for scrapping it.

In the case of HPSD's policies, it might be said that an alternative social reality is beginning to emerge and challenge the established order. GLBTIQ adolescents who are demanding equal rights, representation, and safety in America's schools personify this alternative reality. However, their demands are at odds with the firmly held beliefs and social institutions of the established heterosexist order. Thus, a space must be created at the local level, within the schools and other public fora. It must empower all those involved to debate the merits of such policies and to build broad-based community support so that the policies can be more effectively implemented down the road.

Note

1. These philosophical foundations were the conceptual framework from my dissertation.

7

How the Various Sides in This Debate Make Meaning of the Policies

A S I INTERVIEWED PARTICIPANTS ON BOTH SIDES of this issue, it became apparent that they understood the policies differently. Not only did advocates and opponents have differing conceptions of what the policies entailed, but teachers, administrators, and school board members understood the policies' intentions differently from one another and from community members. While some staff members wholeheartedly embraced the policies, others rejected them as either having no importance or, worse, having negative consequences. The biggest difference was that district staff who opposed the policies thought it was inappropriate for schools to address "social issues," like sexual orientation, and felt that schools should instead focus on "academic excellence."

School Board Members and Staff Who Oppose the Policies or the Mention of Sexual Orientation in the Classroom

The arguments expressed by these individuals[1] include many of the same concerns that were laid out in chapter 2, on the history of the policies' adoptions. Briefly, these arguments are:

- "sexuality of any kind should not be a part of the curriculum";
- "homosexuality should not be promoted in the schools";
- "the district is telling us we have to value homosexuality";
- "GLBTIQ students are already protected under the law—they don't need special treatment or special rights";

- "spelling out protected classes in the policies balkanizes people";
- "all students deserve to be safe in school, so the policies are unnecessary."

The two teachers, one current board member, and one former board member who expressed outright opposition to the policies all agreed that it is not a purpose of schools to educate students about differences in sexual orientation. In the conversation below, an ex-school board member explains her opposition to the curricular inclusion of homosexuality.

IAN: I'd like to go back to when you were saying schools shouldn't be talking about heterosexuality or homosexuality.

FORMER BOARD MEMBER: Well, I don't think a teacher should be promoting, and I don't really know what the curriculum is in sex education, but if we're talking about literature, I don't think there should be a focus on gay literature because this person is promoting gay issues.

IAN: Let's say you don't offer a gay literature course, but what do you think about the argument that any time you offer any literature, like Shakespeare's *Romeo and Juliet*, it's all about heterosexuality. So even though you're not calling the course "Heterosexual Literature" it's still full of heterosexuality. Do you think that promotes heterosexuality, reading *Romeo and Juliet* and all those other love stories between a boy and a girl?

FORMER BOARD MEMBER: No, I don't think it promotes it. I think it's fine literature and you can also find examples of fine literature written by individuals who are clearly gay, if you're trying to establish some sort of balance without getting into those issues, and still look at different pieces of literature from folks of many different persuasions.

IAN: So with a piece of literature written by a gay person, do you mean an obviously gay story, say about two boys falling in love?

FORMER BOARD MEMBER: You have to be careful there. There's still a majority of taxpayers and parents who will raise hell.

IAN: Do you think that's a good reason not to introduce that kind of literature, though? Wouldn't it be fair to gay kids in the class to also have a gay story represented in the literature selection?

FORMER BOARD MEMBER: Ah. You know everything isn't fair and the educational system is owned and driven by the taxpayers and if the majority of them don't support a certain focus or direction then that's how it goes. But I don't consider that *Romeo and Juliet* promotes heterosexuality even though it is obviously a hetero love story.

IAN: Where would the line get crossed between just talking about something and promoting it? I think most people would say if you had a piece of literature talking about two boys falling in love that would be promoting homosexuality but they wouldn't say that about *Romeo and Juliet*. That seems to be a contradiction.

FORMER BOARD MEMBER: I'm thinking of *The Color Purple* where there clearly is heterosexuality and nonheterosexuality issues. I think that, I don't know. That's a very difficult question. I don't know the answer. All I know is we have to be very careful because people are easily offended and they go crazy and you get a lot of turmoil.

"Schools are not the place to effect social change!" exclaimed a middle school teacher. Another school board member explains, "My line was always that if we strive for excellence in academics, many of those problems [like harassment] will disappear because kids will be busy learning and we will not be stressing the differences and everybody will be engaged in learning." According to these individuals, then, curricular materials that contain gay content teach students about social issues, thus imparting certain values that are best left for parents to teach their children. These opponents, however, do not feel that way about curricular materials that contain heterosexual content. This point demonstrates the normalizing discourse of heterosexual hegemony, where heterosexuality is assumed and goes unquestioned. In the following conversation, a high school math teacher defends his use of heterocentrist word problems.

IAN: What about changing names in a word problem so it might read "Bruce bought David one dozen roses and David gave three to . . ." so it's about being inclusive in your language and not presuming that you're just talking about heterosexual people? Do you do anything like that?

TEACHER: I don't, probably mostly because I wouldn't think of it. . . . Some kids would read that and go, "What's up with this?" If there was a neutral way to do that, that didn't get a reaction either way, and there probably is if I had enough time to think about how to do it, I would probably prefer to try to do something neutral. I understand that stating it in a more heterosexual way could make some people feel uncomfortable. I also think that stating it as "Bruce got David flowers" would make some people feel uncomfortable. I think you need to be careful about who you make uncomfortable and I think also as a math teacher, I don't want to distract from what I'm trying to do. What I want kids to do is the math and not say, "Why is it so and so?" I know that goes both ways but I'm not sure I'd be willing to do that or not. I'd have to think about it.

IAN: Does the topic of homosexuality or gay people ever come up in math classes?

TEACHER: Never has, except when kids use the word "fag" and that's pretty common and when they do that I jump on them right away and ask them to be more careful about their word choice.

IAN: Do you think using only heterosexual examples in word problems is in a sense bringing up the social issue of heterosexuality and positing it as the only option, because you're not giving equal time, or any time, to other lifestyles?

TEACHER: Being a heterosexual white male, I'd like to believe that it doesn't. Frankly, I think a person can drive themselves crazy by always trying to give equal time to everybody. On the other hand, if I have a gay student in my class and they read that [heterosexuals are buying one another flowers in math problems]—I can see that [might be a problem]—but I also hope that they're focusing more on the math part of that. I would like to think the fact that I used what's considered traditional—not because it's better or worse than anything else, just for convenience's sake—I would like to think that's not offensive to anybody. . . . I think a lot of times language is done in a very casual carefree way and I guess if I placed meaning in everything I heard every single day, then I think anybody can find something. I guess I hope that in a math class people would be able to say this is a math problem, I didn't mean anything what ever my words are, I'm just trying to write a math problem. I see your point but I'd like to have a little bit of understanding also that we all use language casually some times and not every single sentence is necessarily meant to be taken in a literal sense.

As is clear in the examples above, these teachers are quick to defend their practice of assuming heterosexuality and presenting it as the only option. When I asked interviewees, "Is it okay to discuss homosexuality in the classroom?" staff on both sides of the issue, but more frequently the opponents, responded that it is not okay to bring up homosexuality out of the blue, but that it is okay if it is "tied in with something in the curriculum" or if students bring it up. Another commonality was that staff often equated talking about homosexuality with talking about the sex act, totally discounting that sexual identities can be discussed without mentioning sexual behavior. The one content area where these individuals said it may be okay to mention sexual orientation was in sex education and health class. As Friend (1993) argues, however, relegating mention of homosexuality to sex education and health classes stigmatizes being GLBTIQ as a "health issue." These teachers rarely considered that GLBTIQ people and perspectives can be infused throughout all content areas, like saying "Bruce bought David one dozen roses" in math word problems, without getting into a discussion of sexual behavior.

Most of these individuals agreed that the policies wouldn't be necessary if we could just treat one another as human beings or if teachers would just treat all their students the same. When asked if the nondiscrimination policy was needed, a middle school teacher replied, "It shouldn't be needed if everybody treated everybody as human beings." Another teacher said he was unaware of what the purpose of the nondiscrimination policy was, but simultaneously claimed it was not necessary. Like the teacher above, this teacher disagreed with what he believed the policy to say and so discounted it as having any relevance for him because "he treats everyone the same."

Along with the expressed ideas of "treating everyone the same" and "respecting everyone," the idea expressed by all of these individuals was that "everyone deserves equal rights." However, when pressed further, it became apparent that, although they professed this idea frequently, they often did not extend it to GLBTIQ people. For instance:

FORMER BOARD MEMBER: I think everyone deserves equal rights.

IAN: Do you think same-sex marriage should be legalized then?

FORMER BOARD MEMBER: No. I do not believe in same-sex marriage.

IAN: If heterosexuals can get married shouldn't homosexuals be allowed to, if you believe in equal rights for everybody?

FORMER BOARD MEMBER: Maybe it's not a right. It's a privilege.

Thus, many opponents believe the policies are unnecessary and end up causing problems, rather than solving problems—for example, by highlighting differences between students, which they believe leads to disunity. They express the beliefs that all students should be treated equally and that nondiscrimination equals treating everyone the same.

Besides the belief that the policies were simply unnecessary, others believed the policies would have negative consequences. Many of these individuals stated that the move to include sexual orientation in the policies is nothing but "political correctness" and that it puts a damper on freedoms of expression and thought. Opponents referred to political correctness as an assault on individuals' rights to hold their own beliefs and values, and to express them publicly. A school board member contends:

> As far as the policy, there are many steps I thought limit freedom of speech for our teachers. . . . There is already an inhibiting force in this country, which is called political correctness. . . . And I understand that political correctness today is what 50 years ago, a hundred years ago, were manners. This is essentially the replacement for old-fashioned manners. This is also the replacement for many people for the tenets of religion. And I am not saying that many things in political correctness are in general right, but the moment you start operating, not based on your judgment, but based on because "Somebody says this" or "One should not say this or that" we are limiting speech.

For this school board member, then, good old-fashioned manners would be better guidance in how we treat one another than a policy that spells out protected classes. The reasoning is that the policy could potentially be abused and thus give rise to frivolous claims of discrimination based on politically correct ideas of how things should be. The board member goes on to give an example of a lesbian student who complained she suffered harassment because her high school literature teacher assigned *Romeo and Juliet*. The board member explains:

> [The student] considered this harassment that she had to read [the book] and that she had to write about it. Well, there is a serious problem because this way we could probably chuck out of the window 95% of the history and literature of the past.

This board member believes that we as a society have lost sight of common sense and are now blinded by political correctness, of which spelling out protected classes in policies is an example. This board member fears that inclusion of sexual orientation in district policy would lead to frivolous claims of discrimination, such as the one above, and that a court of law would use the policy as justification for finding in favor of the lesbian student—that she indeed suffered harassment because her literature teacher assigned a heterosexual love story. According to this board member, the result of such frivolous claims would effectively limit the rights of teachers and other students to hold their private beliefs and to express them, in fear of being found guilty of offending another person with whom they disagree.

The school board member in the above quote hinted at "the way things used to be." Recalling "how things were back in the good old days" was something that almost every opponent did, and not one advocate did. On the topic of teachers' disclosing their sexual orientation to students, an ex-school board member states, "It's just something that would never, never have happened when I was growing up. Teachers wouldn't even tell you what political party they belonged to. I think some things should be private. . . ." In the following conversation, William, a middle school teacher, reminisces about "the good old days."

> WILLIAM: It's so different from when I was growing up. . . . I suppose because of the fact that I don't believe in political correctness. . . .
> IAN: You mentioned political correctness earlier, too, and said it's a problem with social issues. Could you talk about that a little more?
> WILLIAM: I don't feel like people are allowed to have their own feelings about anything anymore. Everybody is supposed to feel the same, everybody is supposed to react the same. . . . I grew up a totally unbigoted bone in my body. I didn't know what bigotry was. . . . When I was in college I had a friend who was black and we got along great all the time until he got with his black friends and then I was a nobody, I was a honkey white, and he turned black. He wasn't just a person. I had trouble with that. Why could we be friends together but we couldn't be friends when you're around your other friends? And so I got to not like certain parts of things yet I feel with political correctness, I'm not allowed to not like those parts. I feel like I have to like everybody the same all the time. I'm sorry, nobody does. I'm allowed to have differences of opinion but I don't feel with political correctness we're allowed to.

This teacher, who reminisces about the good old days, worries that our country is in social decline and that political correctness is one of the reasons. It is interesting to note the implication that his black friend was "white" until he got with his black friends. This point is important, and it comes up in the next chapter. The distinction the teacher is referring to demonstrates the power of the majority to define what constitutes "correct" and "proper" behavior, and how the behavior deemed "proper" by the white and heterosexual majority comes to be equated with "human" behavior. The teacher explained that when his black friend was around other black people, "he turned black. He wasn't just a person."

For this teacher, political correctness entails a loss of power, and it borders on thought control. This teacher feels that because of "politically correct" mandates, from the government and from the liberal popular opinion, people no longer have the right to dislike others and express that dislike; otherwise, they risk being labeled a racist, a homophobe, or a bigot. For him, the inability to express his opinions because of fear of retribution is the same as not being able to hold an opinion privately. In sum, teachers who oppose the policies say the policies conflict with freedom of conscience in that they attempt to change peoples' beliefs and opinions.

Besides believing that the policies violate their right to freedom of conscience, opponents believe an effect of the policies is to legitimate and promote homosexuality. Gay rights advocates sometimes mistake this claim to mean that homosexuality will be promoted over heterosexuality. For opponents whom I interviewed, however, it simply means legitimating homosexuality to the same level as heterosexuality, thus promoting it as a normal and socially acceptable way to live.

Almost all those interviewed believed that class discussions on homosexuality will occur more frequently now that this issue has been pushed to the forefront and because teachers will be stopping and addressing antigay abuse more frequently. Some believe that simply stopping antigay peer harassment may force teachers who oppose homosexuality to agree with and defend homosexuality as being okay. Nancy, a lunchroom supervisor (who is also a member of Concerned Citizens), finds herself in a quandary when faced with addressing antigay harassment. She is unsure of what the policy requires of her in explaining to students why they should not use antigay epithets. Her preference is to stop any sort of name-calling and not get into a detailed discussion of why it is wrong to call others certain names. But she wonders if the policy requires that she go so far as to defend the victim's real or perceived sexual orientation in explaining why the name-calling is wrong. She explains:

> I think it's difficult to determine exactly where to draw the line. It's sometimes easier to address, rather than the specific names that are being called, the actual fact of calling people names. So the particular names that are called are not what the supervisor would address. They would address the general bullying, harassment, and name-calling of any kind. So that makes it a general call, rather than specific. I don't know whether that would be the kind of enforcement that some people are looking for or if they're looking for supervisors to actually stand up for and defend the sexual orientation [of the victim].

Nancy admits, "I definitely have strong religious feelings that homosexuality is wrong behavior." Outrightly defending a student's perceived homosexual orientation would be difficult for Nancy. Thus, staff who oppose homosexuality are put in a quandary: they are expected to halt antigay harassment but feel that doing so in some way defends the student's homosexual orientation—thereby, in their mind, "legitimating a homosexual orientation" as normal and sending the message "It's okay to be gay."

Most opponents acknowledged that antigay harassment of students is a problem at the high school level and should not be allowed. When asked if antigay harassment was a problem in their schools, however, all elementary and middle school teachers replied, "No." They responded that students in elementary and middle school are too young to know their sexual orientation; thus, antigay harassment is only a problem at the high school level, when GLBTIQ students begin identifying themselves as GLBTIQ. This belief demonstrates a mind-set that only openly identifying GLBTIQ students can be the victims of antigay abuse and that no students begin self-identifying as GLBTIQ before high school. It also ignores the facts that some elementary and middle school students come from GLBTIQ families, that elementary students are frequently the victims of antigay abuse, and that gender and sexual identity development begin in early childhood. Several teachers denied that it was a problem at all, and several suggested that students bring abuse upon themselves. One explained, "If people feel intimidated sometimes it's because they let people do that to them and I figure you've just got to get up and do what you've got to do."

Along with a tendency to see antigay harassment as only being a problem at the high school level, elementary and middle school teachers often made a distinction between antigay harassment and name-calling, denying that name-calling is a form of harassment. A middle school teacher explains his belief that name-calling does not necessarily entail harassment:

IAN: Do you think antigay harassment of students is a problem in the schools?
TEACHER: One thing I do hear occasionally is name-calling. I think lots of times the name-calling is just that, it's name-calling. And sometimes it's hard to sort out whether kids even know the implications of what they're saying. They may be repeating things, you know how you pick up those terms without even knowing what they are and they don't know what they mean.
IAN: What are some names you'd hear?
TEACHER: The only one I've ever heard is "fag." I don't think that sometimes when those things are said, they're said to draw a response and all.

In summary, some staff members oppose the policies in general; others oppose what they believe the policies entail or to what they will lead. One of these beliefs is that curricular inclusion of GLBTIQ people and perspectives is an example of teaching social issues. In their minds, teaching social issues imparts values best left for families to teach. In addition, they believe that academics (reading, writing, and arithmetic) can be taught devoid of any values. They also believe that the current inclusion of heterosexual people and perspectives in the curriculum does not legitimate or promote heterosexuality, nor does it impart any values to students about heterosexuality. However, they believe that including GLBTIQ people and perspectives would legitimate and promote homosexuality. They also reason that if we just treated everyone as human beings, policies like these would be unnecessary. Likewise, they continuously affirm that everyone deserves equal rights, but they do not extend it to GLBTIQ people, as I show in the next chapter. They believe that the policies limit freedom of thought and expression by requiring that everyone accept homosexuality as okay; furthermore, they think that this alleged forced acceptance of homosexuality has the subsequent effects of promoting and legitimating homosexuality. Finally, they believe that antigay peer harassment is only a problem in the high schools. They reason that since the elementary and middle school levels have so few (or no) self-identifying GLBTIQ students, then no antigay peer harassment would therefore exist.

Principals, Teachers, Counselors, and Other Staff Who Support the Policies

Not one principal, guidance counselor, intervention specialist, or high school teacher I interviewed expressed opposition to the policies.[2] I do not presume, however, that there were no district staff who flatly opposed the policies. While all of these teachers state support for the policies, several expressed some reservations about curricular inclusion of sexual orientation issues. The biggest difference between advocates and opponents of the policies is that staff who support the policies agreed that schools not only have the right, but also the responsibility, to address social issues and talk about sexual orientation differences with students. These individuals' understandings of the policies varied from simply stopping the name-calling and other forms of peer harassment to equal inclusion, including curricular inclusion, for GLBTIQ students. Meg, an intervention specialist, explains the importance of discussing social issues in school:

> MEG: I believe it's very important to talk about the social issues of what's happening with kids [e.g., kids' relationships with their parents, peers, and lovers]. And if you don't do that, you won't be able to do the other stuff. If you don't get to the social issues, they're not going to be in the place to learn.

IAN: Some people say that schools' sole focus should be on academics and not social issues. What would you say to those people?

MEG: From a psychological standpoint, and a developmental standpoint, and a sociological standpoint, you have to look at what's going on developmentally and psychologically with that adolescent. To just forget that there's so much going on with them, you know, you have to realize that some kids are going to need some mental health.

IAN: Then what would you say to those parents who say, "That's the job of the family. Not the school."

MEG: I can understand that and a lot of times I would love for that to happen. It just doesn't always happen that way. The kids come to school, and there's a lot of stuff going on in their minds and a lot of them just don't go to classes. And then you've got a big problem. And then you can say, "Survival of the fittest. Oh well. What are you going to do? They should be going to class." You can take that stance. But you can also take the stance of, "Well, maybe if they had a place for 45 minutes to just kind of get what's off their mind . . ." then I bet you for the rest of the day they'd be able to function all day in class.

All staff that supported the policies agreed that the policies are needed for a variety of reasons. Many of the staff I interviewed who openly support the policies are willing to proclaim that it is okay to be gay and that GLBTIQ people are a part of society and thus deserving of equal rights. Many of these staff simply accepted that GLBTIQ people exist, that GLBTIQ students are in the schools, and that homosexuality should be normalized—that is, accepted as a normal way of being and living, without any stigma. Many of them also advocated curricular inclusion of GLBTIQ issues. A middle school teacher, who also identifies as a Christian, explained, "I think you just have to make [being gay] not a taboo. It's not about it being secretive and hidden and dirty. It's about it being a part of life just like anything else is." Another middle school teacher explains, "I think that the more exposure people have to homosexuals, [the more] they can just kind of see their normalcy and just relate to that as part of life. We really need to bring in homosexuals and have discussions with [students] at that age." A guidance counselor gives her opinion in the following exchange:

IAN: What would you say to those parents who claim the district is legitimizing a gay lifestyle by allowing class discussions on the topic—that the school is sending the message "It's okay to be gay"?

COUNSELOR: It is okay. I mean, why wouldn't they? It is okay! [laughing] I don't think that because we have it in a policy it makes it legitimate. We're just recognizing a reality as far as I'm concerned.

The understanding of the policies upon which all of these staff agreed was the need to stop all forms of antigay abuse, including name-calling. They disagreed, however, that stopping antigay name-calling would have the effect of promoting homosexuality as an acceptable lifestyle. In sum, while many of the staff who support the policies believe "It's okay to be gay" and that homosexuality is a legitimate lifestyle, they stop short of conceding that the implementation of the policies plays any part in promoting homosexuality as normal and sending the message "It's okay to be gay." In essence, staff who support the policies insist that the effect of the policies is not to change anybody's beliefs about homosexuality. However, this expressed belief seems to contradict the fact that many supporters also proclaim that a purpose of schooling is to shape students' beliefs, as discussed in the next section. In the following interview, a fifth-grade teacher explains how he stops name-calling, and he maintains that doing so does not impart any values.

IAN: Do you consider a student saying, "That's so gay" to be inappropriate?
TEACHER: Oh, yes. We're very strict with that kind of thing. We let the kids know that harassment of any kind is totally inappropriate.
IAN: Do they understand the implication is that gay is bad, therefore, you're bad, that there's something wrong with being gay?
TEACHER: Oh yeah. [Students who are] jocks will use the term against boys who are different.
IAN: At the fifth grade level kids are already making distinctions between jocks and boys who are effeminate?
TEACHER: Oh yeah. Oh yeah. And I don't know if they really understand "effeminate" so much as they know they're different, they're not into sports, they're doing other things.
IAN: So when you have this discussion about why it's inappropriate to call someone "gay," how much do you get into what it means to be gay?
TEACHER: That's a tough one because we can't really start getting into the whole values thing or anything like that. Mostly it will surround that it's inappropriate, it's hurtful, it's something that you don't know anything about, it's no different than calling them a "nigger," it won't be tolerated, and usually that's all it takes. We've never had to take it any further than that.

While staff and others who opposed the policies felt that schools should focus solely on academics and leave discussions of social issues and values to families, staff who support the policies have different ideas about the purpose of schooling. As one of these supporters stated, "It's all about changing norms." Thus, the views of both sides regarding the purpose of schooling radically depart from one another. Staff who support the policies stated, "I want [students] to be respectful of other peoples' ways of life," and "Students need more knowledge about homosexuality. The more information you can get out about differences the more you can educate kids." A high school principal asked:

If a school can't change belief systems then who can? Who in our society is charged with that if the school's not? We don't always like to think of ourselves as the shapers of moral and civic responsibilities and beliefs and things, but that's what [schools] were originally designed to do and we still carry a lot of. We have those charges.

In sum, where these staff members' beliefs most differ from those of opponents is that they all believe schools have the right and responsibility to address social issues and to challenge students' previously held beliefs. Most simultaneously deny, however, that stopping antigay harassment or including GLBTIQ people and perspectives in the curriculum will legitimate homosexuality as normal and thus promote it as "okay" to students. Their other beliefs are that antigay abuse of students is a problem at all grade levels and should be stopped; that it is okay to discuss homosexuality in the classroom; that it's okay to be gay; that homosexuality should be normalized and that schools should play a role in this through curricular inclusion and by inviting guest speakers; that the policies help alter norms, raise awareness, and change peoples' hearts and minds; and, finally, that the policies do not legitimate or promote homosexuality.

School Board's and District
Administration's Beliefs about the Policies

District administrators[3] give the same reasons in support of the policies as do other district staff who support the policies. A school board member explains:

I think it's important that we begin to address [sexual orientation]. I think the biggest thing that's coming for us culturally is, as demographics change, a lot of fears come up about what it is to be an American and what it is to be a member of the community. The more that we can have these discussions the more it will allay those fears—that gay and lesbian people are people.

Based on interviews and videotaped school board meetings, support for the policies exists among every current school board member except for one, who opposes both the spelling out of protected classes in the policies and the phrase "value diversity" in the Diversity Goal. All central administrators interviewed agreed that antigay peer harassment of students is a problem and that the policies are needed to help stop abuse. Except for the one school board member, they also agreed on the necessity of spelling out the protected classes in the policies to send a clear message about what is covered by the policies. A high-level administrator explains, "I don't think you'd have a policy that was as specific as you wanted it to be without including [the protected classes] in there."

By and large, the administrators I interviewed realize a need to be inclusive of GLBTIQ students and families. A school board member recounts:

> A lot of people I've talked to say, "You should just [teach] academics"—old school folks who want it the way it was 50 years ago. I try to tell them, "Hey, the world's not like it was a 50 years ago. It's a lot more complex, kids are more sophisticated, they're exposed to things at younger ages, and they're inquisitive and if we don't deal with that then it's not, we're not serving them in the way that we should."

On the topic of discussing GLBTIQ families at the elementary level, an administrator states, "I would advocate that we say they exist and that we list them as normal in our society. Not right or wrong, not good or bad." In response to the charge that the school would then be legitimating homosexual families by calling them normal, she responded, "They're a part of our reality and my statements don't legitimize anything. What they do is identify the reality in which we live. [GLBTIQ families] exist so why would we deny their existence?" Like teachers who support the policies, high-level administrators who support the policies deny that saying "homosexuality is normal" legitimates and promotes homosexuality.

When it comes to implementing policy, there was at least confusion, and at most disagreement, among school board members over the school board's role in ensuring that policies are implemented once the board adopts them. A school board member who opposed the inclusion of sexual orientation in the Diversity Goal continuously drew a distinction that the school board's role is simply to make policy, not to implement or enforce it; otherwise, the school board risks micromanagement, to which he is opposed. He stated that training should not be necessary in helping staff to understand how to implement a new policy and that staff, as professionals, should be expected to understand and implement policies once the school board creates them. He argued that any implementation of the policy should be left up to program directors and administrators in the district's central administration. However, this case reveals that leaving the implementation of policy up to central administrators leads to a great deal of confusion and inconsistencies in the information that goes down the line to principals, teachers, and other staff. The result is that many district staff are either unaware or unfamiliar with the policies and what they entail. In many cases, staff members' interpretations of the policies were completely dissonant with the school board's interpretations.

Besides not understanding policies, board members apparently believe that there are too many policies to keep track of. Ironically, school board members proved to be unaware of their own policies on two occasions. The first case arose in the summer of 1999, when High Plains Safe Schools Coalition petitioned the school board for "official advisory committee" status, which would put them on the same level as Citizens United against Racism, an official advisory committee that reports to the school board on equity issues for students of color. A member of HPSSC reported that the superintendent and a school board member said there is no precedent for an official advisory committee to the school board, and it was apparently by pure persistence and longevity that CUAR had become a de facto advisory committee. However, I found three school board policies adopted prior to 1969 that allow for and encourage the formation of advisory committees of residents of the district to investigate and report on issues to the school board through the superintendent. Thus, the superintendent's and the board member's response that there was no precedent for the HPSSC to become an official advisory committee was incorrect, as school board policy clearly allows it.

The other case of the district's being unfamiliar with its own policies is the fact that one policy was forgotten altogether—JFH-R: Student Complaints and Grievances, adopted June 18, 1992, which addresses discrimination based on sexual orientation and outlines a procedure for students and staff to follow in settling grievances. At no time during the debate over the nondiscrimination policy in 1994 or during the debate over the Diversity Goal in 1998 and 1999 was this policy ever mentioned.

Further confusion existed over whether or not the nondiscrimination and Diversity Goal policies also protect transgendered students by prohibiting discrimination based on "gender identity." Though gender identity is not listed as a protected class in the policies, one program director stated her belief that transgendered students would be covered under sexual orientation. She contends, "Sexual orientation is such a broad term I'm not sure people understand that it includes transgender issues."[4] Another program director acknowledged that the nondiscrimination policy "doesn't speak directly to that" but that any complaints of harassment against transgendered students would receive the same treatment as other complaints. She adds, "We tried to write [the policy] so that it would be broad enough to encompass everybody's needs."

In sum, the district's position on the inclusion of sexual orientation in the policies and the implementation of the policies are as follows. They believe antigay abuse is a problem in the schools, that it should not be permitted, and that it is necessary to spell out the protected classes in the policies, so there is no question about who and what is covered. They believe the policies protect transgendered students, too, even though "gender identity" is not listed as a protected class. They affirm that GLBTIQ people are a part of society, and the district should acknowledge their existence. They also believe that curricular inclusion of GLBTIQ issues may be congruent with the district's goals, although no formal curricular inclusion exists; that teaching that homosexuality is normal will not legitimate or promote homosexuality; that the policies will not have the effect of legitimating or promoting homosexuality; and that it is up to central administrators to implement policy once the board adopts it.

High Plains Safe Schools Coalition's Beliefs about the Policies

Members of the HPSSC and other advocates see this policy as a civil rights issue. They assert that schools must deal fairly with the topic of homosexuality and with GLBTIQ students and families. One community member contends, "Many gay and lesbian kids can't talk about being gay or lesbian in their families and if they can't talk about it at school, I don't know what's left for them." Members of HPSSC frequently use the phrase "raising awareness." They believe the policies should help raise awareness about the needs of GLBTIQ students and families, with the goal of helping district staff to better serve them. A member of HPSSC explains district staff need "general awareness raising and education and understanding and breaking down barriers."

In every discussion with HPSSC about why schools should care about this topic, the recurring and consistent theme is "safety." For instance, a parent came to the HPSSC for advice on how to get her child's elementary school to include discussions of GLBTIQ families. The parent wanted to know how best to handle teachers and parents who would oppose discussing GLBTIQ families with children. A member of HPSSC told the parent, "You just have to get them to understand it's about safety."

No members of HPSSC ever publicly talk about the policies leading to a "legitimation" or "promotion of homosexuality," though they do acknowledge these potential effects in private. A member of HPSSC talked about normalizing GLBTIQ identities in an interview. She stated:

[Talking about sexual orientation and gender identity] may be more suitable for some subjects than others but it's a piece about supporting and normalizing our youth in that community. And I think that that is a political word—normalizing—because the conservative folks would argue, "That's exactly what you're doing. You have an agenda. You're trying to normalize and I don't have to accept your behavior." But there's a piece about what the nondiscrimination policy really is—are we really allowing these youth to be themselves and be represented in our curriculum? If "no," then we shouldn't normalize heterosexuality. You don't get to legislate for me my identity and gender expression, that's my choice. But you do get to support me in making my choice.

Another member of HPSSC explained, "We want to continue the encouragement of allowing Gay-Straight Alliances in area high schools so that GLBT kids can gain a sense of empowerment and legitimate identity in their schools." Thus, members of HPSSC believe that GLBTIQ students and families must be dealt with fairly; that the policies help raise awareness among staff as to the needs of GLBTIQ students; that the policies are about ensuring safe schools for all students; that the policies may or may not have the effects of promoting or legitimating homosexuality; and that people who oppose the policies are fearful of a "gay agenda."

Concerned Citizens' Beliefs about the Policies

Concerned Citizens, while opposed to the inclusion of sexual orientation in the district's policies, agree that all students should be safe in school, and they acknowledge that GLBTIQ students are often the victims of horrendous abuse. However, Concerned Citizens believe that existing federal and state laws—as well as a nondiscrimination policy that simply states "all students," rather than spelling out protected classes—would be adequate for protecting students from antigay and other forms of peer harassment.

Opponents in this study give morally conservative (Howe 1997) reasons based on libertarian values, more than religious reasons, for opposing the policies. While some opponents stated their religious beliefs as reasons for opposing homosexuality, none gave religion as the sole reason they oppose the policies. In fact, many opponents I interviewed never brought up religion at all. Rather, their arguments for opposing the policies focused on government nonintervention and parental autonomy.[5] As stated, opponents consistently said that "everybody is already protected" and that more laws and policies are not needed. Carol, a Concerned Citizen, asks:

> Don't we already have laws on the books that, "We all are created equal, we all should be treated equal?" Don't we have that in the Constitution, that we're all equal? I really think instead of writing law after law, we've got some good laws.

Similar to staff who opposed the policies because they believe the spelling out of protected classes balkanizes people, Carol goes on to explain:

> The categorization of people leads to stereotyping. [It's] better to teach children to be colorblind and to be blind about peoples' sexual orientation. When we spend all of our time focusing on what makes us different, eventually that is all we see.

Some opponents believe the policy requires teachers to teach that homosexuality is an acceptable and normal way to live. Others acknowledge that nowhere does the policy mandate this assumption; nonetheless, they believe it will be a consequence, whether intended or not. In this belief, they do not differ from the HPSSC. Another concern is that the inclusion of sexual orienta-tion in the policies will open the door for formal curricular inclusion down the road. When asked if the exclusion of GLBTIQ people and perspectives from the curriculum were fair, a Concerned Citizen responded, "Students do not have the right to have their lives represented in the curriculum." Furthermore, claim morally conservative parents, the inclusion of GLBTIQ people and perspec-tives in the curriculum would teach social values on "controversial issues."

All opposing parents agreed that the schools should focus on academics and not address social issues like sexual orientation. For opponents, class dis-cussions on social issues would lead to the schools' imparting values to stu-dents, and they believe the teaching of values is the sole responsibility of par-ents. One opponent explained, "The attempt of the public schools to teach our children about choice-based lifestyles is wrong. The school has no business in replacing the family unit as the sole source for providing children with moral and ethical values." Frank, a Concerned Citizen explained, "It's indoctrination and thought control when the government tells children how and what to think. . . . I have a problem with telling other people that they're thinking right or wrong thoughts."

Opponents believe the policies, and the schools' resulting treatment of GLBTIQ students and GLBTIQ issues, legitimizes homosexuality as an ac-ceptable lifestyle and promotes homosexuality as being as good as, or equal to, heterosexuality. In discussions with opponents, the phrases "legitimate a ho-mosexual lifestyle" and "promote homosexuality" were used interchangeably and essentially mean that schools will be sending the message to students that "it's okay to be gay."

> IAN: So when you say "legitimate homosexuality," does that mean the schools are teaching that homosexuality is okay—that schools are sending the message "It's okay to be gay"?
> NANCY, CONCERNED CITIZEN: Yes, that's right.

Concerned Citizens object to the schools' legitimation of homosexuality, stating that schools "shouldn't promote a lifestyle" and that "advocacy of pos-itive encouragement of lifestyle choices is not something schools should be in-volved in." Carol concurs: "I do not want anyone telling [my kids] that this is an alternative lifestyle that is acceptable and okay and just another choice. To choose the gay life is simply wrong." Frank explains the phrase "promote ho-mosexuality."

> IAN: I've often heard the phrase "Schools shouldn't promote homosexuality." Have you used that phrase or heard others use it and what does it mean to you?
> FRANK: It means homosexuality promoted as a personal choice or alternate

lifestyle. The [Diversity Goal] says we have to value homosexuality. I think the principal reason for my opposing the policy was that government shouldn't be telling us what to value. The government can govern actions but not inner beliefs.

Here the word "promote" is used to describe a purposeful action done with intent—that is, that the government is advocating "valuing homosexuality." Richard, another Concerned Citizen, adds, "The advocacy of positive encouragement of lifestyle choices is not something schools should be involved in."

Concerned Citizens believe that the policies undermine their parental authority. Many of their objections to the policies are framed in what Howe (1997) would describe as rigid parental autonomy rationales. They contend that the policies and the resulting promotion and legitimation of homosexuality undermine parental authority. Concerned Citizens are trying to instill in their children their belief that homosexuality is wrong. They feel the schools are sending the conflicting message to their children that "it's okay to be gay." Thus, these parents are put in a position of having to explain and justify their beliefs to their children, who are hearing contrary beliefs in school. An opponent explains, "You want my three-year-old to value particular behaviors, which I don't want him to engage in. I think parents' rights supersede states' rights."

The beliefs expressed by Concerned Citizens and other opponents of the policy all reflect a core theme of infringement of First Amendment rights of freedom of conscience and speech. Though advocates of the policy continually repeat the slogan of "safety" and state that "the policy is about changing behaviors, not beliefs," many morally conservative parents and district staff continue to complain that they feel like they cannot hold their own beliefs—that the school district is trying to mandate that everybody agrees that "it's okay to be gay." Nancy, a Concerned Citizen, affirms, "It's our right and privilege in this country to have those differences [and] people who have those religious beliefs have every right to have them."

Along with the sentiment that the policies force individuals to change their beliefs is the charge that it is now okay to discriminate against Christians. Frank recounts, "A speaker [for Diversity Day at my child's school] said hateful things about Christians. It seems okay to discriminate against Christians." Many morally conservative parents feel that GLBTIQ and liberal students and parents are given preferential treatment over parents and students with morally conservative beliefs. Moreover, they feel that morally conservative students and their parents are now being discriminated against and that Christians are now being left out of the definition of diversity. As a result of feeling slighted by the school district, some of these parents threaten to pull their kids out of the public schools. Parents who feel disenfranchised from the public schools give the alternatives of private schools and home schools, and one group of morally conservative parents attempted to start a charter school with a strong focus on academics. Carol contends, "I reserve the right as a parent to teach my children my values. We feel like if there ever comes a time that our efforts are being frustrated, that is where we will draw the line and say, 'You cannot have access to our children anymore because we can't trust you.'"

Concerned Citizens affirm they do not hate GLBTIQ people. Their concern is that everybody's rights are respected, including their own rights as parents to instill in their children the belief that homosexuality is wrong. Nancy's basic message is "respect for all people—we all need to be treated with respect." She contends that she and other opponents are not "homophobic." She explains, "I'm not sure that they had a fear of homosexuality as much as they had an emphatic belief that it was wrong."

Finally, Concerned Citizens' beliefs about the policies are congruent with district staff who opposed the policies. Concerned Citizens believe that all students should be safe and that antigay abuse should be stopped; however, they also believe that homosexuality is wrong on religious grounds and that the policies are wrong on libertarian grounds because they violate government nonintervention and parental autonomy. They also believe the policies undermine parental authority by making it difficult to teach their children that homosexuality is wrong. The policies also require teaching that homosexuality is acceptable, thereby sending the message "It's okay to be gay." They believe that the policies will lead to curricular inclusion of homosexuality, that the policies restrict freedom of conscience and speech for those who disagree with homosexuality, and that it now seems okay to discriminate against Christians. Finally, Concerned Citizens affirm they do not want to be seen as bigots and that they do not hate GLBTIQ people.

In conclusion, some of the slogans employed by advocates and opponents seem to agree with one another—that is, "everyone should be safe in school" and "everyone should be treated the same." Where opponents and advocates part company, however, is with the idea that while schools rightly prohibit behaviors (like bullying), they may not attempt to change students' beliefs. The next chapter is an interpretation and analysis of the deep meanings and worldviews underlying each side's slogans, and it explains what the slogans really mean.

Notes

1. Included in this section are data from teachers and school board members who opposed the policies in whole or in part. It is not fair to say, however, that all of those

I quote in this section opposed the policies entirely. Rather, some of them simply opposed the ideas they believe the policies represent while acknowledging that the policies have some practical use, such as prohibiting harassment. I also include teachers who proclaim their opposition to curricular inclusion of homosexuality except in some cases of mention in the health education curriculum. Though the policies do not say anything about curricular inclusion, these teachers, along with many opponents, fear the policies will eventually lead to curricular inclusion and class discussions on homosexuality, thereby legitimating homosexuality as normal and promoting it as being as good as heterosexuality. It is not fair to say that these teachers flatly oppose the policies; however, what they oppose, or fear, is what they believe the policies could lead to. Only two teachers whom I interviewed, both middle school teachers, could be said to flatly oppose the district's policies regarding sexual orientation. I was unable to determine if these two teachers are typical of other teachers in the district who oppose the policies. One elementary teacher and one high school teacher, while not expressing opposition to the policies themselves, expressed opposition to curricular inclusion of GLBTIQ people. All other teachers interviewed endorsed the district's policies, at least in part.

2. Included in this section are six principals, five guidance counselors, and two intervention specialists, along with the fifteen teachers who stated support for the policies.

3. In order to determine the district's conception of the policies, I relied on archival and interview data from school board members, from the superintendent, and from other high-level administrators in the district's central office.

4. The policy would need to spell out "gender identity" to extend protections to transgendered people.

5. Concerned Citizens did not use the terms "libertarian," "nonintervention," or "parental autonomy." These are terms I chose from (Howe 1997) that typify the beliefs Concerned Citizens expressed.

8

Why the Various Sides Support or Oppose the Inclusion of Sexual Orientation in the Policies

BOTH SIDES IN THIS DEBATE AGREE THAT schools can rightfully prohibit certain behaviors (like bullying) on the parts of staff and students. Still, neither advocates nor opponents claim to have clear understandings of exactly what behaviors the policies prohibit and under what circumstances. Furthermore, much of the disagreement lies within the following three issues:

1. the perceived long-term effects of including sexual orientation in school policies;
2. the schools' resultant handling of the topic of homosexuality; and
3. what impact the policies—along with the prohibition of certain behaviors, like antigay harassment—will have in changing individuals' beliefs.

Herein lies the source of contention. While the school can rightfully prohibit and work to change students' behaviors (i.e., harassing behavior), it is not as clear a matter for the school to prohibit and work to change students' beliefs. As will be explained, both sides deny they are attempting to change students' beliefs. However, both sides give many examples of beliefs and values they think schools should teach.

A question I have posed is "Do differences in understanding and competing realities (worldviews) hamper the implementation of the policies?" The answer is "Yes." The main sticking point for staff who otherwise support equity for GLBTIQ students is the concern for the rights of parents who do not want their children to hear "progay" messages and their perception that schools treat homosexuality as a socially acceptable lifestyle. That is, district staff are caught between wanting to provide a safe and supportive classroom for all of their students, including GLBTIQ students, and fearing they will violate the rights of morally conservative parents and students by treating homosexuality as heterosexuality—that is, by implying that homosexuality is equal to, or as good as, heterosexuality.

Both sides, advocates and opponents of the policies, cling to their slogans in attempting to sway the opinions of district staff and others in the community. However, neither side makes any real attempt to understand the deeper meanings of the slogans and ideas that each side professes. In other words, the two groups continue to talk past each other: Concerned Citizens claim that the effect of the policies are to change peoples' beliefs, and the HPSSC claims that the policies simply address behaviors. The sticking point is that Concerned Citizens are correct—HPSSC and others who support the policies really do want to change beliefs. But Concerned Citizens also want to change beliefs, or at least maintain the current normalizing discourse that elevates heterosexuality above all other sexual orientations. Teachers, principals, and other district staff thus find themselves embroiled in a public debate that has not yet been resolved. They are caught between the requirements that they uphold school board policy while at the same time they try to respect the beliefs of their more conservative students' families. For some school staff, the policies represent welcomed change in helping to bring about equity for GLBTIQ students. For others, the requirements of the policies and the wishes of parents are irreconcilable. For many, they simply have unanswered questions, so their modus operandi is to stick with the way things are—that is, nonenforcement of the policies.

The Power of Heteronormative Hegemony

Before I begin to interpret the worldviews of advocates and opponents of the policies, I wish to reintroduce some important concepts from the philosophical foundations I laid out in chapter 6. These concepts guide my interpretation and will aid in understanding from where the opposing sides draw their beliefs. Teachers who support the policies told me that their colleagues who are not as supportive often fail to enforce the policies. For instance, antigay name-calling and other remarks are often ignored. District staff who are unsure of what the policies entail and how to implement them fall back on old practices—that is, ignoring antigay behavior and thereby not enforcing the policies, which effectively reinforces the heterosexist status quo in the schools. This scenario illustrates the power of silence as a way to sanction heteronormative hegemony.

Using Apple's (1993) notion of official knowledge, heteronormativity becomes the official position as to what should get taught and how. It is maintained and reinforced through the heterosexist normalizing discourse of the schools. Further, the dominance, or the coercive power, of the institution of heterosexuality and heterosexual ways of being, coupled with the exclusion of other ways of being (e.g., homosexuality), are relegitimized and transmitted to successive generations of teachers and students (Berger and Luckmann 1966). This transmission of power justifies the assumed superiority of the heterosexual social order not only of schools but of society by giving it a normative dignity while simultaneously hiding the mechanisms by which it asserts itself as the natural order (Foucault 1984). The result is that teachers who do not enforce the policies—either because they are unsure how to implement them or they fear retribution from morally conservative parents—perpetuate the exclusion and abuse of GLBTIQ students as an accepted sociocultural practice by failing to make their classrooms safe and inclusive for GLBTIQ students. The same is true for teachers who are reluctant to include GLBTIQ characters or themes in their literature selection, math word problems, and other lessons. Most teachers continue to assume that all of their students are heterosexual, so they continue to present heterosexuality as the only option. Thus, the tradition of GLBTIQ exclusion from the schools is preserved by both omission and commission; thus, it remains stable, unless it is changed through persistent efforts (Fullan 1991) to institute and normalize—that is, change beliefs about—school policies and practices that challenge heterosexist norms. The HPSD's diversity policies are challenging the previous order of heterosexual hegemony, thus forcing all those involved to "[come] to grips with the *multiple* realities of people, who are the main participants in implementing change" (Fullan 1991, 95). This shifting paradigm means establishing a new order—one that is inclusive of GLBTIQ people and perspectives. The following discussion is an interpretive analysis of the slogans and worldviews of:

1. Concerned Citizens and teachers who oppose the policies,
2. the HPSSC, and
3. teachers who support the policies.

Concerned Citizens: Opposition to Legitimating GLBTIQ Identities as Normal

The inclusion of sexual orientation in the district's policies extends protections to students and staff who are heterosexual, not just those who are bisexual or homosexual. For opponents, however, merely acknowledging that people have different sexual orientations, and that all sexual orientations deserve equal protection under the law, challenges their worldview that heterosexuality is the only and, therefore correct, orientation. Thus, the inclusion of sexual orientation in any policy or law helps legitimate the fact that individuals can have different sexual orientations; thus, it helps legitimate homosexuality as normal. Opponents fear this legitimacy will lead to the promotion of homosexuality as "an alternative lifestyle" that is just as good as heterosexuality.

Carol explained, "I do not want anyone telling [my children] that this is an alternative lifestyle that is acceptable and okay and just another choice. That's completely against my religion." What "legitimation of homosexuality" means for these opponents is that homosexuality is portrayed as being an "alternative" to heterosexuality—that homosexuality is "as good as" or "equal to" heterosexuality. For opponents, then, the implicit message sent by the inclusion of sexual orientation in the district's policies is "It's okay to be gay."

This message challenges their belief that everyone should be heterosexual—as well as their conceptions of proper gender and social roles for men and women—and it signals a change in public support in favor of GLBTIQ people that threatens the natural order of their world. With increased public acceptance of homosexuality, moral conservatives who oppose homosexuality come to be seen as intolerant. In fact, several Concerned Citizens expressed to me their concern that they are now seen as a minority of "bigots." Concerned Citizens now see themselves as a minority whose morally conservative worldviews and value systems are at odds with those of the more liberal and tolerant majority. Button, Rienzo, and Wald (1997) explain that the legitimation and promotion of homosexuality, with the prospect of GLBTIQ people being granted equal marriage rights,

> threatens virtually every social value cherished by religious traditionalists—role differences between men and women, the process of procreation, the raising of children, respect for authority, the practice of self-control, and the development of civic commitment. Precisely because it targets the divinely ordained institution of the family, religious conservatives believe, the pursuit of gay rights threatens "the basic building block of a stable culture." To adopt policies of this nature is seen by religious traditionalists to undermine the essence of our cultural identity. (180)

The perception Concerned Citizens have of themselves as a threatened minority is apparent in their efforts to make themselves appear to be victims in the debate over GLBTIQ inclusion. Opponents continuously refer back to a romanticized version of the past where there was no strife and where everybody got along; however, they totally discount our nation's history of exclusion of various segments of society—non-Protestants and GLBTIQ people alike. Furthermore, opponents now claim that GLBTIQ people are getting special treatment and special rights—that is, they get more rights than they deserve and more rights than morally conservative people. This same argument and similar ones were used to deny civil rights to African Americans (Gates 1964) and women (Zinn, 1995). Apple (1992) explains this sense of loss on the part of moral conservatives. He says, "The subjects of discrimination are now no longer those groups who have been historically oppressed, but are instead the 'real Americans' who embody the idealized virtues of a romanticized past" (28). Apple's comments are congruent with many of Concerned Citizens' comments about "indoctrination" and "thought control."

In sum, morally conservative opponents fear a loss of their way of life and their traditions. Button, Rienzo, and Wald (1997) explain that for moral conservatives, "the pursuit of gay rights threatens 'the basic building block of a stable culture'"(180). The legitimation and promotion of homosexuality, through the district's policies, represent a challenge to their worldview that homosexuality is wrong and should not be taught as an acceptable way to live. For GLBTIQ students in the schools and for GLBTIQ adults in the larger society, however, the legitimation and promotion of homosexuality as normal and acceptable are needed to ensure equality of educational opportunity and equal rights under the law.

Moral conservatives, however, see the district's acknowledgement of different sexual orientations as the first step down a slippery slope to legitimating a homosexual orientation. Even though everybody has a sexual orientation, many opponents equate the inclusion of sexual orientation in the policies with the inclusion of homosexuality because recognizing sexual orientation as a protected class officially acknowledges that people have different sexual orientations, which has largely been ignored by the schools and denied by moral conservatives. An example that demonstrates this mind-set is from the 1998–1999 school board debate over whether the district should "respect" or "value" diversity, where "sexual orientation" was to be listed as a type of diversity. During the debate, opponents often used the term "sexual orientation" where they meant "homosexuality," thus conflating the two. For instance, an opposing school board member is quoted as saying, "People in the community don't value sexual orientation." This misusage demonstrates the normalizing discourse of the majority that everyone is or should be heterosexual— that heterosexuality is a given. Thus, one would not even talk about sexual orientation unless one was talking about something other than heterosexuality—that is, homosexuality.

By instituting these policies, the schools are challenging the superiority of heterosexuality by giving a normative dignity to other sexual orientations. When teachers stop antigay harassment and tell students it is not okay to harass someone simply because he or she is gay, students pick up on the implied message that a person's homosexual orientation does not warrant discrimina-tory treatment. Students will allegedly reason, then, that if GLBTIQ people should not be discriminated against, then they therefore deserve equal rights. This message helps legitimate and promote GLBTIQ identities as socially ac-ceptable and "okay" by removing the stigma and punishment attached to GLBTIQ identities. For instance, students allegedly reason:

> if it's not okay to discriminate against someone simply because he or she is
>   GLBTIQ, and
> if it's not okay to use epithets like "queer" and "fag" to hurt others, and
> if GLBTIQ students deserve the same respect accorded others, and
> if GLBTIQ people deserve equal rights, then
> it must be okay to be gay.

It is precisely this logic that moral conservatives fear most. The chance that students might get the message "It's okay to be gay" is why many morally con-servative teachers refuse to display SAFE ZONE signs that read "This space re-spects all people regardless of sexual orientation, ethnic background, age, religion, disability, and gender." They see the signs as legitimating homosexu-ality through proscribing discrimination against GLBTIQ people. A high school teacher reports:

> I put a SAFE ZONE sign on the office door of all the teachers [in our department] and a Christian teacher took it off. He wasn't comfortable with it because he thinks homosexuality is a sin and he's not comfortable with the wording on the sign. . . . The sign implied it agrees with, or approves of, homosexuality.

For some teachers, posting SAFE ZONE signs and stopping antigay abuse can be seen as acts of defending a homosexual orientation. Fullan (1991) is cor-rect, then, in stating that we must understand where the people who are af-fected by policy change are coming from, in this case, teachers. In other words, we need to see the world through their eyes to understand how the change will be both received and perceived by them. While the district may see the post-ing of SAFE ZONE signs and the curtailing of antigay harassment as positive steps toward encouraging a safe learning environment for all students, morally conservative teachers and parents see them as defending, condoning, and promoting homosexuality.

Besides believing that homosexuality is legitimated and promoted through the practice of stopping antigay peer harassment and posting SAFE ZONE signs, opponents believe that teaching about GLBTIQ people and perspectives ("teaching homosexuality") will eventually "creep into the curriculum" and become legitimated through discussions in the classroom and other school-sponsored programs. Responding to the question "Do you think including sexual orientation in the policy will lead to more discussion of homosexuality in the classroom?" Nancy responds, "Oh sure. Yeah. You open the door and it'll be part of the discussion." In sum, those opposed to the inclusion of sexual orientation in the district's policies are concerned that the ultimate result will be the legitimation of homosexuality as acceptable and the promotion of homosexuality as an alternative to heterosexuality with the message "It's okay to be gay."

The schools' handling of the topic of homosexuality may legitimate it; however, it does not promote homosexuality over other ways of being. All sexual orientations can be presented neutrally, just as different religions can be presented neutrally. For instance:

> When teachers require children to read stories describing a Catholic Indian settlement in New Mexico, the effect is not to inculcate belief in Catholicism. There is no reliable evidence that children who are required to read about different religions or different ways of life are likely to convert to those religions or choose those ways of life for themselves. The assumption that this is the effect of education ignores a simple distinction between teaching students about a religion and teaching them to believe in a religion. (Gutmann and Thompson 1996, 66)

The point is that information on different sexual orientations, like religions, can be presented to students without advocating one over the other. Concerned Citizens, however, do not want the schools to treat homosexuality neutrally, let alone positively ("progay"), as evidenced in their belief that discussions of homosexuality have no place in the schools. They want schools to remain silent on the topic of homosexuality and thus reinforce the heterosexual established order that posits all other sexual orientations as "not normal" and "deviant." Given this scenario, students would continue to be exposed to a heterosexist curriculum, which would thereby reinforce heterosexuality as the only option.

Reconciling Discordant Beliefs through the Use of Slogans

Even though the acts of stopping antigay peer harassment and posting SAFE ZONE posters are seen to endorse or defend homosexuality, all those opposed to the inclusion of sexual orientation in the district's policies agreed that no student should suffer peer harassment, and this fact constitutes opponents' greatest paradox. The dilemma for opponents is that there is no way to stop antigay abuse without sending the message, at least to some extent, that GLBTIQ people should not be discriminated against simply for being GLBTIQ, which they believe helps legitimate and promote GLBTIQ identities.

The way that Concerned Citizens and morally conservative teachers attempt to cover up this discord in beliefs—and lessen any chance of appearing to condone or defend homosexuality while stopping antigay harassment—is to focus on the three slogans that run throughout all their arguments:

1. "We should all be civil toward one another."
2. "Everybody deserves to be safe in school regardless of differences."
3. "We should treat one another as human beings."

Most important, their responses indicate a concern with minimizing differences rather than defining them. For moral conservatives, "equality" means not acknowledging differences between people and not making accommodations for those differences, even if accommodations (like equal inclusion in the curriculum) are necessary to bring underprivileged groups up to the same level as privileged groups. For moral conservatives, to make any accommodations would be to grant "special rights" and to give preferential treatment to one group over another, which contradicts their notion of equality. Moral conservatives consistently talk about "treating others as human beings," which has the effects of *(a)* minimizing differences, so they do not have to acknowledge or appear to defend a student's homosexual orientation, and *(b)* allowing moral conservatives to deny that any accommodations are needed to bring about equal inclusion for GLBTIQ students, who are currently excluded from the curriculum and practices of the school.

When asked, "What things should schools do to provide a safe classroom environment for students who are gay?" Frank, a Concerned Citizen, responded, "First of all, my approach is to state the sentence so that you're talking about safety of *all* students. We have to focus on making it safe for *all* students and not single out any one group." William, a middle school teacher replied:

> I don't like the question because it's limiting to one faction. If you take off the word "gay" then it's an excellent question. It would be for every student. Every student should feel safe, comfortable, and welcoming in the building. [The policy] shouldn't be needed if everybody treated everybody as human beings.

Nancy adds, "There shouldn't be special policies for gay students because they should be treated as everyone else is, with respect. I just think we need to be more civil and more respectful to each other." Besides attempting to minimize difference so that they do not have to acknowledge and appear to condone students' homosexual orientations, these statements are libertarian arguments for government nonintervention. Opponents contend that spelling out protected classes inevitably leads to the exclusion of some types of students. For instance, during the school board debates, opponents asked, "What about fat students or students with bad acne? Don't they deserve protection too?" The implication is that spelling out protected classes reduces safety because it will always exclude some type of student. For Concerned Citizens, it is better to say "all students," rather than list protected classes of race, ethnicity, gender, sexual orientation, and religion.

Slogans—in this case, "treat one another as human beings"—help maintain the status quo through garnering broad-based support for easily defensible ideas, around which everyone can rally. This universal claim supports the established norms and values that, in turn, guide the schooling process and other social processes so that the official knowledge of the dominant group is not called into question. The dominant group's position is that individual differences do not matter; thus, they do not need to be acknowledged because "we treat everyone the same." For this reason, Concerned Citizens frequently say they support equal treatment for all. In reality, however, they oppose equal marriage rights for same-sex partners, and they oppose any attempt to equalize the curriculum by including GLBTIQ people where heterosexuals are already included. Thus, they really only support equal rights and equal treatment for people who share their ideas. Slogans, such as "let's treat one another like human beings," are a strategic use of language that serve to subvert attention from the real issue—that is "we really don't want GLBTIQ people to be treated equally." Such slogans hide the real issue behind a simplistic message with which everyone can agree, based on its face value. Both sides, advocates and opponents, employed this tactic, and I will demonstrate advocates' use of slogans later in this chapter.

History has shown—for example, women's suffrage and the civil rights movement—that unless protected classes are spelled out in policies and laws, saying "all people" is not sufficient.[1] Furthermore, to say "let's treat one another as human beings" ignores that the majority's definition of what it means to be a "good" or "proper human being" excludes people who do not fit their definition. Opponents consistently cited behaviors exhibited by GLBTIQ people and people of color, and said they either disagree with or do not like those behaviors (such as where one teacher said his black friend stopped being "just a person" when he got around other black people). The problem is that they go beyond disagreement or dislike and try to outlaw what makes them uncomfortable. Because the heterosexual and Anglo majority, as well as the social institutions created by them, carry the social power to define and legitimate what constitutes acceptable human behavior, many of the behaviors of minority groups, whether sexual or cultural, get posited as "not normal," "subaltern," and thus "not human." The majority, then, is justified by its own system of values and social institutions in its attempts to limit or regulate those behaviors they deem to be "not human," all the while arguing that they are promoting "proper human behavior" and "civility." In this way, slogans like "let's treat one another as human beings" and "it's best to be color blind" are smoke screens for the coercive power of the majority to define who and what counts as "human" and to deny that differences, like sexual orientation and race, make a difference.

The Purposes of Schooling: "Academic Excellence" versus "Social Issues"

Besides "treating everyone as a human being," another slogan moral conservatives wielded in opposing the inclusion of sexual orientation in the policies and in attempting to prevent any mention of homosexuality in the curriculum, was to argue that schools should "teach academics only and not address social issues," like sexual orientation or religion. The implication is that addressing social issues cannot be done without imparting values—that is, "morals and ethics. Such a position also presumes that the teaching of reading, writing, and arithmetic is value-free, which it is not" (Kumashiro 2001). Opponents see homosexuality as a "moral issue," a "family issue," and also a "religious issue." Teaching values, they claim, is the sole domain of the family and perhaps the church. When asked what he would say if a student raised the issue of discrimination against gay people in a class discussion, an elementary teacher responded:

> We would say, "You know, that's not something we're going to discuss here because we don't get into values and moral issues." Even when we teach sex ed our policy is that anytime moral or value issues come up, we don't deal with them.

For this teacher, merely allowing a discussion on the topic of discrimination against GLBTIQ people risks teaching students values he believes are best left to parents to deal with. This teacher's response supports the moral conservative position that it is too risky to tell students "Discrimination based on sexual orientation is wrong," even though the district's policies demand such instruction. Other opponents responded that teachers "shouldn't influence values in one direction or the other" and that "teachers should appear neutral on topics like sexual orientation." A demonstration of moral conservatives' logic on this point is as follows:

> Addressing social issues (like homosexuality) cannot be done without imparting values.
> Schools should not teach values.
> Therefore, schools should not address social issues.
> *and*
> The teaching of reading, writing, and arithmetic are value-free.

Schools should not teach values.
Therefore, schools should focus on reading, writing, and arithmetic.

Their statements, however, are rife with contradiction and demonstrate the moral conservative dilemma of not wanting to acknowledge or appear to condone homosexuality while still upholding the nondiscrimination policy's requirement of stopping antigay abuse. Many opponents answer that schools should not teach values, but then they go on to say schools should teach "respect" and "nonharassment" and should even teach students to "value other people." Respect, nonharassment, and valuing other people are democratic values upon which all of us can and should agree. Thus, an important distinction to make here is that where moral conservatives say they think "schools should not teach values," what they really mean is that "schools should not teach values contrary to our own." A case in point is the interview below, where a morally conservative elementary teacher maintains that schools should not teach values, but then contradicts himself.

> We don't get into anything that borders on any kinds of moral or religious issues, values, family things, anything like that. . . . We can answer with any scientific facts, general kinds of knowledge, but to get into any sort of values around that, that's not something we talk about here. . . . We try to teach kids in here that everyone has value and that no one should be discriminated against for any reason, that everyone has a right to life, to live it without fear, without having to worry about somebody yelling at them or not letting them have a job for whatever reason. When we talk about the Civil War and talk about slavery issues, even then we don't say this is right or wrong, we just give them the facts. But we also show what was done to those people and that everyone needs to be treated equally and fairly.

Like many other morally conservative teachers and parents I interviewed who are uneasy with schools handling issues of sexual orientation, this teacher is attempting to explain that schools shouldn't teach values. But in the process of doing so, he gives a long list of values he thinks schools should teach, such as:

- "Everyone has value."
- "No one should be discriminated against for any reason."
- "[People shouldn't have] to worry about somebody . . . not letting them have a job for whatever reason."
- "Everyone has a right to life, to live without fear."
- "Everyone needs to be treated equally and fairly."

These are values that everyone can agree on—that is, until sexual orientation enters the equation. At this point, moral conservatives' self-contradictions become clear: it is not the teaching of values that worries moral conservatives but rather the teaching of values contrary to their own. To cover up this dissonance, they call for "treating everybody the same" and for "granting equal rights to everybody." However, they are against curricular inclusion of GLBTIQ issues in the schools, where heterosexual people and perspectives are already included; and they are against equal rights, such as same-sex marriage, for GLBTIQ people in the larger society. Thus, moral conservatives' slogan of "schools should focus on academic excellence and not address social issues" is an attempt to avoid dealing with sexual orientation differences and to avoid sending the message to students that "it's okay to be gay." However, this slogan misses the points:

1. Schools rightfully teach values (which I address in the next chapter).
2. Even the subjects of reading, writing, and arithmetic are value-laden (as Apple [1993] and Kumashiro [2001] affirm).
3. A value-free education does not exist (again, as Apple demonstrated and which I come back to in the next chapter).

Further, though the teacher in the previous interview says that he is able to answer students' inquiries with scientific facts, even science is value-laden (Kuhn 1970) and can be interpreted differently by each individual. A good example is the debate over teaching creationism versus evolution in biology.

Undermining Parents' Authority to Teach Their Children Their Beliefs

Another slogan moral conservatives frequently used was that the district's policies "violate our parental rights," on the grounds that the policies undermine their ability to teach their children that homosexuality is wrong. This is a libertarian appeal to parental autonomy—the view that "moral-political education is a private matter that should be left to parental discretion" (Howe 1997, 109–10). Concerned Citizens contend that when schools discuss differences in sexual orientation, like any "social issue," the effect is to teach certain values that are best left to parents to teach. Thus, their authority as parents to instill in their children their belief that homosexuality is wrong is being undermined by schools that send the message "It's okay to be gay." Carol contends:

> We're just simply not willing to have our efforts to teach our kids our morals undermined. . . . If [parents] feel that sending their kids to public schools is undermining their efforts they're simply going to get out.

Frank believes the policy "risks trampling on peoples' rights," and Colleen believes the topic of homosexuality "shouldn't come up. I think parent's rights supersede state's rights." Another morally conservative parent warns:

> If you continue down this road, you must provide an alternative for families of conscience to leave the schools and go somewhere else to educate our children in academics, not the current popular politically correct lifestyles. You are violating our First Amendment rights to teach our children and to raise them as moral human beings. (Audiotaped school board meeting, May 12, 1994)

Thus, a fear of Concerned Citizens is that the schools will send the message to their children that their parents are wrong for holding antigay beliefs. In response, they are opposed because they see it as a violation of the right of parents to teach their children their beliefs. When it comes to racist beliefs, however, schools are more likely to challenge them, even if it sends the message to students that their parents are wrong for holding those racist beliefs.

> TEACHER: If you start getting into values and those issues [like mentioning when a historical figure was gay] then you start getting into territory where you have people say, "You don't have a right to say that. You're telling me that I'm wrong because I've been telling my child that this is wrong and you said it's right."
> IAN: What if you have a child of Ku Klux Klan members and the child was spouting racist rhetoric in class and . . .
> TEACHER: We'd stop it. It would not be tolerated.
> IAN: What if the child got the message that her parents are racist, that her parents are wrong for having those beliefs?
> TEACHER: Those are the kinds of things that would be stopped, we wouldn't get into, and if the child persisted, the parents would be involved. The principal would be involved. We cannot tolerate that kind of rhetoric from adults or children.

For this teacher it is more important that students get the message "It is not okay to say racist things," even if it risks sending the message "Your parents are wrong for saying racist things." When it comes to disciplining students who make antigay remarks, however, morally conservative teachers do not want to appear to condone homosexuality and thus send the message "Your parents are wrong for having antigay beliefs." Thus, his argument is not so much about the schools' teaching values in general, but more about whose values get taught. The teacher in the interview, by challenging racist ideas but not heterosexist ideas, sends a clear message to students that it is not okay to discriminate on the basis of race but that it is okay to discriminate on the basis of sexual orientation.

A teacher who opposes the policy pointed out earlier that in today's "politically correct" world one can no longer express his or her racist beliefs without being labeled "a racist." Likewise, as public expressions of homophobia and heterosexism become socially unacceptable, people who express their antigay beliefs in public will probably be seen as bigots, too. Concerned Citizens told me they resent being called "bigots" and that they do not fear or hate gays; they simply want to preserve their First Amendment right to freedom of conscience, as well as their rights as parents to teach their children their antigay beliefs. Nancy mentioned that she is disheartened by accusations of homophobia leveled against people who oppose the inclusion of sexual orientation in the policies. I agree with Nancy that moral conservatives are often mislabeled as homophobes, which implies they fear and hate homosexuals. Concerned Citizens certainly did not express any outright hatred or hostility toward GLBTIQ people in my study. The moral conservative position is more appropriately labeled "heterosexist" or "heterocentrist," as it reflects the belief that everyone is, and should be, heterosexual.

Carol claims to have felt anti-Christian bigotry in response to an article in the local paper in which she was quoted as opposing the inclusion of sexual orientation in the Diversity Goal. Carol explains:

> The main feeling I've felt is a feeling of condescension that because I'm a moral person, and I'm trying to live a moral life in accordance with my conscience and the outlines that God has given in the scriptures, that I'm some kind of a narrow minded bigot. Probably the most devastating things have been those three [harassing] phone calls.

Thus, Concerned Citizens like Carol find themselves in a difficult position: they do not see themselves as mean, fearful, or hostile toward GLBTIQ people; rather, they see themselves as nice, moral, and respectful individuals. They want to instill their belief in their children that homosexuality is wrong, and they certainly have the right to do so. Also, they correctly sense that the schools, increasingly, are sending the message that "it's okay to be gay," which conflicts with their beliefs. Furthermore, the implied message to students is "Your parents are wrong for having antigay beliefs." Concerned Citizens, then, think they come off looking like bigots in the eyes of their children and in the eyes of the public, and they do not want to be seen as bigots, as Carol clearly expressed. They simply want to preserve their right to go about their lives, to teach their kids that homosexuality is wrong, and to not be undermined by the schools.

In addition to the morally conservative parents who feel as though the schools are against them, an assistant principal told me that some morally conservative students also claim they are suffering a form of "reverse discrimination" in that they are not allowed to express their religious beliefs in school, some of which are antigay. The assistant principal explains:

We've had complaints from students for several years that it's not acceptable to be openly Christian in this school. You know, Buddhist is fine, Jewish is fine, but openly Christian is not acceptable here.

Public awareness has been heightened by the effects of antigay sentiments and antigay bullying, such as the beating death of Matt Shepard and the school shootings by gunmen who were frequently the targets of antigay epithets. Teachers' awareness has been heightened as well, with their having seen the noticeable effects of antigay peer harassment of students. Given such cause for concern, the district staff now make more attempts to stop and challenge incidents of antigay peer harassment. In fact, they may even demonstrate a bit of over zealousness in how they handle alleged incidents of antigay peer harassment, which might support Christian students' contention that they are discriminated against. During my interviews, district staff were given the following scenario:

Say that in class the topic of homosexuality arises naturally out of the discussion. A Christian student raises her hand and calmly explains, "I believe that homosexuality is immoral and that gays are going to burn in hell." Do you consider that to be harassment and how would you handle that?

Some teachers and principals who were given this scenario responded that this example definitely would be harassment and would warrant punitive measures against the Christian student. An elementary teacher explained:

We would definitely take that child aside and say, "This is not the right place to talk about that. If you have those feelings we'd appreciate it if you wouldn't express them here and that you need to talk to your parents about that and if we have to we'll bring your parents in."

A principal replied, "That would not be tolerated, making that statement. And we would probably call the parents." Other teachers, however, said this example does not constitute harassment. One teacher explained that although she does not think the scenario would be harassment, she still would not tolerate that statement from a student:

TEACHER: Last year we had people from the Rape Crisis Team come and we talked about what is harassment. Under the definition we used in that I would say, "No, that wouldn't constitute harassment because it's not directed at anyone and it's not repeated." I might talk to the student after class and tell them they need to keep those thoughts to themselves and that I'm not trying to change their mind but we don't want to know about it.
IAN: If the school sponsored panels of gay people to come in and talk about what it's like to be gay and their beliefs, why would you tell a Christian student they can't talk about their beliefs?

TEACHER: I think that what we're looking for here is a policy of tolerance and acceptance and one of those examples promotes tolerance and acceptance and the other one doesn't. The people coming in and talking about what it's like to be gay don't say that they don't tolerate or accept anyone. They're just saying, "This is my experience" and sharing their experiences. On the other hand, the Christian student is being intolerant. That's what the difference is for me.

This teacher may be sending a confusing message to students, however, because her statement is somewhat self-contradictory. In prohibiting the Christian student from saying anything negative about homosexuality on the grounds that the Christian student is being intolerant, the teacher, herself, is being intolerant.

A high school math teacher, who was asked if the scenario would entail harassment, responded:

Probably not because if we're discussing it, then there is something implied there that kids should feel safe to share their beliefs. I think if I were encouraging a kid to talk about it then it seems to me you ought to be open to ideas, even ideas that you don't agree with. No, I wouldn't think of that as harassment. On the other hand, if a student in the hall were pointing and said, "You're gonna burn in hell because you're a homosexual!" that's a whole different context and I'd say that's definitely harassment.

A guidance counselor replied:

That's a tough one because someone's giving their opinion. I don't know. It's a class discussion so I don't know if I would call it harassment. Now if they kept saying it and trying to monopolize the discussion or kept bringing it up out of context, then yes, it's harassment.

Thus, district staff have differing opinions of what harassment entails and when student speech amounts to harassment or not. This lack of unity may lead to unequal enforcement from teacher to teacher and may give students the impression that certain teachers are punishing students based on the teacher's own personal biases about homosexuality or religion. Moreover, given that some teachers invite GLBTIQ speakers into their classes, it may also seem to the students and parents who oppose homosexuality that GLBTIQ people are being privileged over Christian students, whose beliefs and opinions are sometimes squelched and excluded from the discussion. Federal guidelines for talking about religion in public schools, however, make it clear that religion can be discussed in public schools, and, indeed, it often is. Religion, including Christianity, is discussed informally among students and formally in class discussions, especially in history, civics, and world religion classes.

Thus, Concerned Citizens feel they are the victims of anti-Christian big-otry. Fraser (1999) concurs this sentiment is commonly expressed by moral conservatives nationwide. He states that members of this group "tend to feel discriminated against. . . . They feel modernity is against them—in matters dealing with sex, crime, pornography, education. . . . many felt themselves to be victims of 'anti-Christian bigotry'" (186). Apple and Oliver (1996) explain that moral conservatives attribute all of the nation's problems to moral decay and that these larger concerns are linked with "what counts as 'legitimate' con-tent in schools" (424). Thus, moral conservatives see the secular public schools as "a site of immense danger" (428). Furthermore, explain Apple and Oliver, "in the minds of conservatives, raising these objections is not censor-ship; it is protecting the entire range of things that are at the center of their being" (429). Congruent with this logic, Carol explained:

> I'm a student of history and in every other society where homosexuality became normal and accepted and just another lifestyle that was one of the signs of its eventual collapse. I don't like what is happening to the family today. I live my life thinking about my grandchildren and great grandchildren and what kind of a life are they going to live? I think for the sake of holding onto the things that I hold dear, morality and a belief in God, that I simply had to speak [at the school board meeting].

Perhaps no other issue raises the concerns of morally conservative individ-uals more than does the legitimation of homosexuality and its presentation as being equal to heterosexuality or as being socially acceptable. The reason is that a heterosexual identity is tied in with many other identities at a fundamental level. To challenge moral conservatives' worldview about the superiority of het-erosexuality is to challenge their worldviews of what it means to be a man or a woman, a husband or a wife, a family, a Christian, and even a human. Thus, as-saults on the normative dignity of heterosexuality are assaults on the core be-liefs, the bottom line, of moral conservatives' identities. A relatively recent body of literature in education known as "queer theory" has taken a postmodern ap-proach in explaining the importance of identity and why the deconstruction of identity can be such a terrifying process (Pinar 1998).

Moral conservatives fear that an effect of the policies will be to give GLB-TIQ students and adults special rights while stripping the rights of moral con-servatives who hold and express beliefs that run counter to portraying GLB-TIQ lifestyles either neutrally or positively. These fears are apparent in moral conservatives' claims about the presumed existence of a national gay agenda. Though most Concerned Citizens did not reference the gay agenda in their in-terviews with me, much of what they said parallels moral conservatives' con-cerns about a "gay agenda" at the national level. In a June 1999 letter on "the gay agenda" I found on the PERSON Project website (Public Education Regarding Sexual Orientation Nationally), California state assemblyman Steve Baldwin states that "gay students are already thoroughly covered by existing law." He goes on to state that the inclusion of sexual orientation in school policies is simply a tactic to promote GLBTIQ lifestyles through hiring quotas for gay teachers and through curricular inclusion of GLBTIQ people and perspectives—all of which portray homosexuality in a positive fashion (Baldwin 2000). Moreover, claims Baldwin, the policies "will freeze all speech that is viewed as 'hostile' by the gay community." Baldwin asserts that a teacher could be fired if he or she "mentions that the Bible considers homosexuality to be sinful behavior"; in addition, a health teacher would not be able to give factual information—such as "Anal intercourse by male homosexuals leads more than any other practice of sex that we know about to the incidence of AIDS"—because it would be seen as presenting homosexuality in a negative light and as being discriminatory against gays. Neither of these claims is tenable, however, as both are examples of teachers' stating factual evidence and not examples of using personal opinion to put gays in a negative light.

Baldwin's letter also touches on themes of pedophilia, homosexuality as a behavioral choice (implying that GLBTIQ people simply need not choose to be GLBTIQ), and the assertion that the average life span of a gay male is shorter than other peoples' life spans. He then asks, "Why would any school district want to send a message to our youth that this life style is OK?" He calls on schools to "bring in counselors who specialize in counseling gay students to return to the heterosexual lifestyle." The problem with these assertions—that homosexuals are pedophiles, that sexual orientation is a personal choice, and that the average life span of a gay male is shorter than for others—is that they are based on false premises that have no scientific validity or basis in the lived experiences of GLBTIQ people.

Concerned Citizens also expressed similar stereotypes and misinformation in this case study. Carol was the most forthright in her stereotypes of GLBTIQ people. She mentioned that the author of a book she read thinks:

> The one thing that all gay and lesbian people have in common is they were molested as children and they become confused about their sexual orientation. [She goes on to explain that GLBTIQ people] suffer from this sexual addiction and it literally overtakes their life. . . . We have devalued our food. We eat white flour; we take the seeds out of our fruits and vegetables and eat all processed and chemicalized foods. [The author of a book I read] believes that this contributes to homosexuality simply because there's just not enough physical there to have a normal heterosexual life. . . . I think a whole generation or two were born in the '40s and '50s and the babies did not bond with their mothers and they were not breast fed and I think that this unnatural beginning of life kind of perpetuated

some unnatural behavior later on. . . . I think there is also some evidence that gay men have not bonded well with their fathers. . . . For the most part [gays] don't reproduce themselves, some do but most don't, and to raise their numbers there's a lot of recruitment going on. . . . [being GLBTIQ] I think leads to a lot of depression and it's just a hard life.

Carol said that for eight years she belonged to a religious right organization, bought one of its books, and received its newsletters. Much of Carol's information about GLBTIQ people came from morally conservative books and organizations. I gave Carol a related example of going to the Ku Klux Klan for information on African American people and asked her if she thought the information she received from the morally conservative organizations was perhaps biased against GLBTIQ people. She responded, "Everybody is biased. God is biased. God is prejudiced against certain lifestyles and behaviors. [These organizations and books] line up with my beliefs and practices as a Mormon." Carol went on to say, "I'm for equal rights under the Constitution, not special rights." I asked her, then, if she supported same-sex marriage, and she replied, "No, because it undermines my religion." When confronted with the prospect that her expressed belief of "equal rights" contradicted her stance on same-sex marriage, she responded:

> I can see where someone would see that as being contradictory. But to have a civilization, and for me civilization is all about children, there needs to be some standard of family life—a husband, a wife, and children. Same-sex marriage frustrates the foundation of society.

Thus, moral conservatives see society's acceptance of GLBTIQ people and GLBTIQ lifestyles as the end to their traditional religious way of life; thus, they give many reasons, most often based on misinformation and fear (Silin 1995), to try to stop GLBTIQ people from attaining equality. They believe the social acceptance of homosexuality will corrupt our society. Though moral conservatives frequently proclaim they believe in equal rights, upon further examination it is clear that they really only want rights for themselves and for those with whom they agree.

Summary of the Interpretation of Concerned Citizens' Beliefs

Since the formation of this country, and still today, Christians have been the dominant religious group, with much sociocultural and political power. On what grounds do morally conservative parents and students claim that they are being discriminated against? My research reveals that these morally conservative students and parents are reacting to a change in public opinion about the acceptability of publicly expressed views that are intolerant of homosexuality. Opponents consistently recalled the "good old days" when people could say and think what they wanted without fear of being labeled a racist or homophobe. Whereas people could publicly express their antigay beliefs without public scorn for being intolerant of differences—and still can to a large extent—it is becoming less socially acceptable to express antigay beliefs in public and in schools. As Carol explained to me, those who do so come off looking like "bigots." Thus, Concerned Citizens and others who are opposed to the inclusion of sexual orientation in the policies feel they can neither hold nor express their antigay beliefs, nor can they instill them in their children, because it is becoming less socially acceptable to hold antigay beliefs. Thus, modernity truly is against them.

Interestingly, Concerned Citizens do not acknowledge that schools currently promote heterosexuality over all other sexual orientations by including, for instance, heterosexual literature and math word problems and by excluding any mention of GLBTIQ people and perspectives from the curriculum. For them, the promotion of heterosexuality as superior seems natural, normal, and thus unquestionable. This rationale could be explained as Concerned Citizens' "reality of everyday life." That is, Concerned Citizens' intersubjective understandings of the superiority of heterosexuality seem self-evident. When called into question by the HPSSC's demanding equal recognition for GLBTIQ students, they are presented with a threat to their worldview and their privilege as heterosexuals. Thus, when GLBTIQ advocates suggest that homosexuality should also be promoted as natural and normal along with heterosexuality, it seems to Concerned Citizens that GLBTIQ advocates are asking for "special rights," when, in reality, GLBTIQ advocates are asking for equal treatment. Moreover, it seems to Concerned Citizens that they are now being discriminated against because their expressed antigay beliefs are coming under scrutiny, whereas it was previously accepted that Christian and other students and teachers could make antigay comments without fear of criticism or punishment.

In sum, an interpretation of Concerned Citizen's slogans and worldviews reveals that Concerned Citizens believe that peer harassment should be stopped but that the inclusion of sexual orientation in the district's policies has the effect of legitimating homosexuality as normal and promoting homosexuality as socially acceptable, thus sending the message to students "It's okay to be gay." They believe schools should downplay differences between people and not acknowledge GLBTIQ orientations and identities, because acknowledgment leads to legitimation. Also, acknowledging a homosexual orientation runs the risk of defending or condoning it. Another way Concerned Citizens attempt to prevent the acknowledgment of sexual orientation differences is to assert that schools should not teach social issues like sexual orientation and should instead focus on academics. Concerned Citizens resent being portrayed as bigots and homophobes in the eyes of the public and in the eyes of their children, who receive conflicting messages about homosexuality from their parents and schools. Concerned Citizens simply want to preserve their rights to hold their beliefs and instill them in their children. They believe their parental rights are being violated. They feel they are being discriminated against and that GLBTIQ people are getting special rights. They believe this discrimination and subsequent favoritism will lead to the social acceptance of homosexuality as normal and will eventually result in the downfall of society.

High Plains Safe Schools Coalition: "It's Just about Safety"

Members of the HPSSC give many reasons why the policies are needed, most often under the slogan of "safety." For instance, HPSSC's main contention is that the policies promote safety for all students and staff who might otherwise be targeted for antigay abuse. Another slogan members of HPSSC often cite is "educate, not just discipline." The HPSSC believes that if students found guilty of antigay harassment are simply disciplined, and not educated as to why antigay harassment is wrong, then the student will not understand why their harassing behavior was wrong and will consequently repeat their behavior. Charles, one of the founders of HPSSC, explains:

> The [nondiscrimination] policy won't work without the education piece. If it's strictly about enforcement issues, it won't work. What can be done at the elementary level to reduce the impact of heterosexism at the middle level? And what can be done at the middle level to reduce the impact of heterosexism at the high school level? There needs to be continuity as kids move through the system or they'll get the impression that the policy's intent is not real.

Dorothy adds:

> The only thing I would change is [to make the nondiscrimination policy] an educational process and not just a punitive process. I really think that some form of restorative justice—educating people—because what we need to do is change peoples' hearts and minds and not only their behavior. I'm really dedicated to changing attitudes. So I think that if the enforcement of the policy could include something about changing, how they might change attitudes, or at least work on changing attitudes, that would be great. [laughing] It would be very progressive!

Roger, a member of HPSSC and a retired schoolteacher who is gay, acknowledges that schools should be helping students overcome their prejudices about GLBTIQ people and homosexuality in general. In the following interview, he explains that it is the district's responsibility to help people become tolerant of gays.

> IAN: You keep bringing up acceptance and changing values. Do you think that's a big part in getting over this [nonacceptance of GLBTIQ people]?
> ROGER: I told you my story about coming out at school and one second grade student said to me, "Ooh, yuck. You're gay." And then he would sit there and every day afterwards I watched him out of the corner of my eye and he would be sitting there staring at me. And I thought, "There's some cognitive dissonance there." He knows that he likes me as a teacher and I'm a good teacher. But [he's been taught that] gay is bad. So he had to resolve in his own mind, "Is this guy good or bad? He can't be both." It was powerful. I could just see, you know, if there's anything that's attacking the homophobia in him saying, "Ooh, yuck. You're gay," it's that process that he was going through trying to reconcile good and bad in his teacher. And that's why I think there has to be role models out there. This is the crux of the matter really. This is the school district's responsibility, to try and help people become tolerant around this issue, accepting around this issue. You can enforce laws and policies, but if you don't change the heart you can still harass gays on your own time, in your own neighborhood. So what's going to be accomplished in the long run unless hearts are changed?

As much as the HPSSC talks about the need to "raise awareness" and "change hearts and minds," they continually downplay, or flatly deny, opponents' contention that the policies will ultimately lead to the legitimation and promotion of homosexuality, although some concede this point privately. Thus, the advocates' public slogan of choice is "safety" because everyone—including moral conservatives—agree that students should be safe in school. A principal who supports the HPSSC concurs, "You're always on safe ground when you're talking about respect and dignifying each human and safety. People are always ready to rally around safety." However, continually arguing for the inclusion of sexual orientation in school policy on the grounds that it will increase safety does nothing to address the concerns of moral conservatives that the policies will legitimate and promote homosexuality; that they will make them look like bigots; and that they will eventually result in the downfall of society. Thus, Concerned Citizens are left feeling that their concerns are being dismissed without being sufficiently addressed.

Members of HPSSC continue to repeat the slogan of "safety" and largely ignore opponents' charge that the policies will legitimate homosexuality. I asked a member of the HPSSC if it was a future goal of the group to try to get GLBTIQ issues included in the curriculum, which opponents claim will ultimately happen. She indicated that right now it is "too dangerous" to talk about that, but perhaps it would be a goal at some point in the future; right now, however, the group's primary goal is safety. She also mentioned that one of the other group members sometimes talks about inclusion of GLBTIQ issues in the curriculum at presentations and trainings for district staff, and she hinted that she wishes the other member would not do that—that the other member is hurting the current and primary goal of safety by bringing up curricular inclusion.

At a recent HPSSC meeting, a member of the parent–teacher organization of her children's school was inquiring how to garner support among staff and parents to incorporate information on GLBTIQ families into the elementary school's curriculum, knowing that some parents would object. A member of HPSSC responded, "Parents who resist do so because they just don't get that it's about safety." The HPSSC member's argument was premised on the idea that if one could just convince opponents that including GLBTIQ issues in the curriculum increases safety, then opponents will understand and agree to the change. For Concerned Citizens, however, "safety" is defined simply as no physical or verbal harassment, without any explanation of why antigay harassment is wrong. For the HPSSC, "safety" is more broadly interpreted to include, for instance, "emotional safety" and "developmental safety," which curricular inclusion of GLBTIQ issues would help establish. Thus, curricular inclusion of GLBTIQ people and perspectives is a part of making schools safe. Until recently, however, the HPSSC still focused on "safety" solely as a "nonharassment" issue and was reluctant to bring up curricular inclusion for fear of backlash from morally conservative parents.

Advocates largely dismiss or deny opponents' charge that the schools are legitimating a homosexual lifestyle. To do so, they feel, would undermine their ability to "get their foot in the door" using their current slogan of "safety." The HPSSC realizes that once the idea of safety (i.e., "nonharassment") for GLBTIQ students has been legitimated and normalized, then they can begin the same process with GLBTIQ curricular inclusion, which would also enhance safety. Thus, the HPSSC currently promotes implementation of the policies as simply "stopping antigay harassment." Dorothy explained this strategy as an "evolutionary process" and an understanding that "you can't do everything at once." She recounted that shortly after HPSSC had formed a relationship with several of the parents in Concerned Citizens, she showed a video to one of the morally conservative fathers—*It's Elementary: Talking about Gay Issues in Schools*, which depicts teachers discussing GLBTIQ people and perspectives with elementary students. Dorothy related that watching the video "mortified him." It was too soon to have shown the video to this parent, who only recently agreed to discussions with HPSSC. Dorothy learned that the process itself "is important" and "takes time." On using the strategy of getting one's foot in the door by focusing on safety, Dorothy reflects, "It's not like we had thought all this through and were trying to be secretive." She explains how the new frontier in HPSSC's advocating GLBTIQ student rights is working with elementary schools: "We didn't know we would do this—it just came to this through the process. There's no agenda."

For the future, the HPSSC acknowledges they would like implementation to include the eradication of antigay bias from the schools, which would entail equal inclusion in the curriculum and practices of the school. (As of January 2003, the HPSSC was completing a resource guide that included GLBTIQ-themed lesson plans for teachers at all grade levels. HPSSC is also writing professional growth workshops for administrators as well as ideas for how to respond to opposition. They intend to distribute these materials, along with GLBTIQ-related books, to each school in the district.)

Rather than paying heed to the notion that the implementation of the policies may ultimately help legitimate and promote homosexuality as normal and okay, the HPSSC consistently couches its arguments in terms of "safety," "creating understanding," and "raising awareness." As explained, however, many staff who oppose the policies feel they are being forced to condone or defend homosexuality in being required to stop antigay harassment and in attending in-services on GLBTIQ students' needs. That is, opponents feel that the policies and ensuing in-services do more than simply raise awareness and understanding—they actually force staff to agree that it is okay to be gay. District administrators and school board members acknowledged that teachers with antigay beliefs are employed in the district and that they have the right to hold those beliefs. They maintained that the purpose of the policies and the in-services on GLBTIQ issues was not to change the beliefs of teachers who may oppose homosexuality. The key point in this issue, however, is that the contest between advocates' and opponents' positions goes unaddressed. The unresolved debate is the idea that the policies merely "raise awareness and create understanding" versus the idea that the policies force "groupthink." As previously explained, the paradox for Concerned Citizens was the discord between agreeing that antigay abuse of students should be stopped while simultaneously recognizing doing so helps to legitimate and promote homosexuality. The paradox for HPSSC and teachers who support the policies is the discord between their professed beliefs that the policies help to "change hearts and minds and raise awareness" while they simultaneously deny that the policies help to legitimate and promote homosexuality as okay in the minds of students.

In sum, an interpretation of HPSSC's slogans reveals that members of HPSSC, like Concerned Citizens, believe all students should be safe in school. Unlike Concerned Citizens, however, they believe the policies are needed to help stop antigay harassment and force equality of GLBTIQ students and families. They also believe a function of the policies and of the schools should be to educate students why antigay harassment is wrong, and not just to discipline students. That is, they want to change students' hearts, minds, and attitudes. They deny that changing hearts and minds will legitimate or promote homosexuality: it simply "raises awareness." Finally, members of HPSSC do not believe they are being "secretive" or "deceptive" but are merely being strategic in pursuing equality for GLBTIQ students.

Teachers: "We Are Not Legitimating or Promoting Homosexuality"

Like the HPSSC, teachers who support the policies deny that in allowing class discussions on GLBTIQ-related topics and in stopping antigay harassment, they are sending the message "It's okay to be gay." In the following interview, a high school teacher denies she's legitimating homosexuality by stopping antigay harassment.

IAN: Do you think antigay harassment of students is a problem in the schools? Why or why not?

TEACHER: I hear remarks like "Fag!" and "That's so gay!" once or twice a week and I stop it and tell the kids to not use those words. If it happens in class sometimes I'll address the whole class about it and explain that it implies that being gay is a horrible thing and to think about how you would feel if you heard someone saying that about you. If you just say, "You need to find a new word," they don't really understand why so I explain it a little bit when I can.

IAN: When you say calling someone fag implies being gay is a horrible thing and that's why we shouldn't call people fag then aren't you, in turn, implying that it's okay to be gay? Some parents would object to that saying you're trying to change their kids' beliefs. How would you respond to that?

TEACHER: I would say I'm not trying to change anybody's mind but what offends me offends me and I get to say what's acceptable in my classroom, that's my domain. If parents or kids feel that way, to a certain extent I don't feel like I have the power to change their minds, but in my classroom they will be respectful to all people.

In another interview, a teacher talks about "raising awareness" but simultaneously denies that raising awareness may have the effect of changing students' antigay attitudes and thus lead to the legitimation of homosexuality as socially acceptable.

IAN: Do you think the policy has made the schools safer, overall, for students? If so, how?

TEACHER: Yes. Just heightened awareness. Hopefully, as these fourteen-year-olds grow into adults that will help society in general.

IAN: Do you think the policy is changing attitudes in that respect?
TEACHER: Yes. I think so.
IAN: Some people think the schools are promoting homosexuality and legitimizing a homosexual lifestyle. What do you think about those claims?
TEACHER: I've certainly heard those claims and I don't think that it is legitimizing it. I do think it is increasing awareness. I would hope that all people would be valued.

One administrator conceded that including homosexuality in the curriculum might have the effect of legitimating it as a topic worthy of discussion, but stopped short of saying homosexuality would be legitimized as socially acceptable.

IAN: If homosexuality were explicitly stated in the curriculum do you think that would help teachers feel more comfortable in weaving it in class discussions?
ADMINISTRATOR: It probably would add some legitimacy to it.

When queried as to the purposes of schooling, teachers who supported the policies agreed that it is a purpose of the school to influence students' beliefs. On this point, their views contrasted sharply from those of Concerned Citizens, who believe only families rightly influence students' beliefs. While many advocates deny that it is a goal of the policies to legitimate homosexuality as normal and promote the idea "It's okay to be gay," some openly state in private that it is, or should be, a goal. For instance, another administrator (who is lesbian) was asked, "Do you think it's a goal, stated or not, of policies like this that homosexuality will be put on an equal level with heterosexuality eventually?" She replied, "I would hope so." A guidance counselor was asked, "What would you say to those parents who claim the district is legitimating a gay lifestyle, that is, sending the message 'It's okay to be gay' by allowing class discussions on the topic?" She replied, "It is okay! I don't think that because we have it in a policy it makes it legitimate."

Though advocates rarely give public credence to opponents' concern that the policies will legitimate homosexuality, evidence suggests that they understand where the opponents are coming from.

IAN: When opponents say they don't think homosexuality should be taught in the schools, what do you think they mean by that? What are they afraid of?
ROGER, HPSSC: They're trying to protect their children from any indication, they want their church teaching to be paramount. They feel like if the schools treat [homosexuality] as though it were just a given in society, without any condemnation, that in a sense it legitimizes it. It says this is something that, because if it's mentioned objectively in the curriculum without any prohibition, they're afraid that that legitimizes it to their kids and so their kids will say, "Oh, it's okay to be

gay." And so the supposition there is that you're on shaky ground because kids can change their sexual orientation if it's legitimized to them. So if the whole thing becomes acceptable by society, parents think their kids will become susceptible to being gay. So they feel like schools teaching it legitimizes it and, therefore, it makes it enticing for their own kids.

In regards to the advocates' paradox, the question is "Why do advocates consistently talk about the need to change hearts and minds (i.e., change beliefs) while simultaneously denying that a potential effect will be to legitimate and promote homosexuality as normal and okay?" My conclusion is that it may be a matter of not wanting to give credence to the opposing side's charges, not wanting to use the language of the other side, and/or not fully understanding what it means to "legitimate and promote" homosexuality. Regarding the latter, the word "promote," especially, is somewhat loaded; for some, it implies the promotion of homosexuality "over" heterosexuality. One interviewee commented that I should use the phrase "affirm homosexuality" rather than the phrase "legitimate and promote homosexuality." For him, the word "promote" means to view homosexuality as being better than heterosexuality. Concerned Citizens, however, consistently told me they meant "promote" in the sense of "promoting homosexuality as being as good as or equal to heterosexuality," which implies that homosexuality is normal, okay, and socially acceptable. Setting aside the potential for not understanding Concerned Citizen's use of "legitimate and promote," many advocates indicated that they understood what that charge meant or they used the concept themselves in my interviews with them.

Both sides agree that the schools may rightfully prohibit certain behaviors (i.e., peer harassment for any reason). Where the heart of the disagreement lies is whether or not schools may rightfully prohibit the expression of certain beliefs; whether they may work to "change students' hearts and minds"; and whether they may teach students certain beliefs, like "GLBTIQ people deserve equal rights" or even "It's okay to be gay."

In sum, an interpretation of supportive teachers' slogans reveals that teachers who support the policies believe schools should shape students' beliefs. Most of them deny that the policies help legitimate or promote homosexuality to students; they believe they are simply raising awareness about GLBTIQ people and perspectives, and why harassment and discrimination are wrong.

Conclusion: The Dawn of a New Social Order

The end result of the contentions between advocates and opponents of the policies is that teachers are caught in the middle: on the one hand, they want to create a safe classroom for all of their students, and they certainly want to foster in their students democratic ideals regarding the proper treatment of others; on the other hand, they need to respect the rights and wishes of all students and their families who hold differing opinions about what a safe and welcoming classroom environment entails. Participants in this research disagreed about the best ways to ensure a safe and welcoming environment. Teachers and parents were asked "What is your conception of a school that is the most fair to all students, and their parents, who come from diverse backgrounds and have differing opinions?" Teachers and parents who opposed the policies typically responded that a "focus on academics allows all to reach their potential and do well later in life"; that we should "insist on civility"; that we should focus on "reading, writing, and quantitative measures of student performance. There's too much social engineering in schools, too many social issues." They also said we should "teach everybody regardless of intellect or race or religion, creed, sexual orientation, whatever [and] give them all the same opportunities"; we should "treat all students the same."

However, teachers and parents who supported the policies typically responded, "Everybody has to be celebrated. Gays need to be acknowledged and need to be a part of the party." We need to "make sure that gay and lesbian parents feel comfortable, which means put into the curriculum appropriate cases, like even in elementary school when you're dealing with families, put in something that makes the kids who have two moms or two dads feel as welcome as the kids who have the standard [heterosexual family]. It's going to have to be put in the curriculum to have an open and affirming school for all parties." Finally, we should "support and love one another, work together. No judgment. It's all about changing norms."

The recurring themes evident among opponents' beliefs are a focus on academics, treating everybody the same, and promoting civility among students. However, what opponents fail to acknowledge is that the schools currently promote heterosexuality through the curriculum and practices of the school. The exclusion of GLBTIQ people and perspectives from the curriculum is not equal treatment. It is neither neutral nor civil.

As evident in the statements of teachers who support the policies and in the private beliefs of the HPSSC, supporters recognize the need for the inclusion of GLBTIQ people and perspectives in the curriculum, and they frequently mention "changing norms" and "changing peoples' hearts and minds." As I address in the next chapter, what most concerns opponents, and perhaps rightly so, is the expressed desire of advocates to change peoples' beliefs.

It should also be pointed out that other teachers' responses fell somewhere in between the two views outlined above, with many teachers expressing pessimism about the probability of their colleagues' being able to make their classrooms safe and welcoming for GLBTIQ students. A high school teacher told me she doubts that many other teachers would be able to create a welcoming classroom environment for GLBTIQ students.

IAN: Are there some principles you think are important in making a school the most fair for all students and their families?
TEACHER: Well the school would have to be filled with people who had that as a value, appreciating those differences and working towards accepting all types of people and learning from all types of people.
IAN: Is there a way to nurture that in staff and students?
TEACHER: If you have a teacher who comes from a background of non-acceptance and rigidity, that's not going to change, especially if that teacher has been teaching fifteen or thirty years. So I'm not very optimistic. The school would have to be a grassroots kind of thing that began with the right people, the right clientele. . . . But in a school the size of [this one], where there's one hundred staff members and many of them are half time and there are six different administrators and you don't even know who some of the faculty members are and administrators have no clue what's going on in the individual classrooms, I think it's almost impossible.

Thus, we should not reduce teachers to mindless automatons who will blindly follow the policy the school board sets forth. It is necessary to understand the points of view of those affected by policy change to understand how the new policy will be understood and implemented. New policies need to be made part of the school's culture through the social interactions of students, teachers, and parents. Teachers consistently told me they wanted more opportunities to discuss with their colleagues the policies and what those policies entail. To do so requires more opportunities for professional development on the topic because those affected by the new policies will need an operational meaning of the change in policy. That is, they will require help in understanding how their personal beliefs might appear to conflict with the policy, what the policies say and require of them, and how to reconcile their beliefs with what the policy entails. On the surface, many teachers seem supportive, and they do acknowledge the need for the policies. Yet, their comments reveal a dissonance between their desire to "raise awareness" and change students' "hearts and minds" with their assertion that they are not legitimating or promoting homosexuality to students. The dilemma for teachers is that their everyday reality of heterosexist hegemony is being called into question by a new order—one that affirms the rights of GLBTIQ students—and one that is being legitimated by the inclusion of sexual orientation in the district's policies and related in-services. Teachers must therefore negotiate between their previously held beliefs and the policies that may contradict them. Fullan (1991) explains:

> Innovators need to be open to the realities of others [in this case, teachers]; sometimes because the ideas of others will lead to alterations for the better in the direction of change, and sometimes because the others' realities will expose problems of implementation that must be addressed and at the very least will indicate where one should start. (95–96)

Thus, in addressing the question "Do differences in understanding and competing realities hamper the implementation of policies?" the obvious answer is "Yes," for several reasons. First, many teachers do not understand what the policies say and require of them. Some morally conservative teachers believe the policies require that they personally agree that homosexuality is okay. Because of their own antigay beliefs, many teachers do not stop antigay abuse, and sometimes they are even the perpetrators. Other teachers do not stop antigay abuse, because they do not recognize it as such; they do not know how to address it; or they do not want to take the time to address it. Some teachers are afraid of appearing to condone homosexuality if they stop antigay abuse. Others may fear reprisal from morally conservative parents. Finally, many teachers do not understand when student speech equals harassment. They may be unfairly silencing students who express their belief that homosexuality is wrong.

All of these scenarios point to the need not only for top-down support from the school board and administration (in the form of policy and education), but also for bottom-up support from the community, as well as from the students and teachers in the schools. During the debates over the policies, school board meetings were well attended, and they allowed people on various sides of the issue to be heard and to try to sway others to their cause. The end result, at least in this case, was broader-based community support for the policies because more people in the community were aware of the policies as a result of the controversy surrounding them. Other public fora include print and television news. The debate over the policies was frequently reported in the local paper, although never made it onto the television news. The policies were also discussed informally among members of churches and various groups like PFLAG. Within the schools, teacher in-services and gay–straight alliances can be two very empowering spaces in which support for such policies can be won. Teachers need to be given the time and the opportunity to sit down and discuss these issues because they don't have the time during the regular school day. Students, especially, can be very powerful when they organize and ask for policies like these.

The need for simultaneously creating top-down and bottom-up support is a rather circular argument in that policies are needed to create these spaces and these spaces are needed to create support for the policies. One way of looking at this issue is to acknowledge the need for making small steps in the direction of making policy and creating support for it. The point is that the broad-based community support needs to be there to make sure the policy is implemented; otherwise, there's no point in having the policy in the first place. As HPSSC strategies show, there are times when it's beneficial to work behind the scenes to get something done; but then again, sometimes it's better in the long run, even if it causes the opposition to mobilize, to have these debates in the community to build the support that will carry the policy through the implementation stage.

In an August 1998 school board meeting, one of the board members pointed out a problem: Not all schools and teachers are enforcing the nondiscrimination policy and stopping antigay abuse. He asked, "Where is the problem? Is it a matter of policies? We need to find out where is the breakdown [between policy adoption and implementation]." He is correct that there is a breakdown in the process somewhere between the board's adoption of a policy, the district's implementation of it, and the staff's enforcement of it. A case in point is, again, policy JFH-R, adopted June 1992, which included sexual orientation but was subsequently forgotten. I discovered this policy toward the end of this research. When I pointed it out to members of HPSSC and the school board, they were surprised they had never heard of it. This is a good example of how policies get adopted and then are lost in history and bureaucratic maneuvering, because broad-based support for the policy was never created in the first place.

Ironically, however, the school board member who pointed out the problem of breakdown in the system goes on to state that simply creating policy is enough and that teachers, as professionals, do not require further training to be able to implement and enforce board policy. That is, teachers should be expected to carry out the wishes of the board, as set forth in policy, because it is their duty as professionals. However, there is incontrovertible evidence presented in this study and other works (Fullan 1991; Sarason 1971, 1990, 1996) that teachers and administrators understand district policies differently and that they either do not understand how to enforce them or simply do not want to. This scenario is akin to giving teachers and administrators a blueprint without any tools. Up to this point, teachers and administrators have not enforced the district's policies as much as they could have because they either disagree with them, do not know how to enforce them, are afraid to enforce them, or do not consider the policies important enough to warrant taking the time to enforce them.

Another example of the district administration's being under the control of, and not understanding the power of, heteronormative hegemony was revealed in the following comment by a high-level district administrator: "But it also takes the people who are being discriminated against to come forward and point out that something is happening and we'll take the corrective actions necessary." This administrator is asking GLBTIQ students who are discriminated against to take it upon themselves to step forward and report the abuse and, in so doing, potentially identifying themselves as being GLBTIQ with the possibility of receiving more abuse for coming out. What this administrator failed to realize is that GLBTIQ students do not feel comfortable reporting incidents of antigay abuse in the normal established channels for reporting incidents of harassment, and with good reason. According to the director of the local GLBTIQ youth support group and several teachers I interviewed, in the past when GLBTIQ students have reported to school officials that they were the victims of antigay peer abuse, they were sometimes revictimized by students, teachers, and administrators who told them it was their own fault. Thus, another protocol for reporting incidents of antigay abuse needs to be implemented. GLBTIQ students who are victims of abuse should rightly report the incident. The district, however, should make the reporting of abuse possible in a way that prevents retribution against the alleged victim.

In conclusion, Concerned Citizens attempt to prevent the legitimation of homosexuality as normal and the promotion of homosexuality as socially acceptable by asserting that their rights as parents are being violated, that schools should focus on academics and not discuss social issues, and that the policies are unnecessary and do more harm than good. The HPSSC, on the other hand, downplays Concerned Citizens' charges and thus continues to focus on the promotion of student safety through the eradication of antigay harassment. In the next chapter I provide a way of evaluating the competing claims of each side and offer a way of getting around the apparent political stalemate over the conflict of violation of rights.

Note

1. See the interview with the ACLU attorney in chapter 9 (158).

9

Conclusion: How to Evaluate the Competing Claims of Violations of Rights

I START FROM THE PREMISE THAT DEMOCRACY and social justice are worthy goals, that the schools' treatment of GLBTIQ students is unjust and inequitable, and that schools should implement nondiscrimination and curricular policies that include sexual orientation and gender identity to help bring about justice and equity for GLBTIQ students. Although Concerned Citizens agree that physical abuse and name-calling of GLBTIQ students are wrong, their main point of contention is that school policies and state or federal laws that include sexual orientation have the attributions of "approving, legitimizing, or increasing the statistical occurrence of same-sex relations" (Cicchino, Deming, and Nicholson 1991, 571) and sending the message that "the religious believer who disapproves of homosexuality is just as bigoted as a racist (whose actions are also prohibited by similar legislation)" (Hills 1997, 1588). In other words, Concerned Citizens believe that a consequence of these policies and laws will be to destigmatize GLBTIQ identity and behavior, thus sending the message to students that being GLBTIQ is as acceptable as being heterosexual. They fear this scenario because they believe it will tempt their children and others to become GLBTIQ. Further, the policies and laws will then stigmatize moral conservatives as bigots when they speak out against homosexuality.

Many school district officials and teachers understand each side's charges and feel caught in the middle. This debate need not end in political stalemate, however. My conclusion does not necessarily reconcile these opposing views, but it does provide a pathway around them by identifying a guiding principle that both sides should accept: the principle that all students have a right to participate equally in discussions of political and social relevance. The requirements of our democracy, with principles like neutrality, provide a legal and democratic framework for evaluating these competing claims between advocates and opponents, and they help give direction in what steps to take to ensure that each side's rights are protected to the greatest extent possible.

It is in the best interests of both sides in this debate (and it is implied in the U.S. Constitution) to accept that certain policies necessarily follow to secure the rights embodied in this guiding principle. First, policies are needed to protect students and staff against discrimination, which often occurs when students and staff disclose their GLBTIQ identities and speak about homosexuality. Second, curricular materials are needed to inform the discussion and help students and teachers wade through the arguments being made.

Thus far I have explained how and why various beliefs become established as social norms, and I have illustrated that advocates and opponents have competing worldviews. I have yet to evaluate the "rightness" or "wrongness" of their opinions or claims of rights' violation. This guiding framework, based on democratic principles, offers a way of evaluating both sides' arguments in an attempt to avoid philosophical and political stalemate.[1]

Hills' Institutional Theory of Antidiscrimination

Roderick M. Hills Jr. (1997), assistant professor of law, explains the government's role in antidiscrimination law that includes sexual orientation. His explanation of the government's role in implementing antidiscrimination law provides a way around the moral conservative charge that government intervention in this respect helps legitimate and promote homosexuality. Though Hills is speaking to the purpose of antidiscrimination law in regulating private enterprise, his theory is a good fit for this case. Because the public schools are government regulated and are not necessarily well suited for solving contentious public debates, such as the social acceptability of homosexuality, Hills' theory applies. Though government may rightly advocate democratic social relations and force individuals and institutions to treat GLBTIQ people fairly in the spirit of the First Amendment, government should not try to force individuals and institutions to agree that it's okay to be gay. The important distinction here is one between public constraints and private beliefs. That is, whereas government rightly constrains some actions of individuals, it is not as clear a matter for government to constrain the private beliefs of individuals. (This point is similar to the contention between Concerned Citizens and the HPSSC: whereas schools rightly prohibit some behaviors, it is not as clear a matter for schools to influence students' beliefs.) Hills—in line with other defenders of neutrality, like Rawls (1971, 1996)—suggests there is no reason to believe the state would be especially well suited to the task of social transformation for greater social equality. Hills argues that nondiscrimination laws should not attempt to force social equality "by legislative fiat," but they should continue focusing on the institutional level (1592). Hills explains the institutional theory of antidiscrimination as "[reflecting] a judgment that . . . private institutions . . . should not enforce their views on some topic by withholding common law entitlements from disfavored groups" (1619–20), such as firing an employee because the employer does not approve of their employee's lifestyle or religion. According to Hills:

> Antidiscrimination laws do not necessarily try to transform social norms; rather, such laws frequently ensure that both sides in the Culture Wars resolve their disputes in the appropriate fora with appropriate procedures while leaving the ultimate resolution of the substantive dispute to private debate. The norm underlying such laws is not advancement of social equality but rather protection of individual liberty from inappropriate use of economic power. (1592)

According to Hills, the effect of antidiscrimination law is simply to "exclude certain decisionmakers . . . [like] employers, insurers, lenders, owners of public accommodations, or lessors of real estate—from exerting an unfair or undemocratic influence over the [public] debates" (1615). That is, government may prevent businesses from discriminating against GLBTIQ people solely on the basis of their sexual orientation or gender identity, but the government in so doing is not attempting to force anyone to agree or believe that being GLBTIQ is okay.

Concerned Citizens argue, however, that they would in turn be stigmatized because of their disapproval of homosexuality. Hills asserts it is not the place of antidiscrimination law to "stigmatize the discriminatory motive as arbitrary, bigoted, or invidious" or to "resolve disputes about whether some characteristic is worthy of respect"; rather, it is merely to "bar certain suspect methods of conducting the debate [such as] discriminatory withdrawal of employment, leaseholds, access to public accommodations, etc." (1616). To demonstrate this point, Hills cites the National Labor Relations Act of 1934— the Wagner Act. Hills states that the Wagner Act:

> Prohibits employers from discriminating against workers who attempt to organize collective bargaining units at their workplace. However, nothing in the Wagner Act's text or its legislative history suggests that the statute was designed to stigmatize workers who embraced the open shop or rejected unionization of their workplace. To the contrary, Wagner vigorously maintained that the Act was intended to protect the employee's right to *reject* unionization. . . . In other words,

the social meaning of the Wagner Act was not that certain goals—opposition to unionization—were illegitimate, but rather that certain means of advancing those goals—paradigmatically, the pink slip—were illegitimate. . . . In this sense, the Wagner Act is analogous to the First Amendment. (1616–17)

That is, the effect of the Wagner Act "was not to resolve the debate about unionization for workers but rather to provide a better institutional setting in which workers could resolve it for themselves" (Hills 1997, 1620). In the case of school nondiscrimination policy, Hills might say that the purpose of including sexual orientation in nondiscrimination policies is not to resolve the debate about the social acceptability of homosexuality but rather to provide a fair and equitable school setting in which students, staff, and parents can resolve it for themselves. The distinction here is that the government, and schools, rightly advocate democratic principles of public equality and inclusion for GLBTIQ people but do not attempt to alter peoples' private beliefs about the social acceptability of homosexuality.

Concerned Citizens may, in turn, feel stigmatized because the law advocates equality for GLBTIQ people, which runs counter to their intolerant views regarding homosexuality. But their claim that they are thus being discriminated against is unfounded, especially when one considers "group disadvantage," which includes the following definitions: social marginalization, such as exclusion from participating in social activities and societal institutions (like marriage); powerlessness in economic, social, and political realms; being stereotyped yet remaining invisible at the societal and cultural levels; and suffering "random violence and harassment motivated by group hatred or fear" (Koppelman 1996, 86). Moral conservatives have no tenable claims to group disadvantage. On the other hand, GLBTIQ people as a group fit the U.S. Supreme Court's indicia of a suspect class (though the Court has yet to recognize GLBTIQ people as such) and can demonstrate a long history of discrimination (Gutierrez 1994, 207).

In sum, Hills asserts there is no good reason to believe that government officials possess the ability to "define, detect, and remedy 'arbitrary' discrimination" (1628). The purpose of antidiscrimination law is to "regulate private enterprise from exercising inappropriate influence in order to ensure that such topics receive fair and democratic consideration by institutions that are better designed to resolve such disputes" (1620), such as "corporations, partnerships, non-profit organizations, charitable trusts, unions, churches, and other nongovernmental organizations . . . in innumerable settings—union elections, sermons, movies, call-in radio shows, lunch breaks, editorial pages, stockholder meetings, law firm retreats, faculty meetings, etc." (1629).

Moral conservatives may still argue, however, that antidiscrimination law that includes sexual orientation sends an implicit message "legitimating" homosexuality as being equal to or as good as heterosexuality. While this message may be a consequence, Hills maintains it is not the purpose of such laws. With antidiscrimination laws that prohibit sexual orientation discrimination in employment, "It might simply enforce *institutional* norms about employee privacy and the proper scope of employers' economic powers," but it does not enforce private beliefs regarding the social acceptability of homosexuality (1621). Hills' rationale for prohibiting employers from firing an employee simply on the basis of being gay is that "employers [like the state] are not well suited for resolving disputes about sexual ethics" (1621). Hills concludes:

> According to this view, the implicit message sent by many antidiscrimination laws, including "gay-rights" laws, is not that certain motives [i.e., beliefs] are improper but rather that certain sanctions or procedures—for example, "termination of employment, eviction or denial of rental opportunities, denial of insurance coverage"—are not good ways to carry on a debate about divisive social questions in sensitive areas like politics, marriage, sexuality, and religion. (1627)

Thus, the intent of antidiscrimination law is neither to send an implicit message "legitimating" a characteristic it is protecting, whether religion or sexual orientation, nor to stigmatize those who hold disapproving beliefs about religion or sexual orientation; rather, the purpose is to prevent the unfair and undemocratic treatment of those who display characteristics that the majority might find objectionable. In other words, the purpose is not to send the message that being GLBTIQ is equal to, or as good as, being heterosexual. The purpose is to send the message that being GLBTIQ, in and of itself, does not warrant discriminatory treatment. Thus, Hills' institutional theory of antidiscrimination is in line with the principles of democracy—nonoppression, reciprocity, neutrality—which do not infringe on individuals' right to hold varying conceptions of the good; that is, whatever private beliefs they choose is just that, *their* choice.

Neutrality: A Guiding Framework

Government cannot favor some citizens over others with respect to access to process and institutions. The government favors equality and will enact laws to make sure that equality between citizens is realized. For instance, nondiscrimination policies and civil rights laws are means to an end to ensure equality between citizens. In this respect, neutrality does not entail "inaction." That is, the government must actively enforce democratic principles and make antidiscrimination laws—like civil rights laws—to ensure equality between citizens. The goal is to give all citizens equal voice and equal opportunities to exercise their political power in deciding for themselves conceptions of the good. The government should not decide their citizens' conceptions of the good, but they should make it so that GLBTIQ people, or any group of people, are not excluded from access to due process and society's institutions. Thus, government neutrality does not mean being silent or inactive as far as the process goes.

A student in a wheelchair requires certain accommodations to be able to use the school building to the same extent that able-bodied students are able to use the school building—a wheelchair ramp and a handicapped accessible bathroom, for instance. Likewise, certain minority groups in society require certain accommodations (or laws) to allow them access to due process and society's institutions, to which the majority already have access and which they take for granted. Granting such access does not violate neutrality; it ensures it. In other words, the government is not favoring one group over the other; they are merely raising oppressed groups to the same level as the majority group.

As far as democracy goes, the government is not really "neutral," because it is in fact advocating a particular point of view: democracy, nonoppressive relationships, and equality between citizens. The government rightly plays a role in promoting the democratic principles upon which it is based. In addition, it is resting on the very values that ensure its existence. Schools, as government institutions, rightly inculcate in students democratic beliefs, like equal rights for all. The distinction is that whereas the government should promote the belief in democratic principles like equality and nondiscrimination, it is not necessarily well suited for promoting beliefs about sexual orientation or religion; therefore, it should remain neutral on such issues.

The Institutional Theory of Antidiscrimination Law: Preserving Students' First Amendment Rights

GLBTIQ students need nondiscrimination policies that include sexual orientation and gender identity to preserve their constitutional guarantees to freedoms of conscience, expression, and association in America's schools. In many cases, GLBTIQ students are neither free to express themselves nor free to associate with other GLBTIQ students because the risk of disclosing their sexual orientation or gender identity and consequently being abused is too great. John Rawls (1996), professor of philosophy and author of several books on social justice, contends that "certain basic liberties are indispensable institutional conditions once other basic liberties are guaranteed; thus freedom of thought and freedom of association are necessary to give effect to liberty of conscience and the political liberties" (309). I extend this quote to GLBTIQ students and contend they need the protection of nondiscrimination policies to preserve their ability to openly self-identify as GLBTIQ people, to function as free and equal beings, and to organize politically. Free expression enables GLBTIQ students

> to create their own groups, communities, and cultures. Absent self-identification, gay people would never be able to meet with one another to form meaningful friendships; intimate relationships; support, lobbying, or educational groups; or, for example, legal-aid organizations. (Rubenstein 1997, 283)

Schools need to be firm in their stance that antigay harassment will not be tolerated—democracy demands nothing less. Implementing and enforcing nondiscrimination policies are the first step. Schools also need to acknowledge and be inclusive of GLBTIQ identities in every other facet of the practices of the school. Moreover, appropriate curricular materials are required to help students and teachers discuss and understand GLBTIQ and related issues (Silin 1995). Schools should not quash discussions of homosexuality in the classroom because doing so interferes with free speech and negates any affirmation of GLBTIQ students' identities. Discussing homosexuality and affirming the rights of GLBTIQ people does not violate the principles of neutrality or reciprocity; rather, it ensures them because schools currently discuss heterosexuality and affirm the rights of heterosexuals. In ensuring a politically stable society, Rawls asserts that "the most stable conception of justice is one that is clear and perspicuous to our reason, congruent with and unconditionally concerned with our good, and rooted not in abnegation but in affirmation of our person" (1996, 317). Thus, a democratic and socially just interpretation of GLBTIQ student equity in the public schools would *(a)* entail an environment free from harassment and physical abuse, and *(b)* acknowledge in the curriculum students' sexual orientations and gender identities—both of which are vital parts of "our person." When schools prohibit discussions of homosexuality or require that homosexuality be mentioned only in a negative fashion, these restrictions would seem to violate students' First Amendment rights to receive truthful information (Tenney 1997). Moreover:

> By including a full range of perspectives about homosexuality where the topic arises in the curriculum, schools would encourage students to develop their own views and opinions. In addition, providing accurate information helps students to understand and respect people who may seem "different," an essential lesson for ensuring stability in our diverse society. (Tenney 1997, 303)

Finally, the point of including sexual orientation in school nondiscrimination policies is to prevent the schools from unfairly discriminating against unfavored groups, like GLBTIQ students, at the institutional level. A goal of the policies is not to force anyone to agree that being GLBTIQ is okay. Again, the distinction is that government and schools may rightly prohibit certain behaviors (i.e., discrimination on the basis of sexual orientation) but should not necessarily attempt to transform individuals' private beliefs about the rightness or wrongness of any sexual orientation or religion. However, schools rightly instill in students the democratic belief that all people deserve equal rights, regardless of sexual orientation or religion.

The Legitimation and Promotion of Homosexuality

Before I apply my guiding framework and discuss the conclusions of this research, one question remains that first needs to be addressed: Will the inclusion of sexual orientation in the district's policies, in effect, ultimately help to legitimate and promote homosexuality as opponents claim? I believe the answer is a strong "probably." History has shown, as desegregation exemplifies, that laws and policies that prohibit discriminatory behavior probably play a hand in transforming social norms and attitudes. Long ago, during the congressional debates on slavery, legislators realized that if they conceded that slavery was a legitimate topic to debate, it would be the first step down a slippery slope that would end the institution of slavery and change society. In their minds, to simply talk about slavery was just too dangerous (Calhoun 1994).

Essentially, this very point is the crux of the matter for this case study. Opponents attribute society's problems to moral decay and lament a romanticized conception of the past where good "old-fashioned values" guided peoples' actions, rather than current "politically correct" dictates. Although it was considered merely impolite to bring up such topics as racism and sexism, homosexuality was completely taboo. Moral conservatives long for the "civil society" of days gone by, but they fail to recognize that what was passing for civility was actually a complex set of power relations that privileged heterosexuals, Protestants, whites, men, and the wealthy, while silencing and disempowering GLBTIQ people, people of color, non-Protestants, women, the poor, and the disabled. What they mistook for "civility" was actually an imposed silence on anyone who would dare speak up and challenge the status quo. Those who did question systems of privilege and oppression were branded "uncivil" and thus dismissed. Opponents of equality for GLBTIQ people often frame advocates of equality for GLBTIQ people as "radicals," thereby giving the dominant heterosexual majority a reason to dismiss and ignore GLBTIQ peoples' claims of unequal treatment. Apple (1992) explains how this process works to "disenfranchise" GLBTIQ peoples' cultural capital while "enfranchising" moral conservatives' cultural capital (26).

Modernity is against moral conservatives, and homosexuality is no longer the taboo subject it once was. GLBTIQ identities are increasingly becoming normalized and celebrated in popular culture, with television shows like *Will and Grace*; in institutions of education, with bachelor's degrees in gay and lesbian studies; and even in some religious faiths that openly welcome GLBTIQ worshippers. We have progressed as a society. Our civility is now being measured in how we recognize systems of power and oppression that silenced people in the past, and in how we work to change established norms so that no one is disenfranchised from society. Those who oppose homosexuality on religious grounds fear this change in public and political opinion that homosexuality is becoming socially acceptable. Opponents fear they are now the ones who will be stigmatized for having intolerant beliefs about GLBTIQ people. On the other side, advocates believe we have not come far enough and that it is still too dangerous to acknowledge that the legitimation and promotion of homosexuality—as being equal to heterosexuality, with equal rights under the law—are the ultimate goals of the GLBTIQ rights movement (i.e., the "gay agenda"). Antidiscrimination legislation and school nondiscrimination policies help ensure neutrality by putting all people on an equal playing field so that no one is disenfranchised from the social, political, and economic processes that affect their lives and their ability to choose for themselves conceptions of the good. In the following section, I have summarized the implications, interpretations, and conclusions of this study. Discussion follows.

1. One way of ensuring educational equity for GLBTIQ students is through nondiscrimination policies that prohibit discrimination based on sexual orientation and gender identity, along with sufficient training and curricular materials for district staff to be able to implement and enforce the policy.
2. The government, including schools, rightly advocate democracy and the equal treatment of GLBTIQ people. In keeping with the spirit of neutrality, the legitimation and promotion of homosexuality as a socially acceptable lifestyle are not goals of governmental antidiscrimination legislation or school nondiscrimination policy. Rather, the goal of such laws is to ensure neutrality by keeping discussions as to the social acceptability of homosexuality out of the hands of government officials and in the hands of the people to decide for themselves.
3. As a secondary consequence, however, the inclusion of sexual orientation in school policies probably helps legitimate and promote homosexuality as being as good as, and/or equal to, heterosexuality, in the mind of the public. It does not promote one over the other; rather, it puts them on equal ground. Even so, raising homosexuality to the same level

of social acceptance as heterosexuality does not violate the principle of neutrality; it ensures it.

4. The legitimation and promotion of homosexuality as being equal to, and/or as good as, heterosexuality probably makes it more difficult for morally conservative parents to teach their children that homosexuality is wrong, thereby undermining their authority. It may even make morally conservative parents look like bigots in the eyes of their children and the more tolerant public. However, the right of morally conservative parents not to look like bigots does not supersede the right of GLBTIQ students to educational equity.

5. Simply including sexual orientation in district policies and talking about homosexuality in class does not force anyone to "value homosexuality." People are free to hold whatever beliefs they want about homosexuality. People may not, however, silence those with whom they disagree. All students have First Amendment rights to freedoms of conscience and expression, and the district's policies do not limit those rights but ensure them.

6. Teachers, likewise, are free to hold antigay beliefs. Teachers may not, however, express their antigay, anti-Christian, racist, or sexist beliefs in the classroom, because of the special relationship between teacher and student. Teachers, as officials of the school, must remain neutral on such issues. In this respect, teachers' First Amendment rights are somewhat limited in the classroom, and rightfully so.

7. Schools should remain neutral on issues of religion and sexual orientation. This neutrality does not mean that schools should exclude these issues but that schools should include multiple views and allow students to express their own opinions on these issues. Schools should not remain neutral, however, on the issue of extending equal rights to all people regardless of their religion or sexual orientation.

8. The policies prohibit certain behaviors and leave beliefs up to the individual to choose. Every person will continue to live his or her life the way he or she wants, to the extent that is possible without violating the rights of others.

How the Institutional Theory of Antidiscrimination and the Principle of Neutrality Apply to Schools

As previously stated, Hills' explanation of the government's role (in this case, the school's role) in prohibiting discrimination based on sexual orientation provides a way around the moral conservative charge that government intervention in this respect helps legitimate and promote homosexuality. Ever since GLBTIQ rights activists organized politically and demanded inclusion of sexual orientation in antidiscrimination legislation, opponents have charged that the result would be the government's endorsement of homosexuality and the legitimation of homosexuality as an acceptable lifestyle (Cicchino, Deming, and Nicholson 1991). Moreover, charge opponents, the message such laws would send—"It's okay to be gay"—would stigmatize those who disapprove of homosexuality as bigots, just as civil rights laws have had the effect of stigmatizing those who openly profess racist beliefs (Hills 1997). One way this debate plays out, then, is a contest between whose beliefs will be most powerful (Foucault 1984) and whose participants will be most stigmatized (Goffman 1959, 1963)—GLBTIQ people, or moral conservatives who publicly disapprove of homosexuality. As my research reveals, the case of High Plains is no different in that the HPSSC wants to eradicate the stigma attached to GLBTIQ identities, and Concerned Citizens do not want to be stigmatized as bigots for teaching their children that homosexuality is wrong. Essentially, moral conservatives see their power slipping away and fear a loss of their way of life. Moral conservatives perceive this shift in power as society's hostility toward their religious expression (Fraser 1999). As evident in the statements of Concerned Citizens in this case study, opponents feel that their religious expression is being stifled and that they are being forced to accept values with which they disagree. Apple (1992) explains:

> Behind the conservative restoration is a clear sense of loss: of control, of economic and personal security, of the knowledge and values that should be passed on to children, of visions of what counts as sacred texts and authority. The binary opposition of we/they becomes very important here. "We" are law abiding, "hard working, decent, virtuous, and homogeneous." The "theys" are very different. They are "lazy, immoral, permissive, heterogeneous." These binary oppositions distance most people of color, women, gays, lesbians, and others from the community of worthy individuals. The subjects of discrimination are now no longer those groups who have been historically oppressed, but are instead the "real Americans" who embody the idealized virtues of a romanticized past. The "theys" are undeserving. They are getting something for nothing. Policies supporting them are "sapping our way of life," most of our economic resources, and creating government control of our lives. (28)

The charges of Concerned Citizens—that the government is "endorsing" or "advocating" a homosexual lifestyle, or that the school district is attempting to "indoctrinate" students with pro-gay beliefs—prove invalid when examined in terms of Hills' (1997) explanation of the institutional theory of antidiscrimination and the principle of neutrality (Rawls 1971, 1996). Hills suggests that the focus of antidiscrimination laws and policies is to ensure neutrality and keep discussions as to the social acceptability of homosexuality out of the hands of the government and in the space of public fora, families, churches, and other nongovernmental organizations. Because of a history of discrimination—social, political, and economic exclusion—the inclusion of sexual orientation and gender identity in antidiscrimination laws is required to ensure a "seat at the table" (Lester 1994) for GLBTIQ people so that all people can resolve for themselves the issue of the social acceptability of homosexuality. To exclude GLBTIQ people from the conversation where their own fate is being decided would not be fair, democratic, or neutral.

At the school level, the inclusion of sexual orientation in the district's policies ensures an equal voice for GLBTIQ students; thus, it provides a fairer institutional setting, where all students can resolve, for themselves, the issue of the social acceptability of homosexuality. Concerned Citizens do not want this possibility for their children, however, because they fear their children might decide that it is okay to be gay. The goal of such policies is to ensure equality of opportunity for all students to take part in the conversations and decisions that affect their lives. Without the backing of the law, school administrators and teachers would not be able to provide a safe classroom environment and would not be able to ensure equal voice to GLBTIQ students, who would otherwise fear the antigay abuse that would follow speaking out in class. Moreover, without the appropriate training and curricular materials, teachers would not be as well prepared to guide such discussions. Spaces for free and open discussion must be opened up within the schools, where students and teachers are empowered to discuss issues that affect their lives.

The goal of such policies is not to send the message "It's okay to be gay." In all fairness to opponents, however, I acknowledge that this might be a secondary consequence—that is, given the chance to engage in dialogue with others about GLBTIQ issues, their children may conclude that it is, in fact, okay to be gay. I further acknowledge that an effect might be that opponents are then seen as bigots. However, in keeping with the spirit of neutrality, the law cannot, and should not, side with opponents simply to prevent them from being seen as bigots. That is, Concerned Citizens have no right not to look like bigots. GLBTIQ students, on the other hand, have the right to equality of educational opportunity. The fact that opponents might appear to be bigots, or that it might be more difficult for them to instill in their children their antigay beliefs, does not override the rights of GLBTIQ students to a seat at the table with an equal voice in this public debate. As stated, the right of a parent not to look like a bigot does not supersede the right of GLBTIQ students to be safe in school. A logical and proper solution to moral conservatives' dissatisfaction with the public schools is to take their children out of public schools and either homeschool them or enroll them in private schools that teach the values they embrace. The public schools must serve everyone, including GLB-TIQ students and students from GLBTIQ families. Moral conservatives have no right to expect that public schools teach their values to the exclusion of others. When it comes to public education, the rights of moral conservatives as well as GLBTIQ students and families must be weighed and balanced against each other in a democratic, fair, and socially just manner.

I would also like to point out, in light of charges of "reverse discrimination" on the part of morally conservative students, that morally conservative students likewise deserve a seat at the table and an equal voice in this debate. If, indeed, morally conservative students are being silenced by an overzealous application of the district's policies, when they are merely attempting to express their beliefs in a way that does not disrupt or create a hostile classroom environment, then this matter deserves serious attention. The fact that district staff had very different understandings of the kinds of speech that constituted harassment indicates that staff need more training and curricular materials on facilitating controversial class discussions and on understanding the rights of students to exercise their First Amendment guarantees to freedom of conscience and expression.

As I described in the previous chapter, I gave staff the scenario of a class discussion where a Christian student gives her opinion that homosexuality is immoral and her belief that gays will burn in hell. Teachers' and administrators' responses ranged from, "This is harassment, and we would call the parents" to "This is not harassment; it's just her opinion." Though schools can rightfully prohibit speech that "creates an intimidating, threatening or abusive educational environment" (U.S. Department of Education 2000a), calling a student's parents in this case would be extreme. One way of establishing speech or behavior as harassment is to prove a pattern and history of abuse with the intent to repeatedly intimidate a single student or group of students. It is also understandable that a teacher's reaction to a student who says something like this in class may also be severe but not necessarily appropriate, especially since the teacher is responsible for maintaining a safe classroom environment for all.

I take a broad interpretation of the First Amendment, and I do not consider this scenario to be an example of harassment. The student is simply stating her religious belief. A statement like "I believe gays will burn in hell" may be offensive to some and may make GLBTIQ students uncomfortable, but the context in which it is said does not fit the U.S. Department of Education's (2000b) description of harassment; that is, there is no context establishing a pattern or history of abuse, and the comment is not directed at any one student. Rather, it is a single incident of a student's expressing her personal opinion to her classmates as part of a class discussion. There is no law against speech simply because someone might find it offensive.

The question that must be addressed, then, is "Where do we draw the line if we limit speech?" Because schooling is compulsory and because public school students are not adults, schools are therefore granted some right in limiting speech (Imber and van Geel 2001). Advocates of greater limits on student speech need to explain why they should make a distinction between public school students and adults, and none of their arguments convince me we need greater restrictions for students. I prefer fewer limitations on student speech so that schools remain a marketplace of ideas; students can then learn how to negotiate competing ideological beliefs, engage in critical thinking, and learn the skills that will be required of them in exercising their rights as adult, voting citizens. More free speech in public schools, not less, is what stimulates freethinking and, thus, free citizens.

So, I opt for a broad interpretation of the First Amendment because I believe it helps foster "democratic identities" amongst students, which is also one of the goals of the institutional theory of antidiscrimination and the principle of neutrality. In taking this broad interpretation, however, schools must set up other protections for students who could potentially be harmed by allowing greater exercise of free speech. To do so demands more professional development for teachers on the topics of learning how to handle students' free speech issues when they come up and helping teachers treat all occurrences of student speech as a "teachable moment." Opening up these sorts of spaces where students and teachers can hold free and open discussions, about the policies, for instance, helps build broad-based support for more effective implementation. If the teachers have established a classroom atmosphere where all of their students understand that no student will be ganged up on, that no student will be discriminated against by the teacher for their religion or sexual orientation, and that all students will have a chance to express their opinions in a respectful manner, then a single scenario such as the one I gave above is not likely to create an intimidating or threatening environment for GLBTIQ students in the class. This is not to say, however, that some GLBTIQ, and other, students might not be made uncomfortable. The U.S. Constitution makes no guarantees about not being made uncomfortable. That is the nature of living under the First Amendment. I believe a broad interpretation of the First Amendment in relation to student free speech is worth it to teach students how to handle situations where opposing sides are sharing their viewpoints, as long as these other protections are guaranteed—for instance, establishing a school culture of safety and respect. An important distinction here is that respecting others' rights does not entail respecting others' opinions. While we should respect the right of others to hold their own opinions, it is not necessary for us to respect their opinions—that is, to agree with them, for we all are entitled to our own opinions.

If, however, the charges of "reverse discrimination" on the part of morally conservative students are simply a matter of their feeling that the district is legitimating homosexuality, then the same response given to Concerned Citizens applies. Morally conservative students have no greater right to have their beliefs and values affirmed by the district than does any other group. Moral conservatives have demonstrated, however, that "they want 'their place at the table' and they want everyone to agree with them. They want a Christian nation and religious freedom. As contradictory as it may seem, they want to have their cake *and* to eat it too" (Watson, as quoted in Fraser 1999, 189). In a democratic government such as ours, however, moral conservatives cannot have their cake and eat it, too. Howe (1997) explains that

> non-oppression is rooted in the requirements of democracy. It must be both applied to and observed by all who make up a political community, which is to say it must be reciprocal. The problem with . . . Christian fundamentalist reformers is that they refuse to embrace reciprocity. They are cultural imperialists who want recognition only for themselves. (71–72)

Thus, moral conservatives rely on a strategic use of language, reflecting popular beliefs about individual rights and liberties, in an attempt to garner support for their cause. They want a Christian education for all of America's students, but they realize that is not possible and that they would be seen as too radical if they asked for it. They intentionally employ the slogans described in the previous chapters to get something more likely—a Christian education for their own children—or at least an education that does not conflict with, or challenge, their morally conservative beliefs.

Why It Is Necessary to List Protected Classes in the Policies

Opponents frequently charge that the law already guarantees equality to all people and that it is bad policy to spell out protected classes in laws and policies. I concede that the spelling out of protected classes in laws and policies—and similarly, in affirmative action laws—may cause resentment on the part of the dominant class, who may see it as special treatment. However, the charge of opponents that the law already applies equally to all people is historically unfounded and is simply a tactic to divert attention from the fact that certain classes of oppressed people have always relied on government intervention to ensure equal application of the law. Cases in point include women's suffrage and civil rights laws. While statements in our Declaration of Independence and Bill of Rights seem to guarantee equal rights for all, this objective is something our country has yet to achieve. Moreover, government intervention in these matters did not violate the principle of neutrality. By ending segregation and by giving women the right to vote, the government was not favoring people of color over whites, or women over men. Rather, the government was attempting to bring people of color up to the same level as whites, and women up to the same level as men, thus ensuring neutrality through equality of opportunity for all people. Ignoring that whites were privileged over people of color, or that men were privileged over women, would not have been a neutral stance to take. In the following interview, a civil rights attorney explains the necessity of spelling out protected classes.

IAN: A lot of people have said to me that we shouldn't be spelling out race, ethnicity, sexual orientation, gender, age, even religion, in these nondiscrimination policies or civil rights laws. We should just say "All people" or "humans." What do you think about that?

ATTORNEY: That is a worthy goal. If that was the way that it had worked out in our human experience, that's great. The fact is that specific categories from civil rights laws otherwise have been passed because of patterns and practices of discrimination that have failed to respect the clear language of the Fifth Amendment and the Fourteenth Amendment. We needed the civil rights act to make sure that the Fourteenth Amendment applied to the states.

IAN: So do you think it's important to spell out those specific classes?

ATTORNEY: I think it's unfortunate that we've had to go to that length. I don't think anyone thinks it's a great idea that you have to be so specific. But you don't get the government to enforce rights, we've found, unless you're more specific. I mean, we had equal rights for a long time but I'm old enough to remember when I was a little kid traveling in the south and there were black and white drinking fountains. What's that about? They had the same constitution we did. We needed a civil rights act to be passed that you need to extend those equal rights specifically to certain categories and we now know that you can't just say that and have gay, lesbian and transgendered people be respected because it just hasn't worked.

Civil Society

Opponents claim that if we could just treat one another in a "civil" manner, then we would not need more laws. Their conceptions of "civility" and "treating everyone the same," however, do not extend to stigmatized groups when such groups ask for parity with the nonstigmatized, such as GLBTIQ couples' asking for the right to legal marriage. But what does it mean to be civil toward other people? Opponents equate civility to "treating one another as human beings," which entails being silent about differences, or being "color blind." Furthermore, members of Concerned Citizens expressed the need to remain "civil" in public debates, implying that "civil" meant "calm, rational, and composed."

However, I would like to offer a different spin on what it means to be civil. If a legislator sits calmly and quietly in her chair as she casts her vote on a piece of legislation that would deny equal rights to a certain class of people, is that being civil? Is the civility of her action defined by *how* she casts her vote or *for what* she casts her vote? I contend that denying a class of people equal rights is not civil, no matter how it is accomplished. Opponents and other politically conservative individuals, however, would have us believe that civility is defined by the act, not the outcome. That is, Concerned Citizens want to impose their own brand of civility with the message "Let's all be nice to one another and not question the status quo."

Thus, charges of incivility are often leveled against advocates for GLBTIQ equality in an attempt to deflect attention from systems of oppression that confer rights on the dominant class while rationalizing the denial of the same rights to the minority. Similarly, charges that "special rights" are being given to oppressed minorities obfuscates the fact that it is the dominant class that has "special rights." For instance, heterosexuals have the "special right" to legal marriage, whereas homosexuals do not. Colorado's Amendment 2, adopted in 1992, is a good example of legislation passed "civilly" through a statewide general election that sought to deny gay, lesbian, and bisexual people due process under the law. Supporters of Amendment 2 "argued that a statewide ban on nondiscrimination policies [was] a necessary barrier to an extreme homosexual agenda" (Calhoun 1994, 453) and claimed the law was needed to prevent gays, lesbians, and bisexuals from obtaining "special rights." The U.S. Supreme Court found Amendment 2 to be unconstitutional. Writing the majority opinion, U.S. Supreme Court Justice Kennedy stated:

> We find nothing special in the protections Amendment 2 withholds. These are protections taken for granted by most people either because they already have them or do not need them; these are protections against exclusion from an almost limitless number of transactions and endeavors that constitute ordinary civic life in a free society. (*Romer v. Evans* 1996)

In this case, the U.S. Supreme Court recognized that the charge of "special rights" was untenable and that Amendment 2 was simply an attempt by moral conservatives, playing on the fears of the heterosexual majority, to prevent GLBTIQ people from challenging the status quo through due process of the law.

Schools Rightfully Teach Values

Concerned Citizens rightfully contend that students should not be harassed for any reason, including their real or perceived sexual orientation. However, they are caught between two sets of conflicting beliefs: one, the publicly expressed belief that students should not be harassed because of their perceived sexual orientation; and, two, their private beliefs that homosexuality is wrong and that homosexuals should not be granted equal rights under the law. Their language and arguments reveal a dissonance between their publicly expressed belief that students should not be discriminated against because of their sexual orientation versus their private belief that stopping harassment based on sexual orientation in effect defends GLBTIQ identities and implies that GLBTIQ people deserve equality. The way Concerned Citizens try to reconcile this contradiction is to argue that schools should not teach any values and should instead focus solely on academics. They label anything they do not want to talk about as a "social issue."

Even here, though, Concerned Citizens contradict themselves by giving long lists of values they think the schools should teach, such as "schools should focus on academics" and "it is the place of the family to teach social issues." However, this position ignores the fact that public education is not, and never has been, value-free, from its earliest inception as an extension of the church (Kaestle 1983). It is more practical and realistic to accept that the process of schooling will ultimately instill in students some values that should be made an explicit part of the curriculum (Kumashiro 2001). Surely, many educators will protest that they have no right to "impose their values on students," but as Noddings (1992) points out, "these same teachers enforce all sorts of rules—sensible and mindless equally—without questioning the values thus imposed" (39). I agree with Noddings that "intelligent adults [like teachers] can and should talk to the children in their care about honesty, compassion, open-mindedness, nonviolence, consideration, moderation" and many other qualities that promote nonoppressive and democratic social relations (39).

When it comes to teaching values, the schools should teach those values that foster democratic social relations—values that are inherent in the district's nondiscrimination policy—such as equality of opportunity to participate in class discussions and to express one's beliefs about sexual orientation; the freedom of association to join a student gay–straight alliance club; and the right to participate equally in other school practices. In the case of GLBTIQ students, to do so would first require stopping antigay harassment and other forms of abuse directed at students because of their real or perceived sexual orientation and gender identity; second, it would necessitate the inclusion of GLBTIQ people and perspectives in the curriculum to the extent that heterosexual people and perspectives are already included. Concerned Citizens object to the inclusion of GLBTIQ people and perspectives in the curriculum, arguing that doing so will further legitimize and promote homosexuality as acceptable. Again, the same counterargument applies. School officials and teachers can, and should, remain neutral on the issue of the social acceptability of homosexuality. Simply talking about homosexuality does not promote it over heterosexuality, which itself is also talked about in schools. Similarly, while teachers can teach *about* religion, they should remain neutral and not endorse one religion over another.

Schools should not remain neutral, however, on the issues of extending equal educational opportunity to GLBTIQ students, which is the aim of the district's policies, and of instilling in students the democratic principle of equal rights for all, including GLBTIQ people. While the inclusion of GLBTIQ people and perspectives in the curriculum may have the secondary effect of changing students' beliefs about GLBTIQ people, while it may make it more difficult for Concerned Citizens to teach their children that homosexuality is wrong, and while it may even make Concerned Citizens look like bigots, none of these possibilities is sufficient reason for denying equality of educational opportunity to GLBTIQ students. If a child of morally conservative parents grows up to believe that homosexuality is just as acceptable as heterosexuality, then it is the result of engaging in debate and critical thinking with his or her peers and not the result of indoctrination or thought control by the school. The possibility that their children might come to view homosexuality as being equal to heterosexuality is a possibility that Concerned Citizens want to prevent, even if it violates the rights of GLBTIQ students and families to equal representation and equal protection in the schools.

In helping school officials determine the best direction to take in preserving students' rights in this area, I offer the following from Imber and van Geel (2001, 58), who speak to the spirit of the First Amendment and other democratic ideals:

> A central educational purpose of public schools is to prepare citizens [who] can understand and exercise the right of free speech. This can best be accomplished by letting students exercise their free speech rights at school to the greatest extent consistent with the school's other educational needs.

Gathercoal (1996) adds:

> Individual expressions by students that may be annoying or just an inconvenience should be perceived as a human right. Through reasonable discussions and restraint, school personnel can model tolerance and learn to accept the fact that students will be saying and doing things they would not do themselves. Consequences should be necessary only in the case of a *serious* disruption. Student rights are properly denied when their actions infringe on the property and well-being of others. (38–39; Gathercoal's emphasis)

In sum, GLBTIQ students, like all students, have constitutional protections for their right to express their ideas and opinions on topics like sexual orientation and religion as long as such expressions do not create an intimidating or hostile learning environment. Moreover, students should have the right to associate with whomsoever they choose. For GLBTIQ students, who would otherwise choose to associate with other GLBTIQ students, freedom of association is seldom a possibility because the majority of GLBTIQ students remain closeted and fearful of disclosing their sexual orientations and gender identities.

The rights of individuals to engage in deliberation with others and come to their own conclusions are the hallmarks of a free society and extend to students in our schools (*Tinker v. Des Moines Independent School District* 1969). Morally conservative parents, however, believe in what they feel are God-given truths about homosexuality and do not want their children to come to their own conclusions on this topic. Concerned Citizens have the right to their own opinions. The beauty of the First Amendment is that we need not agree with the opinions of others—that is, we also are entitled to our own opinions. Thus, Concerned Citizens' charge that the district's policies infringe upon their First Amendment rights does not hold up. Concerned Citizens have a right to their antigay opinions. They do not have the right to force their antigay opinions on others. Concerned Citizens counter, then, that the district is forcing progay opinions on students and teachers. Again, this claim does not hold up. The inclusion of sexual orientation in the policies ensures neutrality so that all students can come to their own opinions on the topic of homosexuality. The district's policies, in including sexual orientation, rightly reflect democratic values of equal representation and equal protection. Concerned Citizens have no right for their own religious beliefs to be reflected in the district's policies to the exclusion of others' beliefs. The district's policies prohibit discrimination against any religion and any sexual orientation. An important distinction here is that merely holding antigay beliefs does not make Concerned Citizens bigots. To avoid bigotry, however, Concerned Citizens should neither expect everybody else to agree with their beliefs nor abuse their political power and voting privileges to deny equal rights to those with whom they disagree.

Furthermore, the district's policies help ensure students' and employees' First Amendment rights by giving all members of the school community equal voice without fear of retribution. Again, I must make the distinction that the goal of the district's policies is not that Concerned Citizens' kids will come to see homosexuality as equal to heterosexuality. The goal is that Concerned Citizens' kids will come to see GLBTIQ people as deserving equal rights, just as people of different religions deserve equal rights. The question about the social acceptability of homosexuality, then, is left up for the individual student to decide for herself or himself, with the guidance of his or her family and church. The question about extending equal protection under the law to certain classes of people, however, should not be left up to individuals to decide. Everybody deserves equal protection under the law. Though Concerned Citizens also express this belief, upon further questioning, it becomes apparent that they do not really mean it. They want rights only for themselves and not for those with whom they disagree. Nothing in the policies forces students or staff to agree that it is okay to be gay. Teachers and students are free to hold whatever beliefs they want, as granted in the First Amendment. The policies simply prevent teachers and students from treating GLBTIQ students unfairly and discriminatorily, based on antigay beliefs they may hold. That is, the policies prohibit certain behaviors and leave beliefs about homosexuality up to the individual to decide. The one belief that the policies rightly instill in students is that all people deserve equal rights.

I want to be very clear in that I am asking the schools to teach democratic principles like equality and reciprocity. I am not suggesting that the schools teach or require students to "value" homosexuality. Indeed, I believe the High Plains School District erred when it retained the language "value diversity" in its Diversity Goal because it borders on, and may even cross the line in, asking people to "value" differences in sexual orientation, with homosexuality being among them. I agree with Concerned Citizens that "respect diversity" would have been a better choice, but not because of some inherent semantic meaning to the word "respect." Given that Concerned Citizens are against equal rights for GLBTIQ people, they do not "respect" differences in sexual orientation. Rather, in simply conceding to Concerned Citizens and changing the Diversity Goal to "respect diversity," the district may have been able to avoid a protracted public controversy and may have prevented resentment on the side of Concerned Citizens, which only pushed them to fight back harder. The lingering resentment of that debate still spurs Concerned Citizens on to contest the district's handling of anything related to sexual orientation or gender identity.

Similar to Apple and Oliver (1996), my research reveals that the public debate that erupted over the language in the Diversity Goal may have given the more moderately positioned citizens the impression that the district was in fact trying to change peoples' beliefs about homosexuality, which pushed them in the direction of agreeing with Concerned Citizens. Had HPSSC conceded that "*respect* diversity" was sufficient (instead of pushing for the language "*value* diversity"), it may have prevented much of the resentment now being expressed about the district's handling of sexual orientation issues. I am left to wonder what inroads could have been made in garnering Concerned Citizen's support for the policy had the school board allowed them to take some ownership over the language contained therein. I believe a mistake that the High Plains Safe Schools Coalition made was to pursue this war over words and demand that the district retain the language "value diversity." And I must admit that, at the time, I supported HPSSC's position, but I have now changed my mind as a result of this investigation. There is no way to be sure, however, if and how Concerned Citizens would have backed off their opposition had the school board let them have their way.

A personal struggle for me in conducting this research (among others I describe in the epilogue) was that part of me wanted HPSSC to be honest about the possible long-term effects of including sexual orientation in school policies, rather than dismiss Concerned Citizens' charge that the legitimation and promotion of homosexuality as socially acceptable would be ultimate effects. Another part of me realizes that transformation may more easily occur when those advocating change act strategically, instead of putting everything on the table at once. The strategies employed by HPSSC pay heed to the importance of this process, as Dorothy, president of HPSSC, explained in chapter 4.

Conceding that such policy may, in effect, ultimately play a hand in the legitimation and promotion of homosexuality does not weaken the stance of advocates that such policy is needed and desirable in preserving equality of educational opportunity for GLBTIQ students. Nor would the legitimation and promotion of homosexuality require that anybody embrace and personally value homosexuality. Every person will continue to live his or her life the way he or she wants, to the extent that is possible without violating the rights of others. An impatient part of me wants HPSSC and other similar groups to move beyond the slogan of "safety" and help the public understand that what Concerned Citizens really oppose are equal rights for GLBTIQ students in social, cultural, political, and educational realms. Having completed this research, however, the more patient part of me now more fully comprehends the words of John Dewey, with which I opened part II—that changing "long-established institutions" is a slow and complicated process.

Conclusion

School nondiscrimination policies that include sexual orientation and gender identity ensure neutrality through prohibiting the exclusion of GLBTIQ students' voices. Given the current inability of GLBTIQ students to speak out because of fear of retribution, coupled with the exclusion of GLBTIQ people and perspectives from the curriculum, schools have not assumed a neutral stance. Not talking about GLBTIQ people and perspectives, when schools currently talk about heterosexual people and perspectives, does not equal neutrality—it equals exclusion. Neutrality requires that GLBTIQ students be afforded the same educational opportunities afforded heterosexual students. One way of ensuring this equality is through nondiscrimination policies that prohibit discrimination based on sexual orientation and gender identity, along with sufficient training and curricular materials for district staff to be able to implement and enforce the policy.

The inclusion of sexual orientation in the district's policies also helps bring about and ensure neutrality in the sense that it gives a legal guarantee to GLBTIQ students that they may exercise their First Amendment rights to freedom of conscience and expression. Moreover, the district's policies guarantee that *all* students have this right, including morally conservative students. All students have the right to express their opinions in school, but no student has the right for his or her expressed opinions to go unchallenged by others. Such is the nature of living under the First Amendment. In other words, morally conservative students have the right to express their antigay beliefs in school as long as they do not create a hostile or intimidating environment. Likewise, GLBTIQ students have the right to express their progay beliefs as long as they do not create a hostile or intimidating environment. Neither side, however, has the right to have their opinions go unchallenged by the other side. Reciprocity ensures neutrality. Currently, GLBTIQ students are not ensured a safe school environment, where they can express their opinions to the extent that other groups of students can.

I believe it is fair to acknowledge that such policies may, and probably will, have the effect of helping to change peoples' hearts and minds (i.e., their beliefs) about the social acceptability of homosexuality. The main point, however, is that the policies help students understand that *all* students, including GLBTIQ students, deserve equality of educational opportunity and equal rights in general. To this, Concerned Citizens cannot legitimately object, because the rights they would deny GLBTIQ people are the same rights that allow them to object in the first place. To avoid hypocrisy, Concerned Citizens need to respect the rights of GLBTIQ students and truly support equal rights for all people, even those with whom they disagree.

Concerned Citizens may rightly teach their children, within their homes and churches, that homosexuality is wrong. I concede that their ability to do so may be undermined by schools that teach students that GLBTIQ people deserve equal rights. However, claiming that the district's policies undermine their ability to teach their children their beliefs is an attempt to extend their parental authority into the classroom, and to this, they have no right. Schools also have a responsibility to GLBTIQ parents and students. If moral conservatives are dissatisfied with public education, then they have the right to homeschool their children or enroll them in private schools that teach their morally conservative values.

The district's policies do not favor one group of people over another; they simply put all individuals on equal legal footing. In this way, the district ensures neutrality and leaves it to parents on all sides of the issue to teach their

Epilogue: My Reflections on This Research

I WAS INTERESTED IN DOING THIS RESEARCH for three reasons: to share with others the lessons learned by the High Plains Safe Schools Coalition; to understand moral conservative opposition to school policies that include sexual orientation; and to cut through the emotion and rhetoric with well-reasoned and well-grounded logic. I believe I have accomplished my goals in this respect. However, something much more amazing happened as a result of this research—I was transformed in a myriad of ways.

One of the most interesting findings of this case was that religious rhetoric was less important than libertarian principles for Concerned Citizens. While their fundamental objection to homosexuality was grounded in religion, their public arguments opposing the district's policies were grounded in libertarian arguments. Such arguments had common themes, such as nonintervention on the part of schools and government, as well as parental autonomy. Is this a new tactic for Concerned Citizens to try to distance themselves from other opponents who come from a position of extreme religious intolerance and seem blatantly hateful and bigoted? It may be, which gives further credence to the opponents' fear that it is becoming less socially acceptable to express antigay sentiments. Thus, they couch their arguments in terms of "rights." This maneuver is interesting and warrants a closer look.

Apple and Oliver (1996) likewise report that in a similar contest over school curricula, conservative opponents "were quite surprised to find themselves identified as part of the Right" because they thought of themselves simply as "hardworking citizens" and "ordinary people who wanted the best for their children" (435). I asked Nancy, one of the Concerned Citizens who often gave libertarian rationales, if she thought other moral conservatives—like Carol, who gave more extreme religious views—in a way "hurt" what Concerned Citizens were able to accomplish in garnering public support for their position. Nancy answered, "Yes, I do feel that those type of radical and intolerant statements hurt the 'cause.' The name calling, the slogans and the polarization are not going to get either side of this argument anywhere" (personal communication, April 7, 2001).

Another interesting finding from this case was evidence that fundamentalist Christian students may have valid reasons for claiming they are being discriminated against. One assistant principal in the district who is openly supportive of GLBTIQ students is investigating this claim on behalf of Christian students in her school. Thus, I do not question the motives or biases on the part of the assistant principal. If it is the case that morally conservative students are being discriminated against, this scenario would make for an interesting study and would further point to the need for more training on how to identify harassment and implement the district's policies.

A third finding gives credence to Rofes' assertion that "approaches to conflict among children and youth which are predicated on actions by outside authorities or adult threats may be effective in keeping homophobic comments out of the classroom discourse, only to have them proliferate in areas outside adult policing" (2000, 57). Several teachers in this case mentioned that although they hear antigay comments from students less frequently nowadays, they believe that antigay bullying has been "pushed underground" and that students continue to hurl antigay epithets when outside the earshot of teachers. Rofes (2000) thus calls for models of antiheterosexism education that are fully peer-based and peer-initiated. He suggests that current "patronizing and infantilizing" school-based programs, which require adults to impose their authority over students, often lead to the formation of oppositional youth cultures (Davidson 1996). Other teachers in this case mentioned the apparent success of peer-based models of education, such as Restorative Justice, where committees of students act as judge and jury for their peers accused of harassment. Thus, students learn about democratic principles firsthand, and since students are accountable to other students in this instance, they do not form oppositional identities to imposed adult authority. Likewise, Berv (2002) calls for a "substantive valuing of diversity," which emphasizes interpersonal relationships and a sense of community among students.

Whether or not the district's policies truly have created a safer environment for GLBTIQ students has not yet been resolved and was not within the scope of this research to determine. Because teen sexuality, let alone sexual orientation, is such a highly contentious issue, and because it is difficult to have such research approved (Macgillivray and Kozik-Rosabal 2000), I doubt that the district would approve such a proposed study.

Finally, this research implies many directions for other researchers who want to build on this work. In my opinion, what is needed is education on human sexuality, gender identities, transgenderism, intersexuality, sexual orientation differences, and GLBTIQ people and perspectives. Teachers and other staff simply do not have the background knowledge on these topics to be able to discuss them effectively with students. While there has been a movement in recent years on the part of school counselors to learn more about these topics, relegating these issues to the domains of "mental health" or "counseling" further stigmatizes GLBTIQ identities. Schools of education must include these topics in all preservice teacher coursework in meaningful ways that break down the heteronormative discourses that maintain heterosexuality as the only option. To the extent that heterosexual people and perspectives are already included, the representation of GLBTIQ people and perspectives should be included in math word problems, literature selections, history and civics, science (Smith and Drake 2001), and other content areas. Numerous organizations and individuals can provide such resources (too numerous to list here), but I would recommend starting with the Gay, Lesbian, and Straight Education Network (GLSEN), the largest organization in the United States working to end antigay bias in schools. They can be contacted through their website at www.glsen.org.

Surprises I Encountered in Conducting This Research

When I began interviewing participants, I was surprised that they often conflated the nondiscrimination and Diversity Goal policies. I thought district staff would be more knowledgeable about district policy: they were often unaware of one or the other, or they thought they were the same policy. Another surprise was the potential for Christian students to be unfairly silenced by an overzealous application of the policies and by teachers who do not understand what types of student speech constitute harassment. I believe this issue needs to be taken very seriously. All students' voices need to be heard and their speech protected. Teacher preparation programs must do a better job of helping preservice teachers facilitate difficult class discussions and preserve all students' First Amendment rights.

I was also surprised that I got "sucked into" Concerned Citizens' illogic. After interviewing them, listening to their comments from taped school-board meetings, and writing about what they told me, I became so submerged in their reasoning that it started to make sense to me, and I was blind to some of the inconsistencies and contradictions in what they were saying. I didn't realize this until one of my academic advisors on my dissertation committee pointed out, after reading a draft of my dissertation (which became this book), where I was missing disparities between what Concerned Citizens were saying and what they were actually doing. It was then that I realized I had been accepting some of what they were saying at face value, which blinded me to their contradictions. I then had to mentally step back and look at the data anew to see what I had missed.

Similarly, I was surprised how I had bought into the rhetoric and emotions around the Diversity Goal debate on "valuing versus respecting diversity." At the time of those debates in 1998, I was a member of HPSSC, and I addressed the school board as to why they should retain the language "value diversity." I have since changed my mind and now believe that "respect diversity" would have been better, for reasons I discuss in chapter 9.

Finally, I was surprised at the feelings I developed for some of the morally conservative participants, especially Colleen and Nancy. They are very nice folks. This experience was a good reminder of how people can maintain productive relationships even though they disagree on some fundamental issues.

Conflicts I Encountered in Conducting This Research

In conducting this research, I encountered conflicts as well. I had to decide if I would "give away advocates' secret" by stating that advocates really want more than just safety—they want to change peoples' beliefs. This is a primary strategy of those working for safe schools, and I fear that moral conservatives will use this information to fan the flames of hysteria. Another conflict was a fear of pointing out that the HPSSC and other advocates do not understand the slogans and worldviews of moral conservatives. In pointing this out, I thought I risked alienating myself from the HPSSC. Now that many members of HPSSC have read earlier manuscripts of my book, however, this does not seem to be a concern for them.

I am also concerned over how my book may affect my employment, now and in the future. I am currently a K-12 teacher and will be starting a new teaching assignment in August 2003 in Mexico, a staunchly Catholic country that is behind Europe and the United States in granting rights to GLBTIQ people. During the 2002–2003 school year, however, I disclosed to all of my 7th grade students that I am gay. Most of them had already figured it out and for the others it was a "non-issue." Thus, I don't fear problems from students as much as I fear backlash from parents in the community, one of whom called my assistant principal to complain that I was discussing "gay issues" in my classroom and wanted to know if he could then bring his church group in to discuss the Christian perspective. My assistant principal handled the situation by telling the parent to take his request to the district office and that was the end of it. I don't think being "out" will be a problem if and when I pursue employment at the university level, but it still concerns me a bit.

A final conflict was whether or not to use Spanish pseudonyms for Latino participants. Many of the participants in this research are of Mexican descent. I originally wanted to use Spanish pseudonyms for Latino participants but thought that I would be making it easier to identify them. To protect Latino participants and to prevent undue attention on a Latino district employee, I thus settled on Anglo pseudonyms for all participants in a global attempt to better protect peoples' identities.

What I Have Learned From This Research That I Didn't Already Know

The first lesson I learned was how to conduct the necessary research and how to analyze data. A fear I have is that academic research like this probably does not have much potential for transforming public opinion and helping bring about equity for GLBTIQ students. Instead, prepackaged, emotive, and value-laden sound bites and slogans are probably more effective at swaying popular opinion. It is my hope, however, that this book will be used by others working in this area to help inform this public debate so that we can move beyond slogans and other rhetoric.

At first I believed that HPSSC was being just as dishonest about its agenda as were moral conservatives. I learned, however, that it wasn't as much a matter of dishonesty as it was a tactical maneuver and even just a part of the process of discovery for members of HPSSC as they became active in this debate. Dorothy, the president of the HPSSC, and I had many long and informative talks about this very issue. I learned what moral conservatives mean by "legitimate and promote homosexuality," and I came to a better understanding of moral conservatives' libertarian rationales, rather than religious reasons, for opposing equality for GLBTIQ people. I also learned a great deal about how the First Amendment can apply to schools and to the importance of democratic deliberation, and how it can affect schools and the political process in general. This last lesson is perhaps the one I hold most dear.

Participants' Critiques of My Study

In March 2001, I distributed drafts of my nearly completed research to one member of Concerned Citizens, Nancy, and to several members of HPSSC.[1] The following are their comments copied directly from their e-mails.

Where Nancy, a Concerned Citizen, Agreed with My Findings

- "I was not surprised to find that you were a gay young man. I tried very hard not to prejudge the situation, but I was pretty sure that your interest in the topic was personal. I think that you made a valiant effort to be objective, but as you said yourself your own personal experiences and your passion for the issue were obvious, but, in my opinion, did not detract from your presentation."
- "Thank you for your comments [in appendix A] describing the concerned citizens. It was well done and fair."
- "Very interesting discussion on social and educational change, I particularly like the quote from Fullan [referring to where Fullan asserts that "innovators (of policy) need to be open to the realities of others . . ."]
- [Referring to a section of a previous draft of this manuscript where I describe the significance of my research and reference the beating death of Matt Shepard.] "I found this discussion very interesting. I am not just surprised but quite shocked that anyone would think that on some level we could accept what was done to Matt Shepard. Why should we hold schools and teachers responsible? None of them should have taught these young men that violence was O.K. To me I can see no extenuating circumstances that in anyway justifies what was done to this young man."
- "We [Concerned Citizens, HPSSC, and school board] spent a lot of time arguing over the wording of a policy but did not follow through with guidelines as to how the policy was to be implemented. So we are back to where we were in the beginning, everyone with their own interpretation of how this should happen. In all fairness to all of the students in the school district, we need to outline guidelines and procedures to ensure the safety of the students." [The district recently did this. See appendix F.]

Where Nancy, a Concerned Citizen, Disagreed with My Findings

- "I am concerned when the only religious group that you mention are the Mormons. . . . it is the only Christian denomination which is named in your report and seems to set them up as targets. It is an unintended result and really doesn't add to the discussion."
- [Referring to my assertion "the right of morally conservative parents not to look like bigots does not supersede the rights of GLBTQ students to safety and inclusion in school."] "Why bigot? It is not that they are concerned about being perceived to be bigots, it is that they do not perceive themselves to be bigots, but to be people who have a different perception

of the behavior. Is it possible to allow those who have an honest disagreement with the behavior and/or principles to be accepted as well as GLBTIQ people?"

- [Referring to the section The Social Construction of Reality in chapter 6.] "Religious groups are not advocating social action, norms or justice. They feel they get their direction from God, both those that support and those that reject homosexuality. I didn't like the word 'superior' in the last paragraph and it appears to me that any norm privileges itself by virtue of majority acceptance. What level of acceptance is given to other minorities? Are we looking at acceptance or accommodation?"

Where Three Members of HPSSC Agreed with My Findings

- Marge said she had an emotional reaction to my book and that it really affected her. She said she was up all night reading it and got back to me the next day with five pages of comments and grammar corrections.
- Dorothy thought my discussion of religious expression in public schools was a helpful comparison. She also enjoyed chapter 6.
- Another member of HPSSC said, "I think you were insightful in your analysis of both sides. Neither side says exactly what they mean. I really like Hills' theory [chapter 9]. It makes a compelling argument and provides a rationale for including these issues."

Where Two Members of HPSSC Disagreed with My Findings

- Referring to chapter 3, where I describe the HPSSC's tenuous role of advocating for GLBTIQ students and families while trying to remain a "friend" of the district, Marge pointed out that I presented only one side of the story—that of Roger's. I have included Marge's story, which now balances that section.
- Dorothy offered several corrections on historical items.

Notes

1. As I discuss in appendix A, an important step critical ethnographers take is to test their analyses and interpretations by presenting them to those who were studied and asking, "Did I accurately portray you and your opinions in my work?"

Appendix A: On the Making of *Sexual Orientation and School Policy*

Doing Critical Ethnography

IN STUDYING HOW POLICY DESIGNED TO ENHANCE school safety and equity for GLBTIQ students is promoted, adopted, and resisted, my statuses as a member of the High Plains Safe Schools Coalition (HPSSC) and a substitute teacher in the High Plains School District (HPSD) greatly informed this research and facilitated my access to the various populations from which I drew interviewees. Also, because I was an openly gay high school student, I have firsthand knowledge and experience of what it is like to be a victim of antigay peer harassment and to receive little or no support from teachers or administrators. Thus, my experience as an abused gay adolescent, along with my involvement in the HPSSC and the HPSD over three years, rekindled my passion for this topic of educational equity for GLBTIQ students. For me personally, this research was an attempt to make the world a better, and more just, place to live, and seemed like a logical way to proceed in so doing.

The main thing that sets this research apart from much of the other research is that I do not pretend to be a disinterested researcher with no agenda. I drew on the "critical paradigm" (LeCompte and Schensul 1999a) to inform my role as researcher. I do not believe that researchers should refrain from influencing decisions. My agenda was to shed light on this debate, to better understand moral conservative opposition, and to make recommendations about how best the opposition can be educated or outwitted. Controlling for bias and researcher subjectivity were concerns in this study. I handled this conflict of interest by stating my biases up front (in this book, but not during interviews). While interviewing Concerned Citizens, I attempted to remain aware of my own subjectivities. I wanted to understand their points of view and rationales. This task was not difficult for me, and I allowed myself to be "steeped" in their logic to the point where it took a while for me step back from it and begin to see it objectively. This was a good learning experience and made this research stronger.

Thus, I took the position of "researcher as advocate," and doing so affected my study in two ways. One, I have strong opinions on the topic of GLBTIQ student safety and what democracy demands of schools in creating a safe learning environment for GLBTIQ students. My opinions are expressed throughout my research; I believe I have tempered them with well-reasoned arguments based on democratic principles and have grounded them in empirical data.

Second, because I am an openly gay man, a member of the HPSSC, and an outspoken advocate for equal rights, I expected that some members of Concerned Citizens would recognize me and not want to speak with me, or they would be overly cautious in answering questions if they did agree to be interviewed. While some participants who opposed the policies seemed guarded during interviews, none gave me any indication they knew of my involvement in the HPSSC. One of them asked me what my personal interest was in this topic, but none asked me directly if I was gay, and I never volunteered that information.

I believe that many of the people I interviewed presumed I was gay, and some of them may have tailored their responses as a result, especially those who felt they might put themselves in a compromising position by telling me they do not support GLBTIQ student inclusion. The fact that several participants were very guarded, even though they signed a consent form guaranteeing their anonymity, demonstrated to me the fear and apprehension around this contentious issue and how it affects school employees in doing their jobs. All members of HPSSC I interviewed knew I was gay, as did several of the teachers and administrators I interviewed.

This research was conducted in the city of "High Plains" between May 2000 and April 2001. I changed the names of the city, the school district, the community groups, and individuals involved to protect their privacy. Overall, the residents of High Plains are of Anglo descent; middle to upper-middle class; and a high percentage are college-educated. According to 2000 U.S. census data, High Plains has a population of 94,673: 88.3 percent, white; 1.2, black; 0.5, American Indian, Eskimo, or Aleut; 4.1, Asian or Pacific Islander; 8.2, Latino (of any race); and 3.5, other. Of people twenty-five years and older, 66.8 percent had a bachelor's degree or higher, and the median family income for 2000 was $70,257. High Plains is home to over thirty churches and other religious organizations.

The city of High Plains has a reputation as a liberal town, and this reputation does have some basis in fact when compared to the rest of the state, which is more politically conservative. The community of High Plains has a relatively long history of supporting equal rights for GLBTIQ people and a well-established GLBTIQ community. In the early 1970s, the High Plains City Council added sexual orientation to the local nondiscrimination ordinance prohibiting discrimination based on sexual orientation in the areas of employment, housing, and public accommodations. However, the amendment was repealed by popular vote the following year. In 1987 sexual orientation was put back into the local nondiscrimination ordinance by popular vote, demonstrating that a majority of voting residents supported protections for gay, lesbian, and bisexual people. In 2000 High Plains city council members voted unanimously to extended legal protections to transgendered people by prohibiting discrimination based on gender identity. High Plains also has a fair number of well-established institutions for GLBTIQ residents, such as a GLBTIQ retail gift shop, a community coffeehouse, a nightclub, two GLBTIQ dance groups, a community nonprofit organization that hosts GLBTIQ Pride Week, twelve churches and a synagogue that openly welcome GLBTIQ individuals, and a lesbian-owned bookstore. High Plains is also home to a large university that has a GLBT resource center, offers a certificate in LGBT studies, and hosts several GLBTIQ student and faculty groups.

The High Plains School District subsumes not only the city of High Plains, which is the district seat, but much of the county. The county as a whole has different demography from the community of High Plains. Countywide 2000 census statistics are lower than for the community of High Plains along the lines of *(a)* median family income ($70,257 for High Plains compared to $55,861 countywide) and *(b)* persons twenty-five years or older with a bachelor's degree or higher (66.8 percent for High Plains compared to 52.4 percent countywide). Several communities in the eastern part of the school district, mostly Anglo, have the reputation of being more conservative. Indeed, many of the parents who opposed the school district's policies regarding sexual orientation live in the eastern part of the county.

Data Collection

The information in this book was collected in a variety of ways, and the book in general is best categorized as an ethnographic case study, utilizing participant observation, semistructured interviews, document and artifact retrieval, and a personal journal. The big questions I had, and that guided this research, helped define HPSSC's ability to promote enforcement of the district's policies.

My research questions also illustrated the different sides' understandings of the policies, their worldviews about homosexuality, and their beliefs regarding the effects of including sexual orientation in school policy. The research questions are divided into three categories:

I. Competing realities:
   A. What are the worldviews people bring to this issue?
   B. Do various individuals and groups understand the policies differently based on the worldviews they bring to their understandings, and what are those differences?
   C. Are teachers' and community members' understandings of the policies congruent or dissonant with the way the school board and administration understand the policies?
   D. Do differences in worldviews and competing realities hamper the implementation of the policies?
II. Social and political factors:
   A. What specific events, attitudes, and other local factors either facilitated or hampered the implementation and enforcement of the policies and how?
III. Patterns and themes:
   A. What are the precise differences and congruities between and among the various groups' concerns about the policies?
   B. How do the sociocultural patterns and themes from this case study compare with those in Button, Rienzo, and Wald (1997)?
   C. Can this information give other school districts a clearer sense of how best to implement similar strategies and avoid some of the same pitfalls identified in this study?

High Plains Safe Schools Coalition meetings and HPSD school board meetings, where the district's policies were topics of discussion, were the sites of my participant observation. In the HPSSC meetings, I participated as a member. I recorded situations and events as they happened, as well as the language and ideas expressed in dialogues, which later allowed me to identify the explicit and tacit goals, themes, and worldviews of the group. As a member of HPSSC, I also had access to the minutes of the meetings and was on the group's e-mail listserv. Participating as a member allowed me access to much deeper levels of information because the other group members came to trust me, and shared information with me that they might otherwise have kept to themselves.

I conducted interviews with informants who were most visible in the promotion of, adoption of, and resistance to the district's policies. Interviews were face-to-face and took between forty-five minutes and two hours, depending on how much the participant had to say. I audiotaped interviews when the participants agreed to it, which all but two participants did. Questions on the survey instrument (see Macgillivray 2001) were open-ended and thus facilitated answers that were unique to the individual's circumstances. My sampling was purposive and criterion-based (LeCompte and Preissle 1993; LeCompte and Schensul 1999a): I selected individuals who were involved in, or affected by, the district's policies because of the nature of their work, or I selected those who were involved because it was an issue that was personally important to them. Most of the community individuals interviewed in this case were selected through reputational case selection, which entails the researcher's "[asking] community experts to name others who—because of their reputations—are known to be the best examples of the kind of people the researchers want to study" (Schensul, Schensul, and LeCompte 1999, 240–41). My connections with individuals in the community who are considered the "local experts" on GLBTIQ student safety (HPSSC, the county health department, the university's GLBT resource center) directed me toward potential interview subjects who represented various positions. I also utilized chain referral selection, also known as "snowball sampling" (LeCompte and Schensul 1999a, 55) by querying research participants as to whom else they thought I should interview. Finally, I curtailed my sampling when I started getting repetitive information.

Interview participants included seventeen teachers, twelve former and current administrators, three former and current school board members, five guidance counselors, two intervention specialists, seven members of the High Plains Safe Schools Coalition, and four members of Concerned Citizens (the community group who opposed the inclusion of sexual orientation in the district's policies). I interviewed only four members of Concerned Citizens because much of the data I collected from opponents came from audio- and videotaped school board meetings where they spoke against the district's inclusion of sexual orientation in the policies. To decrease the chances of nonresponse for this survey, I worked with individuals in the High Plains School District and community who helped me identify and contact other potential participants. My connections in the community and with teachers in the school district proved useful in increasing support.

Finally, no students or other minors were interviewed for this research. This research does, however, include information from GLBTIQ students in the High Plains School District who were members of a GLBTIQ youth support group sponsored by the county health department. During this research I became acquainted with the youth group's facilitator, who relayed to me details of antigay abuse these youth suffered in their schools.

The information I gathered from teacher interviews greatly informed this study, as teachers have the most contact with students and are held accountable by not only district administrators but also parents. First, I contacted teachers who, through their reputations, I knew were involved in this issue (either pro or con), and I asked them who else they thought I should interview. In addition, a teacher I subbed for agreed to forward an e-mail letter to the teacher e-mail listserv explaining my research and asking for volunteers to be interviewed. This e-mailed request for participants generated some discussion on the district's listserv. One teacher was suspicious of my motives and sent a query to the listserv asking others if they had any information on who I was and why I was conducting this research. A teacher whom I had interviewed about two months prior responded that I was to be "trusted" and that my motives were "nonbiased." The teacher who was suspicious turned out to be an ardent supporter of including sexual orientation in the district's policies and feared I was a member of the opposition. When she learned who I was and about my involvement in HPSSC, she apologized to me in a subsequent e-mail.

Teachers and administrators are expected to uphold school board policies, including those with which they disagree. This reason may have been why I had difficulty finding teachers and administrators who openly opposed the district's policies that include sexual orientation. Teachers who opposed the district's policies and who agreed to be interviewed were guarded, except for William, whose comments in chapter 7 lend great insight into conservative political beliefs. I presume that other teachers who opposed the district's policies either feared speaking out or distrusted my motives in doing this research. William told me he first consulted a school board member as well as the district's director of research and evaluation before agreeing to be interviewed. He feared reprimand for speaking out against the school board's policies that include sexual orientation. The school board member and director of research and evaluation assured William he had the right to speak his mind. That assurance, combined with the fact he was nearing retirement, gave him the confidence to say in the interview that he did not support the policies, even though he was guaranteed anonymity by me.

As administrators are responsible for seeing that the business of the school district is well done, while also being accountable to parents in the community, they were a rich source of data for informing this study about the influence of local politics on policy decision making. None of the administrators I interviewed said they opposed the policies. I do not take this sentiment to mean that not one administrator in the district disagreed with the school board's inclusion of sexual orientation in its policies. Again, those administrators who may disagree with the policies may feel it is too risky to admit their disagreement publicly. The principals I interviewed were aware of the problems faced by GLBTIQ students. One principal had addressed the issue with his staff and students, which brought him under fire from morally conservative parents and a state legislator, who thought he was advancing a "pro-gay agenda."

Guidance counselors and intervention specialists are often involved in cases of antigay abuse and had much firsthand knowledge around this topic. Intervention specialists, in this case, were social workers employed by the school district to assist students at risk of dropping out. One intervention specialist I interviewed, Meg, who counsels several gay and lesbian students at her school, was very forthright in her opinion that schools have the responsibility to talk to kids about the social issues in their lives as a way of supporting their social and psychological development into well-adjusted adults. All of the counselors and intervention specialists I interviewed were very aware of the isolation and harassment GLBTIQ youth face in America's schools and agreed that schools needed to do more to curtail antigay abuse.

Former and current school board members have been caught in the middle between advocates and opponents of any GLBTIQ-related topics being addressed in the schools, including the district's policies. Thus, school board members provided good insight into the community battles that were waged inside and outside of the school board meeting room. One former and one current school board member opposed the inclusion of sexual orientation in the district's policies. One of them, Colleen, the former school board president, is politically conservative but also happens to have a gay brother. Thus, my interview with her lends great insight into how someone who sees both sides of the issue struggles to make sense of her own political beliefs and personal values.

Members of the High Plains Safe Schools Coalition (HPSSC) constitute a crucial part of the population of this study. I worked closely with two key players in HPSSC in identifying other potential interview participants and sites for data collection. These two individuals, Dorothy and Roger, are both retired schoolteachers. Dorothy is also the mother of a gay son, and Roger, who taught in a small conservative neighboring community, came out as a gay man to his students the year he retired. Dorothy and Roger have been two of the most active members of HPSSC since the group's inception, although Roger has since limited his participation. They agreed to work closely with me on this project because of their dedication to improving school safety for GLBTIQ students.

I expected Concerned Citizens to be the most reticent group to participate in this study, but they turned out to be just as willing to participate as those who supported the policies. There may have been some mistrust here, though, as two members of this group, Frank and Richard, did not consent to be tape-recorded during interviews. No other participants in the study declined to be tape-recorded. I do not believe that any of these individuals knew of my involvement with the HPSSC. Carol asked me what my personal interest in the topic was but did not come right out and ask me if I was gay. I learned after conducting this research that another member of Concerned Citizens, Nancy, with whom I worked closely, was not surprised to later find out that I was gay (see the epilogue). During the research she presumed I had a personal interest in this topic, but she never asked me about it, and it did not seem to affect what she said, as she was very forthright during our interviews. Members of the HPSSC have developed working relationships with some of these opponents. I took advantage of these established relationships in gaining entrée to Concerned Citizens. Two parents from this group, Nancy and Carol, were willing to work closely with me, and this research benefited tremendously from their comments and participation. Both Nancy and Carol are Mormon and share many of the same views. While they are acquainted with each other, by fact of living in the same community and sharing the same religious background, they did not work closely with each other to oppose the policies. Nancy worked more closely with the core group that made up Concerned Citizens, including Frank and Richard. Carol acted on her own, separately from Concerned Citizens, but I include her as a part of the group because she shares the same beliefs and goals of the group.

Citizens United against Racism (CUAR) is an official advisory committee to the school board, composed of individuals who advocate institutional equity for students and district employees of color. Members of HPSSC formed a relationship with this group, as described in chapter 3. Two members of CUAR were interviewed regarding their group's collaboration with High Plains Safe Schools Coalition.

I also interviewed two attorneys, who gave specialized legal opinions on this topic. One attorney from the American Civil Liberties Union was involved in negotiating the language of the associated regulations to High Plains School District's nondiscrimination policy. The other attorney works for the city of High Plains and was interviewed regarding the city's jurisdiction over the school district.

Documents I collected during this research included letters to the editor and other local newspaper clippings; internal documents of the High Plains Safe Schools Coalition, detailing their history and activities as an organization; School Climate Surveys recently completed by the HPSSC in the district's eight high schools; letters to district administrators, and other public documents of the High Plains School District that pertain to the policies; and a letter to the school board from Concerned Citizens recommending their proposed changes for the district's Diversity Goal. The rationale for collecting these written documents was that they provided a historical and chronological picture of how public debate around the policies unfolded in the community and how it was handled by the school district.

I reviewed one audiotape and four videotaped school board meetings from the debates on the nondiscrimination policy and the Diversity Goal. These tapes are kept in the superintendent's office and are available for review by the public. The videotapes were extremely useful in my data analysis, insofar as giving me a better sense of the "big picture" and worldviews from which individuals spoke.

I also kept a "reflexive journal," in which I carried on a conversation with myself to record insights, ideas, working hypotheses, unanswered questions, and uncertainties as they occurred to me. I was interested in tracking my personal feelings, as I expected doing so to be somewhat of an emotional journey for me, given my background as an abused gay adolescent. I wondered how my personal feelings on this topic would affect my involvement in, and ability to, analyze this research. In retrospect, my concerns about my ability to remain objective, and that this research would be an emotional journey for me, did not play out. While I felt great passion and drive in conducting this research, I believe I was able to identify my reactions and remain balanced in my analysis and presentation of the findings. Many of the ideas and conclusions in this book came to me while I was writing in this journal.

I regarded much of the follow-up as "fine-tuning" and corroborating my findings and analyses with participants and other researchers, such as Karen Harbeck (1991, 1997) and Arthur Lipkin (1999), as well as with other members of my dissertation committee, all of whom brought their own strengths to my research. When I completed this research, I was interested in finding out what members of HPSSC and Concerned Citizens would say about how I portrayed them.

An important step critical ethnographers take is to "test" their analyses and interpretations by presenting the final work to those who were studied and asking, "Did I accurately portray you and your opinions in my work?" A dilemma arises, however, when those studied disagree with the interpretations of the researcher. When such disagreement happens, the critical researchers must decide if they made mistakes in their analysis or if the participants they studied are unable to see themselves objectively (which begs the question whether the researchers are able to see their subjects objectively). For instance, when people are asked about their eating or exercise habits, they will often give inaccurate information about themselves because, in their own minds, they would prefer to think of themselves as making healthy choices. Accurate data is obtained, however, when they are observed over a period of time and their choices are recorded and analyzed using a set of criteria that defines what "healthy choices" are.

Members of the HPSSC and one member of Concerned Citizens reviewed my completed research, and minor adjustments were made based on their comments, which I have included in the epilogue. A point of contention that arose in regards to how I portrayed the HPSSC was that I perceived them to be somewhat dishonest in their claim that they were advocating the policies only to improve "student safety" and not to advance some further agenda. Dorothy, the president of HPSSC, and I had many long discussions about this issue, and she helped me to realize, as I explain in chapter 3, that it was not that HPSSC was trying to be secretive or dishonest; rather, it was more of an "evolutionary process," where the group started out focusing on student safety but eventually expanded into other areas, like including GLBTIQ issues in the curriculum.

A point of contention that arose from Nancy, a member of Concerned Citizens, was her concern that the only religious group I mention in my work is Mormons. Nancy believed that this would set Mormons up as targets. I considered removing any references to the fact that both Nancy and Carol are Mormon, but then I decided that it was too important a piece of information to exclude. Nancy was also concerned about some of my word choices (see the epilogue), but I did not make any changes based on her comments, because I took it to be a simple matter of disagreeing over semantics. On the whole, though, Nancy agreed with my findings and said, "Thank you for your comments [in this appendix] describing the Concerned Citizens. It was well done and fair."

Thus, in several instances, I used the feedback from my participants to critically examine my interpretations, and I made corrections to some of my previous conclusions. Mostly, however, the follow-up interviews and observations helped me clarify facts and historical items. Following up also gave many participants the opportunity to ensure that I was presenting their stories as they remembered them, despite the fact that I also corroborated my findings with physical evidence, like videotaped school board meetings.

My aims for the analysis (see appendix B) were to identify the themes, slogan systems, official knowledge, and worldviews evident among participants. These helped explain the nature of resistance to the policies in the High Plains School District. One of my goals was to demonstrate the deep meanings and the real intent of the often-masked superficial rhetorical slogans of groups on both sides of the debate. I also attempted to identify points of misunderstanding and breakdowns in communication between school personnel who affected the success of implementing the policies. I was also concerned with whether or not my findings would accurately represent the empirical reality of this case and whether or not my findings would be valid in other settings (see appendix C). Finally, while my study does not reconcile the opposing points of view, it does offer a way of evaluating them in helping other districts more effectively deal with opposition to school reforms that would help bring about safety and inclusion for GLBTIQ students.

In summary, this research is an ethnographic case study of the implementation of, and resistance to, school district policies that include sexual orientation in the High Plains School District. This book focuses on the adoption and implementation of two HPSD policies: one, a nondiscrimination policy; and, two, the Diversity Goal of the district's Strategic Plan, a three-year plan that outlines priorities for the school district. Both of these policies include sexual orientation. This case study also focuses on the efforts of two local community groups: first, the High Plains Safe Schools Coalition (HPSSC), whose objective is to ensure compliance with the policies; and, second, Concerned Citizens, who enacted resistance to the policies and who are made up of a loosely organized group of morally conservative parents, as well as other individuals in the community and employees of the High Plains School District, who oppose the inclusion of sexual orientation in the policies.

A community's local history, politics, people, and other factors all have an effect on the implementation of, and resistance to, policies that include sexual orientation. This research design is meant to explicate all of the factors that affected HPSSC's ability to advocate the inclusion of sexual orientation in their school district's policies. This research design illustrates the reasons why moral conservatives opposed the inclusion of sexual orientation in the policies. Finally, I draw on the critical paradigm to inform this research because of its concerns with social justice and objectivity of the researcher, which are especially important in cases like this, where two opposing sides make competing claims against the other.

Appendix B:
Methods of Data Analysis

Coding and Item-Level Analysis

CODES WERE DEVELOPED BASED ON THE ITEMS THAT became apparent in the item-level analysis (LeCompte and Schensul 1999b). Thus, the coding and item-level analysis stages were done more or less concurrently and in a dialectical fashion using QSR NUD*ST Vivo software. Coding was not attempted until sufficient interviews and audio- and videotaped school board meetings had been transcribed for me to develop appropriate and inclusive codes.

Item-level analysis involved speculating about the information contained in the interviews and school board meetings, in an inductive process where "events, behaviors, statements, or activities . . . stand out because they occur often; are crucial to other items; are rare and influential; or are totally absent, despite the researcher's expectations" (LeCompte and Schensul 1999b). Item-level analysis was used at all stages of the analytic process. I began item identification and coding by first focusing on either single words, or two- or three-word phrases. For instance, I coded any word or short phrase that was linked to an informant's expressed belief about homosexuality. I quickly found, however, that doing so produced an unwieldy morass of information. I abandoned that strategy in favor of coding complete sentences and chunks of interviews so that I could more easily identify what the informant was getting at, based on the context of the chunk of data coded. Doing so produced a more manageable amount of coded data and items that were more easily categorized hierarchically into patterns.

Pattern Level of Analysis

The conceptual framework of my dissertation, which I have included here as chapter 6, suggests that groups adhere to certain normalized beliefs according to their collective identities and legitimated or nonlegitimated social statuses. The associations of certain groups with various expressions and beliefs, which I had coded as items, became apparent at this level of analysis, and I organized them hierarchically into patterns using the coder in QSR NUD*ST Vivo software. This stage of analysis entailed systematic ways of looking at the coded items to identify patterns. "Pattern level analysis involves organizing related items (or indicators of a variable) into higher-order patterns.... Eventually, patterns are organized into structures ... and, finally, linked to theories from various paradigms that help to explain their existence" (LeCompte and Schensul 1999b). Patterns emerged through the following avenues: declaration by informants, the frequency with which they occurred, because something was obviously missing, because of similarity in responses, because of co-occurrence, because they appeared as sequences, and because they appeared in congruence with prior hypotheses (LeCompte and Schensul 1999b). Patterns "popped out" once I organized and grouped the items in QSR NUD*ST Vivo's coder and began writing about them using the ideas expressed in my conceptual framework. For instance, after I had coded items of the informants' expressing nostalgia for "the good old days" and expressing concerns about "political correctness," I observed a pattern that these two items *(a)* were most often expressed together, *(b)* were made in relation to each other, and *(c)* were made only by those informants who also expressed opposition to the inclusion of sexual orientation in the district's policies.

Structural Level of Analysis

"Structural or constitutive analysis involves linking together or finding consistent relationships among patterns, components, constituents, and structures" (LeCompte and Schensul 1999b). During this stage of analysis, a clear portrait began to develop of the questions under study and of the official knowledge and worldviews of participants. This stage entailed my assemblage and integration of constituent parts of the data, either inductively or deductively, and sometimes a combination of the two. I did so by arranging and reorganizing coded items into patterns and then structures. For instance, the pattern just described (informant's mentioning nostalgia for the good old days, along with concerns over political correctness) was linked to other specific perspectives held by informants. For instance, only those expressing opposition to the inclusion of sexual orientation in the district's policies mentioned "the good old days" and "political correctness." All of the specific perspectives helped create an overall picture (a structure) that constituted the worldviews of those opposed to the inclusion of sexual orientation in the district's policies (see table B.1 for an example of how I arranged some of Concerned Citizens' statements into groups of items and patterns, and an overall structure). Moreover, the patterns were congruent with prior hypotheses about moral conservative beliefs, such as those explicated by Fraser (1999). Thus, many of the patterns and structures that emerged out of this research confirmed those of others. The structural level of analysis was also useful in identifying those social and political factors that either facilitated or hampered the implementation and enforcement of the policies.

TABLE B.1
Item, pattern, and structural levels of analysis, based on an interpretation of the slogans and worldviews of Concerned Citizens and teachers who oppose the policies.

Items	Patterns	Structure
Schools teach values, like "It's okay to be gay," with which morally conservative parents do not agree.		
Schools send the message to students that "Your parents are wrong for holding antigay beliefs."	Violations of parental rights.	
Schools undermine parents' ability to teach their kids homosexuality is wrong by teaching that "It's okay to be gay."		
Moral conservatives believe homosexuality is wrong.		
Moral conservatives speak publicly about their antigay beliefs.	Reasons for being seen as bigots.	
The more liberal public sees moral conservatives as intolerant.		
Assaults on Christians' core beliefs.		
Assaults on Christians' identities.		

(Continued)

TABLE B.1   (Continued)

Items	Patterns	Structure
Forbidding those who disagree with homosexuality from speaking out against it.	Discrimination against Christians.	Threats to Christian hegemony.
Preventing moral conservatives from holding antigay beliefs.		
Giving GLBTQ people special rights.		
GLBTQ people are confused about their sexual orientation.	Reasons why the social acceptance of homosexuality will lead to the downfall of civilization as we know it.	
GLBTQ people suffer from sexual addiction.		
GLBTQ people don't reproduce themselves—they recruit.		
Being GLBTQ leads to depression.		
There needs to be some standard of family life—a husband, wife, and kids.		
Same-sex marriage frustrates the foundation of society.		

Theme Analysis

Spradley (1980) explains a cultural theme as a "cognitive principle [which] is something that people believe and accept as true and valid; it is an assumption about the nature of their commonly held experience." My conceptual framework (chapter 6) states that we must be able to understand the nature of reality and the meaning that groups and individuals bring to their understandings of social situations. Thus, theme analysis helped me identify meanings, beliefs, and worldviews that individuals and groups hold. Ways of identifying themes included the following: uncovering tacit or explicit meanings in folk sayings and other expressions (which I did by putting them in my own words and by asking participants, "Is this what you mean?"); looking for relationships between beliefs; and immersing myself in the data until themes emerged. I did so using the coder in QSR NUD*ST Vivo software. Not only did I code while transcribing the interviews, I read through each interview several times, coding each time, to make sure that I did not miss any important information or miscode any data. This process allowed me to become so familiar with my data that I could pinpoint which informant said what when I realized I had accidentally forgotten to reference some quotes used in this report. In the one or two cases where I could not identify to whom a quote belonged, the information was easily retrieved using QSR NUD*ST Vivo's search function.

Constant Comparison and Analytic Induction

LeCompte and Schensul (1999b), drawing on Glaser and Strauss (1965), describe "constant comparison" as a strategy where the researcher constantly compares the language used by those being studied, paying special attention to names or identifiers, relationships, behaviors, settings, actors, "and other dimensions of cultural life." The researcher is then able to make inferences about any differences and develop a set of consistent identifiers. LeCompte and Schensul explain:

> The stream of behavior or language is recorded and then separated into discrete concepts using constant comparison. The items are then "chunked" into categories. Subsequent steps link the categories into concept or theoretical constructs that, in turn, permit selection or development of theories that the researcher can use to explain what was observed in the field [or the interviews and school board meetings, in this case].

Using QSR NUD*ST Vivo's coder, I constantly compared the language of each group of interviewees (members of HPSSC, members of Concerned Citizens, teachers, and so on) within and between groups. I then coded slogans, beliefs, and worldviews, which allowed me to come up with a set of consistent identifiers for each group. Finding that members of each group could be identified based on similarities in slogans, beliefs, and worldviews demonstrated that I had identified the deep meanings of beliefs for each group. There were, however, anomalies, which are discussed next.

LeCompte and Schensul (1999b) explain "analytic induction" as a "specialized form of comparison" in that "its principal feature is its emphasis on a search for negative or disconfirming cases." Most important for this research, analytic induction alerted me "to variance within [my populations] and to nuances and dimensions of meaning and perception that would be ignored were a systematic search for such differences not done" (LeCompte and Schensul 1999b). That is, searching for disconfirming cases to the set of identifiers I had created for each group forced me to dig deeper into the worldviews and slogans for each group and get to the root of each informant's frame of reference. Not only did this search help me identify worldviews I did not anticipate, it strengthened my findings in that I was forced to go to a deeper level in confirming that the set of identifiers I had created for each group was indeed appropriate. For instance, both advocates and opponents in this case consistently said they supported equality for all people, including GLBTIQ students, and that everyone should be treated the same (a common slogan on both sides). These expressed beliefs seemed to contradict many of the actions of opponents, however. Thus, I was forced to dig deeper and query informants about exactly what they meant, and I asked them to give examples. Upon further questioning, I revealed that while opponents express the belief in equality for all, they do not consider denial of equal rights to GLBTIQ people to conflict with their belief of equality for all people. Had I taken their statements at face value, I would have been led to believe that they support equal rights for GLBTIQ people, which they do not.

Appendix C: Validity and Reliability

STRATEGIES I USED TO ENHANCE INTERNAL VALIDITY and minimize observer effects during interviews included:

- attempting to establish a minimal level of trust (most teachers and community members I interviewed—except two teachers who expressed opposition and two members of Concerned Citizens who refused to be audiotaped—showed no hesitation about being forthright with their opinions);
- addressing and answering any concerns the participant might have had about participating in the research;
- clarifying any ambiguity in questions by providing more detailed explanations and examples; and
- "member-checking" recorded data for accuracy by asking interviewee, "Is this what you said/meant?" (Schensul, Schensul, and LeCompte 1999)

A final threat to internal validity, called "observer effects" (creating a researcher–informant relationship within the community that could seriously affect the setting or results), was accounted for by carefully documenting what that relationship was and what its effects were. "Construct validity," another concern, is "relevant to the questions researchers ask in interviews. It involves the degree to which the questions or measures used really assess what they are assumed to measure" (Schensul , Schensul, and LeCompte 1999, 275). Construct validity was thus accounted for by making interview questions as easy to understand as possible, putting them in simple language, and providing examples. I tried to avoid the use of specialized jargon, and I explained words and concepts (like "GLB-TIQ") that I thought interviewees might not be familiar with. I also broke the survey instrument into different categories and explained to participants when we were moving into a new category and what the category was about. When asking informants to recall events, I often gave historical context to help jog their memories. Finally, the survey instrument was piloted with my first two informants. Those first two interviews took longer than expected, which pointed out the need to trim some of the original interview questions. I completely deleted several questions that turned out to be redundant. In subsequent interviews, I simply skipped over questions that I determined were not pertinent to the informant's position. After piloting my instrument, I was confident that it would work well, and I incorporated the data from those first two pilot interviews into my research.

This study included certain "selection effects," although they were not a concern. I realized that because I was relying heavily on participants to volunteer their time and effort in my research, the potential existed for my research to attract members of polarized groups—that is, individuals who felt highly motivated by this topic, either pro or con, and individuals who may have had their own personal agenda that they wished to confirm in my research. However, it was precisely those people whom I sought for the study—individuals who felt highly motivated by this topic, who were the most involved in the public debates around the district's policies, and who ultimately provided me with the richest data.

I attempted to enhance external validity by making my study comparable with other studies. I did so by not developing idiosyncratic terminology to describe the special situation of my research site. That is, I started with the terminology and theoretical frameworks already developed and used by researchers doing related work, and I adjusted or enhanced them to suit the needs of my particular case study. Another threat to external validity is a failure to document the unique historical experiences of the case study site and the groups in the study. I accounted for this threat by providing historical information about the setting and other factors that make the setting and the people involved unique—that is, personalities, connections with district officials, sexual orientation, and so on.

Reliability was less of a concern than validity for this research because of the unique nature of this case study. However, I attempted to enhance the analogs for reliability (replicability)—that is, comparability and translatability (LeCompte and Preissle 1993)—by doing the following:

- describing clearly both the nature and the context of [my] relationships with the study population and the research site, [thus providing a clear basis for comparison with other groups or settings];

- Clarifying and describing clearly who the study's key informants were, the groups they represented, and the status positions they held in the community in the study.
- Making clear how and where observations were made.
- Providing details of sampling techniques.
- Defining concepts, constructs, domains, factors, and variables clearly.
- Clarifying methods and procedures for analyzing ethnographic data. (Schensul, Schensul, and LeCompte, 1999, 288–89)

Finally, Howe and Eisenhart (1990) make an excellent point: The fact "that research might possess internal validity is insufficient" for justifying the value of doing the research (7). Another important rationale for educational research, they maintain, is the worth of the research for improving educational practice. I believe this research has great worth for informing the growing discourse on safety and equity for all students in America's schools.

Appendix D: HPSD's Nondiscrimination Policy

High Plains School District
File: AC
Adopted: date of manual adoption
Revised: May 26, 1994
Associated Regulation: AC-R
Associated Exhibit: AC-E1

Nondiscrimination

THE BOARD AFFIRMS THAT there shall be no discrimination against anyone in the school system on the basis of race, age, marital status, creed, color, sex, disability, or national origin.

The High Plains School District will not tolerate discrimination, harassment, or violence against anyone, including students and staff members, regardless of race, ethnicity, gender, sexual orientation, age, disability, or religion.

LEGAL REFS.: Civil Rights Act of 1964, as amended in 1972, Title VI, Title VII Executive Order 11246, as amended by Executive Order 11375
Equal Opportunity Act of 1972, Title VII
Education Amendments of 1972, Title IX (P.L. 92-318)
45 C.F.R. Parts 81, 86 (*Federal Register*, June 4, 1975; August 11, 1975)
Vocational Rehabilitation Act, Section 504

C.R.S. 22-20-101 *et seq.*
C.R.S. 24-34-301 through-306
Americans with Disabilities Act of 1990
CROSS REFS.: ACA*, Nondiscrimination on the Basis of Sex (Compliance with Title IX) GBA, Equal Opportunity Employment (and Affirmative Action)
JB, Equal Educational Opportunities

End of File: AC

Appendix E: Diversity Goal Statement with Beliefs from Strategic Plan

---

Statement

Value Diversity and Promote Understanding

Beliefs

1. All human beings have inherent worth.
2. All students, regardless of race, ethnicity, gender, sexual orientation, age, disability or religion, deserve a quality education.
3. HPSD will not tolerate discrimination, intimidation, harassment or violence based on race, ethnicity, gender, sexual orientation, age, disability or religion.
4. Healthy school communities respect differences, welcome diversity and promote cultural plurality.
5. Racial, ethnic and cultural diversity should be evident across all employee groups and central administration.

Appendix F: Associated Regulations That Support the Nondiscrimination Policy

*N*ote: I have inserted italicized comments based on my interview with the ACLU attorney. The ACLU asked the district to incorporate language directly from the U.S. Department of Education's guidelines on "Developing a District's Anti-Harassment Policy" (U.S. Department of Education 2000a, 2000b). The concern was that these regulations could be found to be unconstitutional if challenged in court, so the district added ACLU's suggestions to preserve students' First Amendment rights.

High Plains School District
File: AC-R
Issued: May 11, 1995
Revisions: June 8, 2000

Nondiscrimination

In affirming that there shall be no discrimination, harassment, or violence against anyone in the school system, the Board of Education intends this regulation to define what constitutes a violation of the Board's nondiscrimination policy and to provide processes to prohibit discrimination, harassment, and violence. This regulation is further intended to delineate procedures to resolve conflicts that arise and to ensure accountability.

Introduction

1. It is recognized that discrimination or harassment complaints by students or adults may arise from actual or perceived situations and circumstances of discrimination.
2. It is the intent of these procedures to assure that discrimination or harassment complaints are resolved in a timely, orderly, and equitable manner that serves to fulfill the intent of the Board policy against discrimination. All administrators are required to make a conscientious effort to fully understand the nature and basis of any discrimination or harassment complaint and resolve it or refer it to the appropriate source for resolution in a timely manner.
3. The filing of a discrimination or harassment complaint will not be used as a basis for actions that adversely affect any party's standing in the school system.
4. The School District will support teachers and administrators in promoting high standards of academic scholarship in a safe, nonthreatening environment that respects the potential of each student without regard for individual differences. Students will have an opportunity to participate in discussions advocating nondiscrimination. Staff development aimed at the elimination of harassment and discrimination will be provided to all employees in the School District.
5. Support services, such as school counseling, and the nondiscrimination school liaison are available for students who experience discrimination or harassment.

Definitions

1. Harassment
   Behavior toward students or adults based, in whole or in part, on race, ethnicity, national origin, gender, sexual orientation, age, disability, or religion which interferes with a person's school performance or creates an intimidating, hostile, or offensive school environment. *[The ACLU attorney I spoke with recommends the insertion here of wording regarding a "pattern or history of behavior" in helping to define harassment.]*
2. Sexual Harassment of Personnel
   Unwelcome sexual advances, requests for sexual favors, or other sex-based verbal or physical conduct where
   a. submission to such conduct is explicitly or implicitly made a term or condition of an individual's employment;
   b. submission to or rejection of such conduct is used as the basis for decisions affecting an individual's employment benefits; or

c. such conduct has the purpose or effect of unreasonably interfering with an individual's employment by creating an intimidating, hostile, or offensive work environment.

3. Sexual Harassment of Students

Verbal, visual, or physical sexual or gender-based behavior that occurs when one person has formal or informal power over the other and

a. such behavior creates an intimidating, hostile, or offensive educational environment; or

b. such behavior interferes with an individual's educational performance or adversely affects an individual's learning opportunities.

4. Violation or Suspected Violation of the Nondiscrimination Policy

It is a violation of the nondiscrimination policy if, on District property, in District vehicles, or in connection with any District program, activity, or event, a District employee or student

a. makes demeaning remarks (such as by name-calling, slurs, or jokes) directly or, depending upon the circumstances and context, *[The ACLU attorney explained it was this phrase "depending upon the circumstances and context" with which the ACLU was most concerned that the regulations should contain. Adding this phrase allows for a broader interpretation and helps protect students' constitutional rights.]* indirectly; intimidates; or physically threatens or harms an individual on the basis of race, ethnicity, national origin, gender, sexual orientation, age, disability, or religion;

b. harasses an individual on the basis of that individual's race, ethnicity, national origin, gender, sexual orientation, age, disability, or religion;

c. displays visual or written material with the purpose or, depending upon the circumstances and context, effect of demeaning the race, ethnicity, national origin, gender, sexual orientation, age, disability, or religion of any individual or group;

d. damages, defaces, or destroys the property of any individual because of that individual's race, ethnicity, national origin, gender, sexual orientation, age, disability, or religion; or

e. excludes any qualified individual from participation in, denies any qualified individual the benefits of, or otherwise discriminates against any qualified individual in connection with any District program, activity, or event on the basis of the individual's race, ethnicity, national origin, gender, sexual orientation, age, disability, or religion.

Processes to Prohibit Harassment and Discrimination

The administrator/department head of a school/department is responsible for communicating to students, staff, and parents the nondiscrimination policy and the procedures to resolve conflicts and for creating a safe, nondiscriminatory school/work environment. The department supervisor is responsible for the same duties in regard to the employees in his or her department.

At the beginning of each school year, the educational and employment nondiscrimination policy and regulation to resolve conflict (AC-R/AC-E1), shall be disseminated to employees, parents, students and volunteers in the following manner:

1. By inclusion in the staff handbook;
2. By inclusion in the student school handbook;
3. By inclusion in student-parent informational handbook;
4. By inclusion in the HPSD web-site;
5. By posting in school offices, halls, and student gathering areas.

Procedures to Resolve Conflicts

Any adult who witnesses a violation of the nondiscrimination policy is expected to take reasonable action to stop the violation at the time the violation occurs, and to report the incident to the appropriate personnel. Students who witness or know of a violation or suspected violation of the policy are encouraged to promptly report to the school principal or another adult staff member. Confidentiality will be maintained throughout the process, with information made available only to persons having a legitimate educational interest in the records of the proceedings.

Procedure

When a violation or suspected violation of the nondiscrimination policy occurs, the Board policies and regulations provide the following procedures for dealing with an alleged violation:

Students:

| ACA Nondiscrimination on the Basis of Sex (Compliance with Title IX) | ACB Nondiscrimination on the Basis of Disability Under Section 504 and the Americans with Disabilities Act | JFH Student Complaints and Grievances (regarding violation of Board policies or school rules) |

Employees:

| ACA Nondiscrimination on the Basis of Sex (Compliance with Title IX) | GBCC Sexual Harassment of Personnel | GBM Staff Complaints and Grievances (regarding violation of Board policies or regulations) |

Public:

| KL Public Complaints | KLB Public Complaints About the Curriculum or Instructional Materials or Strategies |

Any violation or suspected violation of the nondiscrimination policy, AC, that is not addressed by the procedures specifically provided above, shall be handled by the following complaint procedure.

Every effort shall be made to resolve the complaint at the lowest possible level below.

Level I: Informal Complaint to Administrator/Supervisor. Students, employees, or members of the public who have personal knowledge of a violation or suspected violation of the nondiscrimination policy that does not fall under the specific procedures listed above, shall initiate a review by contacting the building principal or supervisor as soon as possible after the alleged violation. Students may also report to a teacher or counselor on the school's staff who will act or arrange for a staff member to act as the Student Grievance Liaison. The principal or supervisor shall investigate any allegation of violation of the nondiscrimination policy, and attempt to resolve the matter informally by facilitating a discussion between those involved. If the alleged violation is based upon the conduct of the principal or supervisor of the complainant, the report should be made to that person's immediate supervisor.

In determining whether there has been a violation of the nondiscrimination policy, the principal or supervisor should consider all the facts, the surrounding circumstances, the nature of the behavior, the relationships between the parties involved, and the context in which the alleged incident occurred. *[The ACLU requested the district incorporate this paragraph, which was borrowed from the Minnesota School Board's policy, again to preserve students' constitutional rights.]*

Level II: Formal Written Complaint to Administrator/Supervisor. If the matter has not been informally resolved, the complainant may submit the Report Form for Alleged Discrimination, Harassment, or Violence (Form AC-E1) to the principal or supervisor within twenty school days of the alleged act of discrimination. The form will also advise the complainant about persons who are available to assist the complainant in the process. The principal or supervisor shall make, or shall designate another to make, such additional investigation as necessary to determine the complete facts involved. Any person investigating a complaint at this level is expected to have appropriate training in investigating and resolving complaints of discrimination. He or she shall make a written report within ten school days from the date the written complaint is received. The report shall be made on the Alleged Discrimination, Harassment, Violence Follow-Up Report Form (AC-E2) and shall contain the specific findings and conclusion as to the alleged violation of the nondiscrimination policy. Any report that contains the name of a District student shall be considered an educational record and shall be kept confidential pursuant to state and federal public records laws.

Level III: District Level Formal Complaint. If resolution is not achieved, the complainant may file a written appeal within ten days of review of the Level II report at the District level (Executive Directors of Elementary or Secondary Education). The written appeal shall state, with specificity, the reasons and facts that support the disagreement with the Level II decision. The appropriate Director at the District level shall have ten days to review the records of the complaint and investigation and to issue a written decision.

Level IV Formal Written Complaint to Superintendent/Designee. If the issue has not been resolved by the Level III decision, a final appeal may be made to the Superintendent of Schools or designee within five days of receipt of the Level III decision. The Superintendent shall have twenty days to review the record of the complaint and investigation and to issue a written decision as a final resolution of the complaint. Policy KL (Public Complaints) and its associated regulation (KL-R) provide a procedure for District patrons to pursue complaints concerning the application of this policy.

Nondiscrimination Regulations Flow Chart

The Nondiscrimination Flow Chart will be placed in the student-parent handbook, teacher handbook, and on posters that will be placed in all District buildings (see table f.1).

Special Provisions

1. Failure on the part of the student/parent/employee to initiate and/or follow up on a complaint in a timely manner may result in the complaint being considered abandoned. A complaint must be filed within twenty school days of the alleged violation of the nondiscrimination policy.
2. In general, students and employees shall continue attendance at school and pursue their studies or employment, as directed, while complaints are pending resolution.
3. Records of an ongoing investigation shall be kept confidential pursuant to state and federal law.

Procedures to Ensure Accountability

As part of the annual goal setting in the area of cultural plurality, the staffs in each school and department are expected to develop measurable goals to promote nondiscrimination. Consistent with the District's performance evaluation instrument for administrators that assess each administrator's efforts and success in implementing the District's policies and goals, the evaluations of principals and heads of departments shall include consideration of the implementation of this policy and regulation and related goals.

TABLE F.1
Nondiscrimination Regulations Flow Chart

Level	Decision Maker	Respondent Action	District Action
I	School principal or immediate supervisor	Report as soon after event giving rise to claim	Resolve informally utilizing District's disciplinary regulations (inappropriate behavior will constitute disciplinary actions). (See HPSD File: JG for reference.)
II	School principal or immediate supervisor	If not resolved at Level I, file a formal written complaint within twenty school days after event giving rise to claim	Report findings (ten working days) A. No violation of District Policy; B. No violation of District's Nondiscrimination Policy; however, inappropriate behavior by respondent (disciplinary action may be taken); or Violation of District Nondiscrimination Policy (disciplinary action must be taken).
III	District executive directors (elementary, secondary)	File a written appeal within ten days of review of report at Level II	Written decision sent within ten days of appeal which may: affirm; reverse; modify; remand
IV	Superintendent or designee	File a written complaint within ten days of appeal of Level III	Written decision within twenty days of appeal which may affirm; reverse; modify; or remand. The Superintendent's or designee's decision is final.

Cross References:

IB	Academic Freedom
IGAC	Teaching About Religion and Religion in the Schools
IGDB	Student Publications
JF	Student Rights and Responsibilities
JFC	Student Conduct
JG	Student Discipline
JGD/JGE	Student Suspension/Expulsion

End of File: AC-R [AC-R]

NONDISCRIMINATION POLICY/REGULATIONS (AC-R)

POLICY:
The Board of Education affirms that there shall be no discrimination against anyone in the school system on the basis of race, age, marital status, creed, color, gender, sexual orientation, disability, national origin, or religion.

REGULATIONS/PROCEDURES:
The purpose of the regulation is to:

1. encourage respect for diversity,
2. prohibit discrimination, harassment, and violence
3. outline procedures to resolve conflicts that arise, and
4. ensure a measure of accountability to this policy and its regulation.

A report form is available to students and parents in each school's office for reporting alleged discrimination, harassment or violence. The following procedures are to be followed when the principal of a school or the head of a department receives report of any such incident:

Level	Decision-Maker	Respondent Action	District Action
I	School principal or immediate supervisor	Report immediately after event giving rise to claim	Resolve informally utilizing District's disciplinary regulations (inappropriate behavior will constitute disciplinary actions). (See HPSD File: JG for reference.)
II	School principal or immediate supervisor	If not resolved at Level I, file a formal written complaint within 20 school days after event giving rise to claim	Report findings (10 working days) A. No violation of District Policy; B. No violation of District's Nondiscrimination Policy; however, inappropriate behavior by respondent (disciplinary action may be taken); or C. Violation of District Nondiscrimination Policy (disciplinary action must be taken).
III	District executive directors (elementary, secondary)	File a written appeal within 10 days of review of report at Level II	Written Decision sent within 10 days of appeal which may: • affirm; reverse; modify; remand
IV	Superintendent or designee	File a written complaint within 10 days of appeal of Level III	Written decision within 20 days of appeal which may affirm; reverse; modify; or remand. The Superintendent's or designee's decision is final.

Special Provisions

1. Failure on the part of the student/parent/employee to initiate and/or follow up on a complaint in a timely manner may result in the complaint being considered abandoned. A complaint must be filed within 20 days of the alleged violation of the nondiscrimination policy. (Unless otherwise stated, "days" means working days.)
2. In general, students and employees shall continue attendance at school and pursue their studies and employment, as directed, while complaints are pending.
3. Records of an ongoing investigation shall be kept confidential pursuant to state and federal law.

The civil rights law prohibits retaliation against a student or employee who files a complaint.

Note: This poster was created upon adoption of the associated regulations, District Policy AC-R. This poster was to be printed on goldenrod stock and hung in all district buildings.

Bibliography

Anderson, D. A. "Lesbian and Gay Adolescents: Social and Developmental Considerations." *The High School Journal* 77, nos. 1 and 2 (1994): 13–19.

Apple, M. W. "Do the Standards Go Far Enough? Power, Policy, and Practice in Mathematics Education." *Journal for Research in Mathematics Education* 23, no. 5 (1992): 412–31.

———. *Official Knowledge: Democratic Education in a Conservative Age.* New York: Routledge, 1993.

Apple, M. W., and A. Oliver. "Becoming Right: Education and the Formation of Conservative Movements." *Teachers College Record* 97, no. 3 (1996): 419–45.

Arriola, E. R. "The Penalties for Puppy Love: Institutionalized Violence against Lesbian, Gay, Bisexual and Transgendered Youth." *The Journal of Gender, Race, & Justice* 1 (1998): 429–70.

Baldwin, S. "The Real Agenda." Accessed at www.libertycaucus.com/Articles/gay.htm. 2000.

Berger, P. L., and T. Luckman. *The Social Construction of Reality: A Treatise in the Sociology of Knowledge.* New York: Anchor Books, 1966.

Berv, J. "Listening to the Students: The Three Rs of Student-Centered School Improvement." Doctoral dissertation in progress, University of Colorado, Boulder, 2002.

Besner, H. F., and C. I. Spungin. *Gay and Lesbian Students: Understanding Their Needs.* Washington, D.C.: Taylor and Francis, 1995.

Blumer, H. *Symbolic Interactionism: Perspective and Method.* Berkeley, CA: University of California Press, 1969.

Bourdieu, P. "Cultural Reproduction and Social Reproduction," in *Power and Ideology in Education,* edited by Jerome Karabel and A. H. Halsey. New York: Oxford University Press, 1977.

Boy Scouts of America v. Dale, 000 U.S. 99-699, 2000.

Buckel, D. "Legal Perspective on Ensuring a Safe and Non-discriminatory School Environment for Lesbian, Gay, Bisexual, and Transgendered Students." *Education and Urban Society* 32, no. 3 (May 2000): 390–98.

Button, J. W., B. A. Rienzo, and K. D. Wald. *Private Lives, Public Conflicts: Battles over Gay Rights in American Communities.* Washington, D.C.: CQ Press, 1997.

Calhoun, E. "Voice in Government: The People." *Notre Dame Journal of Law, Ethics & Public Policy* 8, no. 2 (1994): 427–66.

Casper, V., and S. B. Schultz. *Gay Parents/Straight Schools: Building Communication and Trust.* New York: Teachers College Press, 1999.

Cicchino, P. M., B. R. Deming, and K. M. Nicholson. "Sex, Lies, and Civil Rights: A Critical History of the Massachusetts Gay Civil Rights Bill." *Harvard Civil Rights-Civil Liberties Law Review* 26 (1991): 549–631.

Colín v. Orange Unified School District. 83 F. Supp. 2d 1135 (2003).

Committee on Adolescence, American Academy of Pediatrics. "Homosexuality and Adolescence." *Pediatrics* 92, no. 4 (1993): 631–34.

Cullen, D. "The Rumor That Won't Go Away. Jocks Say Littleton Killers Were Gay, but Friends Deny It." Accessed at www.salon.com. (April 24, 1999).

D'Augelli, A. R. "Developmental Implications of Victimization of Lesbian, Gay, and Bisexual Youths." In *Stigma and Sexual Orientation: Understanding Prejudice against Lesbians, Gay Men, and Bisexuals,* edited by G. M. Harek, 187–210. Thousand Oaks, CA: SAGE Publications, 1998.

Davidson, A. L. *Making and Molding Identity in Schools: Student Narratives on Race, Gender, and Academic Engagement.* New York: State University of New York Press, 1996.

"East High Gay/Straight Alliance v. Board of Education." *The Lambda Update* 17, no. 1 (Winter 2000): 24–25.

Foucault, M. "Truth and Power." In *The Foucault Reader,* edited by P. Rabinow, 51–75. New York: Pantheon Books, 1984.

Fraser, J. W. *Between Church and State: Religion and Public Education in a Multicultural America.* New York: St. Martin's Press, 1999.

Friend, R. "Choices, Not Closets: Heterosexism and Homophobia in Schools." *Beyond Silenced Voices: Class, Race, and Gender in United States Schools,* edited by L. Weis and M. Fine, 209–35. New York: State University of New York Press, 1993.

———. "Heterosexism, Homophobia, and the Culture of Schooling." In *Invisible Children in the Society and Its Schools,* edited by Sue Books, 137–66. Mahway, NJ: Lawrence Erlbaum Associates, 1998.

Fullan, M. *The New Meaning of Educational Change* (with Suzanne Stiegelbauer). 2nd ed. New York: Teachers College Press, 1991.

Garofalo, R. R., C. Wolf, S. Kessel, J. Palfrey, and R. H. DuRant. "The Association between Health Risk Behaviors and Sexual Orientation among a School-Based Sample of Adolescents." *Pediatrics* 101, no. 5 (1998): 895–902.

Gates, R. L. *The Making of Massive Resistance: Virginia's Politics of Public School Desegregation, 1954–1956.* Chapel Hill, NC: The University of North Carolina Press, 1964.

Gathercoal, F. *A Judicious Philosophy for School Support Personnel.* San Francisco: Caddo Gap Press, 1996.

Giroux, H. A. *Theory and Resistance in Education.* London: Heinemann Educational Books, 1983.

Glaser, B., and A. L. Strauss. *Awareness of Dying.* Chicago: Aldine, 1965.

Goffman, E. *The Presentation of Self in Everyday Life.* New York: Doubleday Books, 1959.

———. *Stigma: Notes on the Management of Spoiled Identity.* New York: Simon & Schuster, 1963.

Greene, S. "Trench Coat Mafia Teen Describes School Life Filled with Taunts, Abuse." *The Denver Post,* April 24, 1999, 1A, 15A.

Gutierrez, F. J. "Gay and Lesbian: An Ethnic Identity Deserving Equal Protection." *Law & Sexuality* 4 (1994): 195–247.

Gutmann, A., and D. Thompson. *Democracy and Disagreement.* Cambridge, MA: The Belknap Press of Harvard University Press, 1996.

Harbeck, K. M., ed. *Coming Out of the Classroom Closet: Gay and Lesbian Students, Teachers and Curricula.* New York: Harrington Park Press, 1991.

———. *Gay and Lesbian Educators: Personal Freedoms, Public Constraints.* Malden, MA: Amethyst Press and Productions, 1997.

Heath, S. B. *Ways with Words: Language, Life, and Work in Communities and Classrooms.* Cambridge: Cambridge University Press, 1983.

Henkle v. Gregory. 150 F. Supp. 2d 1067 (2003).

Hills, R. M., Jr. "You Say You Want a Revolution? The Case against the Transformation of Culture through Antidiscrimination Laws." Review of *Antidiscrimination Law and Social Equality. Michigan Law Review* 95 (1997): 1588–1635.

Howe, K. R. *Understanding Equal Educational Opportunity: Social Justice, Democracy, and Schooling.* New York: Teachers College Press, 1997.

Howe, K., and M. Eisenhart. "Standards for Qualitative (and Quantitative) Research: A Prolegomenon." *Educational Researcher* 19, no. 4 (1990): 2–9.

Hunter, J. *Culture Wars: The Struggle to Define America.* New York: Basic Books, 1991.

Imber, M., and T. van Geel. *A Teacher's Guide to Education Law.* 2nd ed. Mahwah, NJ: Lawrence Erlbaum Associates, 2001.

Kaestle, C. F. *Pillars of the Republic: Common Schools and American Society, 1780–1860.* New York: Hill and Wang, 1983.

Kielwasser, Alfred P., and M. A. Wolf. "Silence, Difference, and Annihilation: Understanding the Impact of Mediated Heterosexism on High School Students." *The High School Journal* 77, nos. 1 and 2 (1994): 58–79.

Koppelman, A. *Antidiscrimination Law and Social Equality.* New Haven, CT: Yale University Press, 1996.

Kozik-Rosabal, G. "'Well, We Haven't Noticed Anything Bad Going On,' Said the Principal: Parents Speak about Their Gay Families and Schools." *Education and Urban Society* 32, no. 3 (May 2000): 368–89.

Kuhn, T. S. *The Structure of Scientific Revolutions.* Chicago: The University of Chicago Press, 1970.

Kumashiro, K. K. "'Posts' Perspectives on Anti-Oppressive Education in Social Studies, English, Mathematics, and Science Classrooms." *Educational Researcher* 30, no. 3 (2001): 3–12.

Lambda Legal Defense and Education Fund. "Colín v. Orange Unified School District." *Lambda Update* 17, no. 2 (Summer 2000): 26.

———. "Docket." *Lambda Update* 18, no. 1 (Winter 2001): 26–37.

LeCompte, M. D. "Standing for Just and Right Decisions: The Long, Slow Path to School Safety. *Education and Urban Society* 32, no. 3 (May 2000): 413–29.

LeCompte, M. D., and J. Preissle. *Ethnography and Qualitative Design in Educational Research.* 2nd ed. San Diego, CA: Academic Press, 1993.

LeCompte, M. D,. and J. J. Schensul. *Designing and Conducting Ethnographic Research.* Walnut Creek, CA: Altamira Press, 1999a.

———. *Analyzing and Interpreting Ethnographic Data.* Walnut Creek, CA: Altamira Press, 1999b.

Lester, J. S. *The Future of White Men and Other Diversity Dilemmas.* Berkeley, CA: Conari Press, 1994.

Lipkin, A. *Understanding Homosexuality, Changing Schools: A Text for Teachers, Counselors, and Administrators.* Boulder, CO: Westview Press, 1999.

Macgillivray, I. K. "Educational Equity for Gay, Lesbian, Bisexual, Transgendered, and Queer/Questioning Students: The Demands of Democracy and Social Justice for America's Schools." *Education and Urban Society* 32, no. 3 (May 2000): 303–23.

———. "Implementing School Non-discrimination Policy That Includes Sexual Orientation: A Case Study in School and Identity Politics." Doctoral dissertation, University of Colorado, Boulder, 2001. *UMI Dissertation Abstracts,* microform no. 3005076.

Macgillivray, I. K., and G. Kozik-Rosabal. "Introduction." *Education and Urban Society* 32, no. 3 (May 2000): 287–302.

Macoby, E. E., and C. N. Jacklin. *Psychology of Sex Differences.* Palo Alto, CA: Stanford University Press, 1974.

Martin, W. *With God on Our Side: The Rise of the Religious Right in America.* New York: Broadway Books, 1996.

Marty, M. E. *Education, Religion, and the Common Good.* San Francisco: Jossey-Bass, 2000.

Money, J., and A. A. Ehrhart. *Man and Woman, Boy and Girl: The Differentiation and Dimorphism of Gender Identity from Conception to Maturity.* Baltimore, MD: John Hopkins University Press, 1972.

Morris, M. "The Pleasant Hill Public School District Has Agreed to Pay $72,500 to a Former Student Who Alleged He Was Sexually Harassed by Other Students Who Thought He Was Gay." *Kansas City Star,* August 9, 2000.

Nabozny v. Podlesny, 92 F. 3d 446 (7th Cir. 1996).

Noddings, N. *The Challenge to Care in Schools: An Alternative Approach to Education.* New York: Teachers College Press, 1992.

Owens, R. E., Jr. *Queer Kids: The Challenges and Promise for Lesbian, Gay, and Bisexual Youth.* New York: Harrington Park Press, 1998.

Pankratz, H. "2 teens 'who felt powerless.'" *The Denver Post,* April 14, 2002, 3B.

Perrotti, J., and K. Westheimer. *When the Drama Club Is Not Enough: Lessons from the Safe Schools Program for Gay and Lesbian Students.* Boston: Beacon Press, 2001.

Pinar, W. F., ed. *Queer Theory in Education.* Mahwah, NJ: Lawrence Erlbaum Associates, 1998.

Provenzo, E. F., Jr. *Religious Fundamentalism and American Education: The Battle for the Public Schools.* New York: State University of New York Press, 1990.

Rawls, J. *A Theory of Justice.* Cambridge, MA: The Belknap Press of Harvard University Press, 1971.

———. *Political Liberalism.* New York: Columbia University Press, 1996.

Reis, B., and E. Saewyc. "Eighty-Three Thousand Youth: Selected Findings of Eight Population-Based Studies As They Pertain to Anti-Gay Harassment and the Safety and Well-Being of Sexual Minority Students." Accessed at www.safeschools-wa.org. 1999.

Remafedi, G. "Fundamental Issues in the Care of Homosexual Youth." *Medical Clinics of North America* 74, no. 5 (1990): 1169–79.

Rofes, E. "Making Our Schools Safe for Sissies." *The High School Journal* 77, nos. 1 and 2 (1994): 37–40.

———. "Rethinking Anti-Gay Harassment in Schools." *Democracy & Education* 13, no. 3 (2000): 52–59.

Romer v. Evans. 116 S. Ct. 1620 (1996). *Writ of Certiorari,* U.S. Supreme Court, May 20, 1996, no. 94-1039.

Rotheram-Borus, M. J., and M. I. Fernandez. "Sexual Orientation and Developmental Challenges Experienced by Gay and Lesbian Youths." *Suicide and Life Threatening Behavior* 25 (1995): 26–34.

Rubenstein, W. B., ed. *Cases and Materials on Sexual Orientation and the Law.* 2nd ed. Saint Paul, MN: West Publishing Company, 1997.

Sarason, S. B. *The Culture of the School and the Problem of Change.* Boston, MA: Allyn and Bacon, 1971.

———. *The Predictable Failure of Educational Reform.* San Francisco: Jossey-Bass Publishers, 1990.

———. *Barometers of Change: Individual, Educational and Social Transformation.* San Francisco: Jossey-Bass Publishers, 1996.

Savin-Williams, R. C. *Gay and Lesbian Youth: Expressions of Identity.* Washington, D.C.: Hemisphere, 1990.

Saxe v. State College Area School District, no. 99-4081, slip op. (3rd Cir. February 14, 2001).

Schensul, S. L., J. J. Schensul, and M. D. LeCompte. *Essential Ethnographic Methods: Observations, Interviews, and Questionnaires.* Walnut Creek, CA: Altamira Press, 1999.

Sears, J. T. "Educators, Homosexuality, and Homosexual Students: Are Personal Feelings Related to Professional Beliefs?" *Coming Out of the Classroom Closet: Gay and Lesbian Students, Teachers, and Curricula,* edited by Karen M. Harbeck, 29–79. New York: Harrington Park Press, 1992.

———. "Crossing Boundaries and Becoming the Other: Voices across Borders." In *Curriculum, Religion and Public Education: Conversations for an Enlarging Public Square,* edited by J. T. Sears and J. C. Carper, 36–58. New York: Teachers College Press, 1998.

Sears, J. T., and J. C. Carper, eds. *Curriculum, Religion and Public Education: Conversations for an Enlarging Public Square.* New York: Teachers College Press, 1998.

Sears, J. T., and W. L. Williams, eds. *Overcoming Heterosexism and Homophobia: Strategies That Work.* New York: Columbia University Press, 1997.

Silin, J. G. *Sex, Death, and the Education of Children: Our Passion for Ignorance in the Age of AIDS*. New York: Teachers College Press, 1995.

Smith, M. U., and M. A. Drake. "Suicide and Homosexual Teens: What Can Biology Teachers Do to Help?" *American Biology Teacher* (March 2001), at www.nabt.org/journal.html.

Spradley, J. P. *Participant Observation*. Fort Worth, TX: Holt, Reinhart, and Winston, 1980.

Telljohann, S. K., and J. H. Price. "A Qualitative Examination of Adolescent Homosexual's Life Experiences: Ramifications for Secondary School Personnel." *Journal of Homosexuality* 26, no. 1 (1993): 41–56.

Tenney, N. "The Constitutional Imperative of Reality in Public School Curricula: Untruths about Homosexuality as a Violation of the First Amendment." In *Cases and Materials on Sexual Orientation and the Law*, 2nd ed., edited by W. B. Rubenstein, 303–7. Saint Paul, MN: West Publishing Company, 1997.

Thompson, M. *Gay Soul: Finding the Heart of Gay Spirit and Nature*. San Francisco: Harper Collins Publishers, 1994.

Tinker v. Des Moines Independent School District. 393 U.S. 503 (1969).

U.S. Department of Education Office of Civil Rights. "Part I: The Fundamentals: A Comprehensive Approach to Eliminating Harassment and Hate Crime." Accessed at www.ed.gov/offices/OCR/archives/Harassment/fundamentals1.html.

U.S. Department of Education Office of Civil Rights. "Part II: Step-by-Step Guidance: Developing the District's Written Anti-Harassment Policy." Accessed at www.ed.gov/offices/OCR/archives/Harassment/policy1.html.

Warner, M., ed. *Fear of a Queer Planet: Queer Politics and Social Theory*. Minneapolis, MN: University of Minnesota Press, 1993.

Zinn, H. *A People's History of the United States: 1492–Present*. New York: Harper Perennial, 1995.

Index

About the Author

Ian K. Macgillivray received his Ph.D. in foundations of education from the University of Colorado, Boulder. An expert at understanding opposition to school policies that include sexual orientation, Dr. Macgillivray coedited a special issue of *Education and Urban Society* dedicated to sexual orientation and gender identity in America's urban schools. He has also authored professional papers, articles, and book reviews; and he has presented numerous professional workshops and conferences on GLBTIQ issues in education. He is a consultant for school districts that want to make their schools safe and equitable for GLBTIQ students. Dr. Macgillivray currently teaches high school biology at American School Foundation, A. C. in Mexico City, Mexico. He can be reached at gurv001@yahoo.com or 2523 54th Avenue, Greeley, Colorado, 80634.